# THE FRONTIER POLICY OF THE DELHI SULTANS

AGHA HUSSAIN HAMADANI

ATLANTIC PUBLISHERS & DISTRIBUTORS

*Published by*
**ATLANTIC PUBLISHERS & DISTRIBUTORS**
B-2, Vishal Enclave, New Delhi-110027
Phone: 5413460

*Sales office*
4346/4C, Ansari Road, Darya Ganj,
New Delhi-110002
Phone: 3273880



*Printed in India at*
Mehra Offset Press
New Delhi

## PREFACE

The history of the Sulṭāns of Delhī has been dealt with by several scholars who have attempted to analyse the internal factors that affected the rise and fall of the early Muslim empire. However, enough attention has not been given to the external relations that caused recurrent menace to the Delhī Sulṭāns. The existence of the Delhī Sulṭānate largely depended upon the manner in which the rulers met the challenge from the West. The result was the evolution of a definite frontier policy to contain the invaders, which took time to develop. The present study attempts to analyse the many-faceted problem of the frontier and explains the factors which were responsible for the shifting boundaries of the Delhī Sulṭānate. The introductory chapter, therefore, defines the frontier of the Delhī Sulṭānate in relation to the contemporary historical cross-currents. It also discusses the source material that is available in manuscripts and published forms. The second chapter deals with the important issue of how the Delhī Sulṭānate, especially during the time of Quṭb al-Dīn Aibak and Iltutmis̲h̲, became an independent entity in contrast with the earlier G̲h̲orid empire. The birth of the Indian frontier resulted in direct confrontation with the then dominant power in Central Asia, the Mongols. The third chapter explains the Mongol threat and concentrates on the ways in which the successors of Iltutmis̲h̲, particularly Sulṭān Fīrūz S̲h̲āh, Sulṭāna Raẓia, Sulṭān Bahrām S̲h̲āh and Sulṭān Mas'ud S̲h̲āh, met this threat in continuation of the earlier frontier policy. The fourth chapter is related to Balban's frontier policy as a Na'ib and then as a Sulṭān. It was Balban who for the first time, reframed the frontier policy on an effectively pragmatic basis which successfully checked the Mongol incursions. The fifth chapter examines how the K̲h̲aljīs under 'Alā al-Dīn, taking advantage of Balban's success, advanced to the west and consolidated the position of the Delhī Sulṭānate beyond the Indus. The sixth chapter discusses the policy under the Tughlaqs and the manner in which they cleared the way for the Delhī Sulṭānate to meddle in the Central Asian affairs. The Khurāsān expedition of Sulṭān Muḥammad bin Tughlaq was one aspect of this advance frontier policy. The rise of the Timūrids in Central Asia, however, changed the whole situation and shattered the Delhī Sulṭān's frontier policy. Specially after Timūr's invasion, Delhī began to follow the line of the Timūrids. The conclusion brings out the fact that the old 'frontier' policy of the Delhī Sulṭānate came to an end within a period of one hundred and fifty years until in A.D. 1526 the Mughals under Bābar invaded India. The 'frontier' lost its meaning during this period and became a part of the Central Asian empire of the Timūrids.

The present study is substantially based on my Ph.D. dissertation written under the supervision of Professor Emeritus, Ahmad Ḥasan Dānī, I would like to take this opportunity to thank him for his inspiring guidance without which this work would not have been accomplished in its present form. Thanks are also due to many other scholars: The Faculty members of the History Departments, Quaid-i-'Aẓam University, Islāmabād and Muslim University 'Alīgaṛh (India); and librarians both in Pākistān and outside, who provided me with ideas and leads to various research materials. It was because of their kindness and cooperation, and of those numerous persons who helped me in one way or the other that I was able to complete this work. Among them, however, I would like to make an exception by mentioning Professor Shaikh 'Abdur Rashīd, former Dean of the Faculty of Arts, Muslim University 'Alīgaṛh and Professor of History at Punjāb University, Lāhore, who, despite advanced age and illness, helped me whenever I needed his guidance, and Dr. Ṭāriq Raḥmān for valuable suggestions in the final editing of the manuscript.

I must record my grateful appreciation of Quaid-i-'Aẓam University and the University Grants Commission, Islāmabād, for providing me financial assistance during my research. I am also indebted to Dr. Waheeduzzaman, Director, National Institute of Historical and Cultural Research, Islamabad, for accepting the present volume as a publication of the Institute. I am also thankful to Mr. Shafqat Amīn and Mr. M. ʿAẓeem Bhaṭṭī of the Institute for their keen interest while the book was in the process of printing. And thanks, finally to my family members for putting up with this and much else besides: especially to my wife and our children – Sāghar, Shāzia, Nayyar, Nāzia and Sattār – who had to take the strain of my absence from home with unstinting forbearance.

Agha Ḥussain Hamadānī

## CONTENTS

## ILLUSTRATIONS

# TRANSLITERATION

| | | | |
|---|---|---|---|
| ا | a | ش | sh |
| ب | b | ص | ṣ |
| پ | p | ض | ẓ |
| ت | t | ط | t̤ |
| ٹ | ṭ | ظ | z̤ |
| ث | s̤ | ع | ‘ |
| ج | j | غ | gh |
| چ | ch | ف | f |
| ح | ḥ | ق | q |
| خ | kh | ک | k |
| د | d | گ | g |
| ڈ | ḍ | ل | l |
| ذ | z dh | م | m |
| ر | r | ن | n |
| ڑ | ṛ | و | w |
| ز | z | ہ | h |
| ژ | zh | ء | ʼ |
| س | s | ی | y |

Vowels: short a, i, u

long ā, ī, ū, e, o

# ABBREVIATIONS*

| | | |
|---|---|---|
| *E.I.* | | *Encyclopaedia of Islām*, 2nd edition |
| *F.M.* | (Text) | Fakhr–i–Mudabbir, *Adāb al–Ḥarb wā Shuja'ah* |
| *F.S.* | (Text) | 'Iṣāmī,*Futuḥ–us–Salāṭīn* |
| *F.S.* | (Trans.) | 'Iṣāmī, *Futuḥ–us–Salāṭīn*, (Trans.) Aghā Mahdī Ḥusain |
| *H.S.* | (Text) | Khwand Mīr, *Ḥabīb–us–Siyar* |
| *I.A.* | (Text) | Ibn al–Asīr, *Al–Kāmil fit–Tārīkh* |
| *I.A.* | (Trans.) | Ibn al–Asīr, *Al–Kāmil fit–Tārīkh*, (Trans.) Elliot and Dowson |
| *I.B.* | (Text) | Ibn Batūṭah, *Reḥla* |
| *I.B.* | (Trans.) | Ibn Batūṭah, *Reḥla*, (Trans.) H.A.R. Gibb |
| *I.C.* | | *Islāmic Culture* (Hyderabād, Deccan). |
| *I.H.Q.* | | *Indian Historical Quarterly*, (Calcutta). |
| *I.K.* | (Text) | Amīr Khusraū, *I'jāz–i–Khusravī* |
| *I.M.* | (Text) | 'Ain al–Mulk Multānī, *Insha–i–Mahrū.* |
| *J.A.S.B.* | | *Journal of the Asiatic Society of Bengal* (Calcutta). |
| *J.C.A.* | | *Journal of Central Asia* (Islāmabād) |
| *J.I.H.C.* | | *Journal of Indian History Congress* (Calcutta) |
| *J.P.H.S.* | | *Journal of the Punjab Historical Society* (Lahore) |
| *J.R.A.S.* | | *Journal of the Royal Asiatic Society* (London). |
| *J.T.* | (Text) | Rashīd al–Dīn Faẓlullah, *Jami'ut–Tawārīkh* |
| *J.T.* | (Trans.) | Rashīd al–Dīn Faẓlullah, *Jami'ut–Tawārīkh*, (Trans.) A.J. Boyle. |
| *K.F.* | (Text) | Amīr Khusraū, *Khaza'in al–Futuḥ*, |
| *K.F.* | (Trans.) | Amīr Khusraū, *Khaza'in al–Futuḥ*, (Trans.) Muḥammad Ḥabīb |
| *K.G.N.* | (Text) | Dunī Chand,*Kai-Gohar–Nāma* |
| *K.T.M.G.* | (Text) | Rashīd al–Dīn Faẓlullah, *Kitāb Tārīkh–i–Mubārak Ghazānī* |
| *M.A.* | (Text) | Shihāb al–Dīn al–'Umarī, *Masālik al–Abṣār fī Mamālik al–Amṣār* |

| | | |
|---|---|---|
| *M.A.* | (Trans.) | Shihāb al–Dīn al–'Umarī,*Masālik al–Abṣār fī Mamālik al–Amṣār,* (Trans.) I.H. Ṣiddique and Qāzī Muḥammad Aḥmad |
| *M.D.* | (Text) | Abul Hasan bin 'Alī Ḥussain bin 'Alī Mas,udī, *Marūj al–Dhahab* |
| *M.D.* | (Trans.) | Abul Hasan bin 'Alī Ḥussain bin 'Alī Mas'udī, *Marūj al–Dhahab,* (Trans.) Elliot and Dowson |
| *M.S.* | (Text) | Maulānā Kamāl al–Dīn 'Abdur Razzāq Samarqandī, *Maṯla–us–Sa'dain wa Majma' al–Baḥrain* |
| *M.T.B.* | (Text) | 'Abdul Qādir Badāunī, *Muntakhab at–Tawārīkh* |
| *M.T.B.* | (Trans.) | 'Abdul Qādir Badāunī, *Mutakhab at–Tawārīkh,* (Trans.) G. Ranking |
| *M.T.T.* | (Text) | Amīr Tīmūr, *Malfūẓāt–i–Tīmūrī* |
| *M.T.T.* | (Trans.) | Amīr Tīmūr, *Malfūẓāt-i-Tīmūrī,* (Trans.) Elliot and Dowson |
| *M.U.J.* | | *Muslim University Journal,* ('Aligaṛh) |
| *P.I.H.C.* | | *Proceedings of Indian History Congress* |
| *P.P.H.C.* | | *Proceedings of Punjab History Conference* (Patiāla) |
| *Q.S.* | (Text) | Amīr Khusraū, *Qiran–us–Sa'dain* |
| *S.A.* | (Trans.) | *Shajrā–tul–Atrāk,* (Trans.) Miles |
| *S.M.* | (Text) | Shihāb al–Dīn Nasāwī, *Sīrat–i–Mangbārnī* |
| *T.A.* | (Trans.) | Niẓām al–Dīn Aḥmad Bakhshī, *Ṭabaqāt–i–Akbarī* (Trans.) De, B. |
| *T.B.* | (Trans.) | Bābar, *Tuzūk–i–Bābarī,* (Trans.) A.S. Beveridge |
| *T.F.* | (Text) | Firishta, Muḥammad Kāsim Hindū Shāh, *Tārīkh–i–Firishta* |
| *T.F.* | (Trans.) | Firishta, *Tārīkh–i–Firishta,* (Trans.) John Briggs |
| *T.F.S.A.* | (Text) | Shams Sirāj'Afīf, *Tārīkh–i–Fīrūz Shāhī* |
| *T.F,S,A.* | (Trans.) | Shams Sirāj 'Afīf, *Tārīkh–i–Fīrūz Shāhī,* (Trans.) Elliot and Dowson |
| *T.F.S.B.* | (Text) | Ẓiā al–Dīn Baranī, *Tārīkh–i–Fīrūz Shāhī* |
| *T.F.S.B.* | (Trans.) | Ẓiā al–Dīn Baranī, *Tārīkh–i–Fīrūz Shāhī,* |

| | | |
|---|---|---|
| | | (Trans.) Shaikh 'Abdur Rashid (Unpublished); Elliot and Dowson |
| *T.H.* | (Trans.) | Abū Raihān al–Berūnī, *Tārīkh–i–Hind,* (Trans.) E.C. Sachau |
| *T.J.G.* | (Text) | 'Ata Muhammad Juvainī, *Tārīkh-i-Jahān Gushā* |
| *T.J.G.* | (Trans). | 'Ata Muhammad Juvainī, *Tārīkh-i-Jahān Gushā* (Trans.) Boyle |
| *T.M.M.* | (Trans) | Mīr Muhammad Ma'sūm, *Tārīkh-i-Ma'sūmī,* (Trans.) Elliot and Dowson |
| *T.M.N.* | (Trans.) | Hasan Nizāmī, *Tāj al-Mā'asir,* (Trans.) Elliot and Dowson |
| *T.M.S.* | (Trans.) | Yahya Sirhindī, *Tārīkh-i-Mubārak Shāhī,* (Trans.) K.K. Bāsū |
| *T.N.* | (Text) | Minhāj al–Dīn Sirāj, *Tabaqāt-i-Nāsirī* |
| *T.N.* | (Trans.) | Minhāj al–Dīn Sirāj, *Tabaqāt-i-Nāsirī,* (Trans.) H.G. Raverty |
| *T.N.K.* | (Text) | Amīr Khusrau, *Tughlaq Nāmā* |
| *T.N.K.* | (Trans.) | Amīr Khusrau, *Tughlaq Nāmā,* (Trans.) Aghā Mahdī Husain |
| *T.R.* | (Trans.) | Mirza Haider Dughlat, *Tārīkh-i-Rashidī,* (Trans.) Ross |
| *T. W.* | (Text) | 'Abdullah Shīrāzī, *Tārīkh-i-Wassāf* |
| *Z.N.* | (Text) | Sharf al–Dīn Yazdī, *Zafar Nāmā* |
| *Z.W.* | (Trans.) | Hājī Dabīr, *Zafar al–Walih,* (Trans.) Aghā Mahdī Husain |

* For the actual edition used, see the Bibliography.

Trans., Shaikh Abdur Rashid & [illegible]
[illegible] and [illegible]

[illegible] Trans., [illegible]
Trans., B.C. [illegible]

[illegible] [illegible]

[illegible] [illegible]
Trans., [illegible]

[illegible] Mir Muhammad [illegible]
Trans., Elliot and Dowson

[illegible]

[illegible]

[illegible]

## Chapter I

# INTRODUCTORY

### I

The Sulṭāns of Delhī ruled in South Asia[1] for over three centuries (A.D. 1206–1526). Their rule covered the periods of the Mamlūks (A.D. 1206–90), the Khaljīs (A.D. 1290–1320), the Tughlaqs (A.D. 1320–1414), the Sayyids (A.D. 1414–1451), and the Lodīs (A.D. 1451–1526). They not only established Muslim rule firmly but also took active steps to defend its frontier against external aggression. The beginning was made by Quṭb al-Dīn Aibak who, after the death of Sulṭān Muḥammad bin Sām,[2] became practically independent in the Indian possessions of the Ghorids. He freed himself from the control of the Shansabānī dynasty of Ghor. It was, therefore, but natural for Aibak to devise a policy to defend territories along the western borderland of his kingdom. The succeeding Sulṭāns of Delhī, who also hailed from Central Asia, became rulers over a considerable portion of the subcontinent. They were initially slaves but soon entrenched themselves as successors to the power of their respective masters. Once they established themselves here, they were cut off from their original homeland by the powers that ruled northwest of the Delhī Sulṭanate. The Sulṭāns were also aware of the hostile designs of the Central Asian powers who aspired to extend their rule and influence into the sub-continent. It was the responsibility of the Sulṭāns of Delhī to defend the frontier of their territory and as a result it was during their rule that a definite frontier policy was evolved.[3]

The frontier policy of the Sulṭāns of Delhī has not received from scholars the attention that it deserves. Several reasons may be adduced for this lack of interest. After the decline of Muslim power in South Asia, the European powers came by sea for trade but soon a power struggle began among them which finally resulted in the British domination over the subcontinent.[4] Thus the commercial relations developed between South Asia and Europe and the importance of the sea route increased. Because of this, attention has not been given to land routes and the connection with Central Asia. A study of Central Asia in recent years has also received less attention from foreign and Pākistānī scholars. Even contemporary chronicles of the Sulṭāns of Delhī did not attempt to give a comprehensive definition of their frontier because they concentrated on the central regions of their empire. Consequently, they paid attention to strengthening their frontier only to the extent that it was necessary for the defence of the kingdom. Therefore, in the absence of material, the present day researcher has no alternative but to turn to traveller's and narrative accounts. The present thesis attempts to study the frontier policy of the Sulṭāns of Delhī as a whole.

The "frontier" discussed in the present thesis, has been deliberately confined to the west so as to understand the evolution of the independent identity of the Delhī Sulṭānate in contrast to its original connection with the Ghorid empire. As the Delhī Sultānate arose out of the expansion of the Ghorid empire towards the east in South Asia, it is pertinent to see how the original state of the Ghorid Sulṭāns got divided after the death of Sulṭān Muḥammad bin Sām[5] and how his territory was apportioned by his officers. In this division, the important question that arose related to the "frontier" between the newly founded states on the border of Pakistān. How and how far the Sulṭāns of Delhī managed to extend their authority westward are important questions. In what way did they involve themselves with the original Ghorid possessions of Ghaznī and how they fared in their western adventure, are issues that are directly related to the establishment of their own independent existence, and particularly the authority, that their own independent rule implied, could extend towards the west. In the beginning, the model of this "frontier" policy could be seen in the developing relations among the succeeding governors of the late Sulṭān Muḥammad bin Sām. It is because of their relations, the power that they could wield and assert, and the authority that they could command, that ultimately decided the way in which the "frontier" would move. Here the word "frontier" is also being used for the power distribution among the governors who, after the death of the late Sulṭān Muḥammad bin Sām, appropriated to themselves the very title of Sulṭān. Thus the original Ghorid power that had barely found extension in South Asia, got divided, or distributed, among the new claimants. It is to the credit of the Sulṭāns of Delhī that the power they inherited was not lost but, on the contrary, was increased in South Asia. It was essential for their own existence to keep a watch on their western neighbours and defend their constantly shifting frontier.

This western "frontier" has been important for South Asia through all periods of history, because this great subcontinent, geographically situated as it is, has always been open to the influence and pressures that came from further afield in Central Asia. It is the shift of events in the history of Central Asia that determined the fortunes of the people living in this geographic zone. And the first illustration of this is found during the early history of the Delhī Sulṭānate. Even when the power structure of the succeeding governors of Muḥammad bin Sām was taking shape, a new historical phenomenon appeared on the Central Asian scene. The Mongol advance[6] into this region and their consequent relations with the Khwārizmian state changed the whole course of history. The Turks in Central Asia were disturbed and many of their tribes[7] found refuge in the subcontinent. In this historical turmoil, the Ghorid state disappeared from the scene.[8] The fugitive Khwārizm Shāh, reorganising his forces, tried to establish himself south of the Hindu-Kush but later made a bid to force a shelter with the Sulṭān of Delhi. However, the then Sulṭān proved to be more tactful. Although the original Ghorid power had come to an end along with the other Amīrates,[9] yet the Delhī Sulṭanate consolidated its power. Now, a question arose for Iltutmish, Sulṭān of Delhī, as to how he should determine his policy towards his western frontier. Actually the policy was to seek a diplomatic solution to the realities of the time. The model of "frontier" determination was now completely changed. In the earlier case the successor states of the original Ghorid state were trying to discover a way for their own mutual relations. In the present case an intruder from Central Asia, being forced by another power behind, was threatening the very existence of the remnants of the Ghorid power. This spelled doom for all those successors who were born outside of that power. Should the Delhī Sulṭānate succeed in retaining its existence and power and then again at what cost? The answer lay in evolving a realistic policy of the "frontier".

However, the Central Asian scene changed further when the Mongols occupied Central Asia,[10] established their power on the Oxus, and following the Khurāsān route onward, overthrew the 'Abbāsids after the sack of Baghdād in A.D. 1258.[11] The original Turkish power was shattered. The western Turks converged to consolidate the Ottoman state while in the east it was the Delhi Sulṭānate that became the refuge for the migrating Turks. What pressure the Mongols brought to bear on these two powers, is a completely new story that belongs to two different historical contexts. The one with which the present thesis is concerned, centres on the frontier regions of the Indian dominions of the Sulṭāns of Delhī. It is surprising to find that the Mongols could sweep overboard the Baghdād power but that in the subcontinent, although they made deep incursions, they could not wipe out the Turkish power from Delhī. This is a long story of hit, advance and withdrawal on both sides, in which the frontier was fluctuating according to the power wielded by each of them. The fate of the frontier was sealed only when the Mongol power got re-allocated among the successors of Chingiz Khān.[12] In the history of the Delhī Sulṭānate the Mongol menace hovered like a ghastly spectre that threatened its existence every moment, but when that power itself got divided, the Delhī Sulṭāns like 'Alā al-Dīn Khaljī and Muhammad bin Tughlaq, made a bid to push their frontier to the west and win diplomatic victory even in Central Asia. It seems that the powers got saturated in the respective hands, and new forces from within the localities emerged to reassert their strength and forge a new form of power sharing. Even within the lifetime of Muḥammad bin Tughlaq the Delhī power was losing its control over its far-flung areas in the subcontinent and, after his death, although Fīrūz Shāh Tughlaq tried to retrieve the power, he was too feeble for any bold adventurous step. On the other hand, Central Asia discovered in the rise of the Tīmūrids a new power that could play a new role in the time to come.

The rise of Amīr Tīmūr[13] in Central Asia is an event of great importance. This was not a sudden event. It was the gradual waning of the Mongol power in this region, and some would like to say that the Mongol power was gradually being shared by the local Turks in the development of the Transoxaniā state[14] that ultimately paved the way for the rise of Tīmūr.[15] It was once again the turn of the Central Asian Turks to reassert their claims, to lay the foundation of a new power by integrating the remaining forces left behind by the Mongols and to seek new direction for its growth. The way lay towards the east in the subcontinent, where the power of the Delhī Sulṭānate, after the death[16] of Fīrūz Shāh Tughlaq, had considerably weakened and the empire had disintegrated. In the eyes of Amīr Timūr this weakening was almost like a loss of the Muslim power[17] and the danger of its passing into Hindū hands. With this realization and declared aim Amír Tīmūr advanced into the subcontinent not only to uphold the Turkish authority but also to claim sovereignty for himself. In this new development the frontier policy, that had been nurtured so long and pursued so tactfully, went overboard and there was a complete inundation of Central Asian power[18] in this wide area.

However, the geographic distance, given the means of communication then existing, was so great that no direct rule could be established. On the other hand the death of Tīmūr caused a further division of power among his sons and their successors. Shāh Rukh's establishment in Herāt disturbed and dispersed the Afghān tribes in the southern part of Afghānistān while Ẓahīr al-Dīn Muḥammad Bābar[19] fled from Farghānā[20] and Samarqand to seek a new fortune in Kābul in A.D. 1501-2.[21] The Arghūns and Tarkhāns moved down from Qandhār into Sind to build Turkish kingdoms for themselves.[22] The Lodī Afghāns, who had migrated originally from the vicinity of Takht-i-Sulaimān, captured power in Delhī.[23] The Yūsafzaī Pashtūns (Afghāns) found shelter in the northern part of the North West Frontier Province. But soon Bābar was to claim the inheritance of his ancestors as he was himself descended from Tīmūr from his father's side. However, the claim could not be established merely by the right of descent and it took nearly twenty five years for Bābar to consolidate his power in Kābul before he could finally make a bid to supplant the Lodīs from Delhī. The western frontier now became flooded by the power of the Chaghātāe Turks, to which group Bābar himself belonged, but modern history has popularly remembered his descendants as the Mughals.[24] With the establishment of the Mughal power in Delhī, the story of the western frontier began a new chapter as the boundary moved towards the Hindū-Kush.

Before any other consideration, it is essential to define the western frontier in its literal sense. In this connection a distinction between "boundary" and "frontier" should be understood first because both terms play an important role in establishing the identity as well as in defining the territoriality of a state. According to Alastair Lamb, ". . . a boundary is a clear divide between sovereignties, which can be marked as a line on a map, and it has, as it were, length but not area, e.g., the Curzon Line between Russia and Poland; the Durand Line between Pākistān and Afghānistān."[25] Explaining "frontier", Mujtabā Rizvī says, "A 'frontier' denotes a region or zone having width as well as length whereas a 'boundary' refers to a line."[26] According to Holdich, ". . . a 'frontier' is but a vague and indefinite term until the 'boundary' sets a hedge between it and the frontier of the neighbouring countries."[27] He further says, " . . no limit is set to a frontier until an actual line is defined by a treaty, every now and then it is generally open to dispute until the boundary is actually demarcated."[28] The distinction between the two terms is thus clear, but in actual use variation is seen. Explaining the frontier in an explicit political sense, Adami says, ". .. . a state frontier is that line which marks the limits of the region within which the state can exercise its sovereign rights."[29] On this particular issue, the views of Sir Norman J.G. Pounds are relevant: "primitive peoples, in general, have simple ideas and concepts. A no man's land separates the territory that is inhabited and used by the tribes from that occupied by the next. This is a frontier in a strict sense, a border zone, unclaimed, unsettled, and unused, into which neither side claims nor exercises an exclusive control."[30] If we apply the views of Pounds to the understanding of the western frontier in South Asia, we find that the "frontier" could be said to be an unclaimed region, inhabited by the local tribes of divergent origins, but actually a no man's land between the authorities of the established neighbouring states. Writing on the "frontier" of the subcontinent, Davis says, "the frontier zone became a sort of *terra incognita* which means no man dared traverse it except under the protection of the armed forces during the British period."[31] This basic principle will be applied to determine the "frontier" policy of the Sulṭāns of Delhī. We will take the "frontier" in its widest sense so as to include a wider geographical belt in the west and then try to see how the boundary of the Sulṭanate has been changing from time to time.

An understanding of the physical geography of the entire western belt is necessary in order to understand the terrain covered by the term 'frontier'. Patricia Kendall writes that "Geography reigns supreme in India. It dictates political boundaries, determines social movements and limits ethnic expansion."[32] In other words, the Geography of South Asia plays a vital role in its history. Speaking of the Geography of South Asia, Holdich states: "Physiographically she is fenced round within a ring of sea and mountains. The north is bounded by the highest and most compact wall of the Himālāya which towers above the plains of Hindustān in a continuous line of snowy peaks and is continued in an unbroken chain of its extensions on the north-east and north-west, reaching right up to the head of the sea on both sides from the foot of which the Peninsula of India which stretches away southwards."[33] Thus geographically South Asia is secluded or shut off from the rest of Asia because of natural barrier of long mountain chains i.e., the Himālāya and its branches, as well as the sea. For a northern invader in the mediaeval age, specially between the 13th and the 14th centuries A.D., a sea route was of little importance. Land routes were also limited. The Himalaya stood like a great barrier in the north. In Spate's words: "The Himālāyas run across the whole of northern India from Assam in the east to modern Afghānistān in the west. They run in a south-east curve all along the northern India and separate it from the Plateau of Tibet, include several ranges of lofty mountains, with deep interspersed valleys. They served the purpose of a great wall of defence and protected India. It has an elevation of twenty thousand feet. Tibet, which, from the point of physical geography includes a large and little known area in Kashmir to the north of the Karākoram range, is a lofty, desolate, windswept plateau with a mean elevation of about fifteen thousand feet. In the parts of it which are situated to the north of the north-west corner of Nepāl, lies the Mansarowar lake, in the neighbourhood of which three great rivers, the Brahmaputra, the Sutlej and the Indus take their rise. This region remains covered with snow."[34] This geographic description explains how these northern Himālāyan chains proved as the greatest fortress for South Asia's security throughout the past ages. Patricia Kendall also comments, "The Himālāyas are contained between the Indus where it bends and enters India on the west, and the Brahmaputra where it makes a similar bend and enters India on the east. In their length of fifteen hundred miles, there are three or four points where a passage into Tibet or C̲hinā is possible. Through these high passes races of Mongolian origin have filtered into Himālāyan valleys and made their homes there. But to an invasion in force the Himālāyas, as thus defined, are an impassable obstacle."[35] In contrast to this northern barrier, the western border presents different features. Spate writes: "The Hindū-Kus̲h, which runs from the Pāmīr in a south-westerly direction, is regarded as a natural boundary of South Asia in the north-west."[36] He further adds: "It is pierced by the numerous passes blocked by snow in winter but in other seasons practicable without great difficulty. Over this Oxus/Indus watershed lies the major passes through which people after people have pressed into the plains of Hindustān, whether impelled by desication in the steppe or by the political pressure of the constantly shifting fortunes of Central Asian wars. Of all the incursions those of prime importance are the organised invasions of the Muslim conquerors."[37] Spate further states: "Safed Koh, Sulaimān, and Kīrthar ranges are generally regarded as the north western boundary of South Asia separating it from the tableland of Irān."[38] Thus the land approaches and gateways to South Asia have always been on the west and north-west, either through the sterile rock ways of southern Balūc̲h̲istān to the Indus Delta, or across the plains of Qandahār to the defiles of lower Sind or from G̲h̲aznī to the Indus valley or from Kābul to Punjāb. These have always been the main channels for the flow of population from Central Asia into the 'golden land of promise' as well as the narrow pathways for the commerce of the past centuries.

'The peculiar situation and structure of the western frontier" according to Holdich, "has, since very early time, been a perennial and permanent source of danger from the other side.'"[39] The frontier remained ill-defined. Spate further makes regional division, "regionally, the whole area falls into three main divisions: i), the hills of north-west frontier,[40] ii) the sub-mountain Indus region including the valley of Peshāwar and the Bannū plain, the Pothwar plain, and the Salt range;[41] and iii) Balūchistān.[42] The study of each of these regions is highly interesting.

**Balūchistān**

It is an extensive plateau of rough country divided into basins by ranges of sufficient height and ruggedness to form obstacle to movements.[43] Holdich divides it into northern and southern Baluchistān, [44] while Spate speaks of its lower highlands and upper highlands.[45] The upper highlands, known locally as Khārān,[46] rise as high as 12,000 feet, with the valley floors about 5,000 feet, above sea-level.[47] The lower highlands include the Makrān and the Chāghi ranges in the west of Balūchistān.[48] "Makrān", according to Ibn Haukal, an 'Arab traveller, "is a vast country mostly desert. It includes long but narrow valleys of very great fertility where date palms grow and fruit is cultivated and have fields of wheat and maize. These valleys run mostly east and west and they are bounded by long rugged ridges of barren rock wrinkled and folded in parallel lines, and often packed in close formation across the wide spaces intervening between them.'"[49] Holdich also states that these parallel ranges sink into Mashkel or Hamun-i-Mashkel also drains the scanty waters of Khārān, the homes of the desert bred of Naushérwāni tribes.[50] According to Spate, "these parallel well-sided ranges are higher than in coastal Makrān, but beyond the Siahān range they are flanked on the north along the Afghān border, by the remarkable recent volcanoes of the Chāghai hills. Round this interior drainage basin, and that of the smaller Hamun-i-Lora, the hill is skirted by great coalescing talus-fans. The basins are floored by wide expanses of bare sun-cracked clay, spreads of black oxidised pebbles and shifting reddish dunes; there seem to be terraces possibly indicating former levels of lakes which are now, except in flood time, nothing but salt incrustations with a few marshy patches and fewer of more or less permanent water."[51] Kureshy says, "towards the east of the lower highlands there lies Sulaimān and Kirthar ranges."[52] "The Sulaimān range", according to Spate, "rises to over 11,000 feet, in Takht-i-Sulaimān[53] from the north, and begins to swing westwards until finally their continuation in the Bughti hills are pointing north-west towards the Quetta node."[54] He further says, "the most striking feature of these ranges is the Kirthar wall, rising from 4,000 feet in the south to nearly 8,000 feet in the north and broken only by a few gorges such as those of the Mūla and the Gāj, now useless for any but local traffic, though the former is relatively easy and was used by one division of Alexander's withdrawing army."[55] There are only three plains, according to S. Aḥmad Kāzi, "the Kachhi plain, the plain of Las Belā and the plain of the river Dasht."[56] Explaining the Kachhi plain, Holdich says, "opposite Jacobābād in Sind, a deep identation or bay in the hills disturbs the symmetry of these parallel flextures, and drives them into curves, pushing back the line of ridges as with a wedge, piling them into huge massifs as the apex. This is the Gandava basin or Kachhi Gandava which opens the way to Quetta."[57] Similarly defining the plain of Las Belā, Holdich further says, "between parting of the ways, where the inner lines of ridge and furrow strike off westward from the outer lies the little alluvial state of Las Belā."[58] The north western section of Balūchistān is desert with an area of Inland drainage, dissipating into Hamun's lake that are generally dry.[59]

This geographical picture drawn by eminent geographers shows the exact nature of a part of the western borderland. Although its few passes were used for movements from Irān and Afghānistān, it generally lay outside the main march of the Central Asian hordes.

### The North Western Frontier Hills

The physical features of this region, which is the second part of the western borderland, are unique. There is a great change of direction between the Karākoram[60] and the Hindū Kush which is controlled at a distance by the hidden outlines of the Peninsular block. The long tongue of Afghān territory in the Oxus valley runs west-east along the top of the arch. The northern boundary lies at 16,000-24 feet, actually on the Hindū Kush,[61] the watershed between the Yarkhūn and Chitrāl rivers (220 miles),[62] the general trend is Northeast-Southwest with a Northerly component,[63] falling from the 25,263 feet of Tirich Mīr in the north of Chitrāl to 5,000–6,000 feet in the Moḥmand hills and the Malākand ridge which separates the Swāt valley from the Vale of Peshāwar. The far north is geologically Himālāyan territory, the rocks of upper Chitrāl are Permo-Carboniferous and Jurassic with large areas of gneiss and granite; but all the human links are with the south.[64] This mountain area is gashed by deep narrow valleys – the town of Chitrāl itself, only 30 miles from Tirich Mīr, is under 5,000 feet. "South of the river Kābul", according to Kāzi, "the north east and south west trend is interrupted by the strong westeast line of Safed Koh range,"[65] which reaches 15,600 feet, in its western culmination, Sikārām, falling to 3,000–5,000 feet, in the hills in the angle between Kābul and Landai river and the Indus. 'This trend", according to Kureshy, "is perhaps a continuation of an outer Himālāyan arch from the neighbourhood of the Jhelum gorges by the Kālā Chitta Pahaṛ, south of Attock."[66] The whole area between the Safed Koh and the Tochi river is a tangle of arid hills up to 5,000 feet, with a general west-east trend cut across from northwest to southeast by the more favoured upper Kurram Valley.[67] Spate has the following to say about this area: "In the Bhittāni country between Bannū and Jandola, there seems to be an arcuate arrangement convex to the west; the spurs of north western hills and of the Salt range nearly meet in the Pezū gap between Bannū and Dera Ismā'il Khān."[68] In the extreme south, Wazīristān, the north-south trends of the Sulaimān begin.[69] "The sinuous strikes", according to Spate, "of this area between the Kābul and the Gomal rivers express, the buckling caused by the meeting. . . of the Himalayas, Hindū Kush and other more western systems of crust movement setting in from three sides against the rigid Peninsular mass."[70] And the habitats of the ever-warring tribes whose political fragmentation corresponds to the extremely broken terrain.[71] This study shows that these hills had remained a basic barrier between Central Asia and South Asia. Hence throughout the ancient as well as the mediaeval ages it was a focus of movements and upheavals.

### The Sub-montane Indus Region

According to Spate, "this region consists of a number of sub-divisions: the three plains of Peshāwar, Kohāt and Bannū, all west of the Indus; the Pothwār plateau, east of the Indus; the Salt range marking off the southern boundary of the region both in Bannū and the Pothwār and cut through by the Indus at the head of the remarkable Kālābāgh re-entrant."[72] The physical features of the first sub-division, which is also called the trans-Indus plains, is of unique importance. According to Cornish, "the valley of Peshāwar forms a great semi-circular lowland of some 2500 square miles hill-girt except along the Indus in the south-east."[73] This region is thus included within the north western hill region. According to Spate, "the side advantages of Peshāwar in the valley of Peshāwar are of much importance as the major portion of the Afghān trade passes through it but its primary importance is strategic."[74] Next is the Kohāt valley which lies higher than Peshāwar and Bannū around 1500 feet, and is much broken by west-east limestone ridges.[75] According to Kāẓi, "the Bannū lowland covers some 1700 square miles and it is entirely enclosed by hills except for the Kurram gorge through the Salt range and the Pezū gap[76] in the south, and into this basin flow the Kurram, the Tochi and numerous hill streams, all much braided and broad boulder-strewn channels dry for much or most of the years."[77] These three plains of Peshawar, Kohāt and Bannū provide a few passes for the immigrants of the Oxus valley to move towards the Indus valley. According to Spate, "the Pothwār plateau, another sub-division, covers an area of 4500 square miles at about 1200–1900 feet, and there are a few outlying spurs of the Salt range in the south, and in the north the Khairi-Mūrti and the Kālā Chitta Dhar with a very open cover of wild olives and bush."[78] In this sub-division, the most favoured area is the Chach, a steppe, some 20 miles by 10 along the Indus north-east of Attock, and really a continuation of the Peshāwar valley.[79] Another sub-division, according to Kāẓi, "is the Salt range,[80] which, due to its general structure, would appear to be that of a monoclinal uplift overwhelmed by lateral pressure from the Himalayan orogeny, so that the southern portion has been depressed under the modern Punjāb plains and overridden on low thrusts by the northern part, leaving a truncated monocline with gentle rises from the Pothwār plateau and the great dissected scrap overlooking the plains. The striking horse-shoe bend round the Indus at Kālābāgh may be controlled in part at least by the underground topography of the Peninsular block and eaten out, as it were, by the Indus."[81] Thus the geography of this third division of the western borderland shows that it occupies pivotal position as regards the defence of South Asia. On the whole, examining the physical features of the western borderland, one understands that it is constituted by the extension of the foothills of the sub-Himālāyas has, therefore, proved a natural fortress for South Asia throughout the ages; Consequently it has exercised the greatest influence in shaping the political history of South Asia.

**North Western Passes: Implications**

The difficulties of access from Central Asia through the lowlands of Bactria and the Oxus to the valley of Kābul lie in the passes themselves. "The Hindū-Kush",[82] according to Holdich, "though the natural boundary of South Asia, has been an effective barrier in the military as well as in the commercial sense."[83] The statement of Holdich is partly true because all the invaders from Central Asia hardly crossed these mountains but detoured around them. According to Spate, "the Hindū Kush forms the north-eastern bastion of the great plateau of Irān, comprising modern Afghanistān,[84] Balūchistān and Irān, which flanks the subcontinent to north-west."[85] Holdich also elaborates, "one route for invaders, from the north west, was from the Oxus valley over the Hindu-Kush to Kabul and thence down the Kābul valley to the Indus."[86] He again says, "another route led from Caspian sea to Herat and thence straight through the mountains to Kābul or by an easier detour skirting the Afghān high lands to Qandhār and then through Ghaznī to Kābul."[87] This was the most frequented route in the Pre-Mughal period. Spate also writes, "between Ghaznī and the Indus lies the Sulaimān range, skirting the Punjāb and Sind, and forming the western frontier of South Asia."[88] According to Raverty, "these mountains are as lofty and imposing as the Pīr Panjāl, but these are not so continuous and are traversed by several routes, which, though difficult, are quite practicable for large armies.''[89] These are the outlets, says Lyall, "through modern Afghānistān by which Alexander the Great and all subsequent invaders have descended upon the low country of modern Punjāb. And any one who, after traversing the interminable hills and stony valleys of modern Afghānistān, has been, on surmounting the last ridge, the vast plains of South Asia spreading out before him in the dusky haze like a sea, may imagine the feelings with which such a prospect was surveyed by those adventurous leaders, when they first looked down upon it from the Asiatic highlands.''[90] P. Saran rightly concludes, "throughout the early Turkish period, the western frontier of South Asia remained very vulnerable, because the conquering hordes from Central Asia were always tempted to cross the Indus and invariably threatened South Asia.''[91] In the north-west, there are several passes across the Hindū-Kush, the importance of which has always been observed. It was through these passes that the invaders poured into South Asia from time to time and established themselves. A brief description of these passes is given below:

**Khyber Pass**

This has been the most frequently used pass which begins near Jamrūd,[92] ten and a half miles west of Peshāwār, and twists through the hills for about thirty three miles in a north-westerly direction till it debouches at Dakka.[93] Describing the origin of the Khyber, Dāni quotes Firishta while mentioning its background and says, "the Afghāns made an agreement with the Hindū Shāhī Kings, by which a few villages in Lāmghān were given to them and they in turn agreed to guard the frontier against the inroads of the'Arabs. They built a fort, called Khyber in the Kohistān to Peshāwar.''[94] The mountains of the Khyber pass form indeed the last spurs of the Safed Koh, as that mighty range sinks down into the valley of the Kābul river. This river rises in the Unai-pass in the south-eastern slopes of the Koh-i-Bābā runs past Jalālābad, and through the Khyber pass to Indus, into which it falls near Aṭṭock.[95] According to Raverty, "this pass has always been the great northern route from Kābul into South Asia. The most important points in this route are 'Alī Masjid, eleven miles from Jamrūd; Landīkotal, the summit of the pass, thirteen miles further; and then Peshawar, eleven miles from Jamrūd."[96] Dani says, "Peshāwar's importance was next to that of Ghaznī until it was taken by Sulṭān Ghorī."[97] According to Raverty, "Peshāwar, lay on the main route from Ghaznī to Indus. Prince Jalāl al-Dīn, being chased by Chingiz Khān, passed through Peshāwar and left the city in the charge of Malik Ikhtiyār al-Dīn Muḥammad 'Alī Kharpost."[98] Raverty further adds, "Sulṭān Mahmud Ghazni came through the Khaibar once."[99] Thus the Khyber pass is of great historical importance and may be considered one of the major passes of the western borderland of South Asia.

**Kurram Pass**

The Kurram river lies between the Paiwar Kotal[100] in the west and the border of the Maranzaī in the east.[101] Its maximum length is seventy two miles. Bounded on the north by the Safed Koh, which separates it from Masūdzaī of Kohāt district. According to Raverty, "from Khost to Kurram, the highest peak of the Kurram river appears to have cut a passage opposite Saḍḍa,[102] and which divides the valley into two parts; Upper and Lower Kurram. Rising in the hill near Aḥmadkhel it flows at first south westward and then sharply to the east entering the Agency of Kurram near Kharlāchī and thence flowing east to Kurram Saddu it turns sharply to the south until it reaches Marekhel, where it curves south-east as far as Thal[103] in Kohāt district. This was the route followed by the Sulṭāns of Ghaznī in their campaigns into India.

Tochī Pass

The Tochī pass is the next gateway of the western borderland that deserves attention. Between the Kurram Valley and the Gomal Valley there is a large block of very rough mountainous country known as Waziristan after the turbulent clan which occupies it.[104] "In the north", according to Malleson, "it is drained by the Tochī, and watershed of the Tochī and its affluents drain two glens known as Bīrmal and Shawāl to the west of the country of the Masūdzaī"[105] The Tochī river, entering Wazīristān in a little west of

Maizer and following in a west east direction to join the Kurram, east of Lakkī, also provides a pass in the western frontier. The physical setting of this pass shows its troublesome route and its turbulent tribes which makes a deep impact on its historical role. This valley is the direct route from Multān to Ghaznī, and about nine centuries ago when that decayed town, Ghaznī, was the capital of a powerful kingdom, it must have often heard the tramp of armed men.

**Gomal Pass**

The next route is callled the Gomal pass. According to Lyde, "this route leads from Dera Ismā'īl Khān to Ghaznī and Qandhār."[106] The physical features of this pass indicate that it leads along the valley of the Gomal river through southern Wazīristān from Murtāẓa and Domandī, on the border of modern Afghānistān and Balūchistān to the Afghān plateau.[107] This is, possibly, the oldest trade route on the frontier. This pass was of great importance when Ghaznī or Ghor were the important historical centres. This historical southern pass was used more frequently in mediaeval period. During the British rule this route was also used, as in the words of a British traveller, "the tribes inhabiting along this route have altogether ten thousand camels of burden belonging to them and trade in all the production of India, and large quantities of indigo are exported annually by them from Multān, Bahāwalpūr, Dera Ghazī Khān to Khurāsān and Bukhāra."[108] But with the growing importance of Kābul, Khyber became more and more popular as it directly linked Peshāwar with Kābul.

**Bolan Pass**

Far to the south of the western borderland lies the Bolān pass which connects Qandhar through Quetta and the Bolān to Sakkhar on the Indus.[109] According to Hughes and Buller, "the tract of country which is known for administration purpose by the name of Bolān pass, extends Rindle to Darwāza inclusive, a distance of about sixty miles, and it is bounded on the east by Thal-Chitrālī, now Sibī district, and on the west by the territory under the administration of the Khan of Kalāt. This had immense strategical importance during the British rule because any possible invasion of Khyber and resistance upon the Indus was followed by a rapid advance from the Bolān."[110] This was so only for the British who were strong in the sea.

Besides the physical geography, it is important to note the historical geography of the area so as to understand the shifting frontier in this part due to different historical and political changes in the area during different periods. It is in this background that a proper understanding of the frontier position during the time of Delhī Sultānate would emerge. As the frontier stands between two neighbouring historical phenomena, it is the development of the historical relations that affect the demarcation of the frontier line. Depending upon the stresses and strains of the neighbouring powers, the "frontier" has to bear all the consequences and it is in the changing fate of the "frontier" that the course of history is partly reflected.

The western frontier of the subcontinent bears the definite impress of these historical changes. The physical geography has never been a barrier to historical developments. In fact, it is the history which has dictated partly the course of alignment and allocation. In this connection, it may be useful to remember the two major directions of historical movemens that left their impress on the "frontier". The first is the southern and coastal movement which mainly affected Balūchistān and Sind, but because of the Rajasthān desert on the east, the movement was rather restricted. Further penetration followed the coastal route to Gujarat. It is rare that the desert route [111]was followed. Such a course is seen as far back as the time of the Bronze Age Civilization[112] when inter-relation with Irān and Western Asia established a particular course. Later the Achaemenians[113] kept Makā (properly Makrān) and Hī (n) dū (probably Indus delta country) as their separate provinces. The same relationship is seen in the time of the Sassānians.[114] However, the most clear picture is obtained when the 'Arab commander, Muḥammad bin Qāsim, extended the 'Umayyid' frontier to the Indus delta country.[115] In all these cases the historical pressure from the west pushed the frontier right upto the desert and further advance follows the coastal route.

In contrast to this southern route, the northern one, which is the second directional movement, has been more potent in history. This northern route has had to take into consideration the great Central Afghān hilly massif that, very often, stood as a barrier for the invaders from Central Asia. The easiest passage was to go round the massif from its west, south to east. It is on this route that Herāt, Qandhār and Ghaznī are situated. The last city stands as a great sentinel towards the subcontinent and the plain path facing south-west towards Qandhār has really been the main entrance towards the east, and hence it is appropriately named in history as *Zamīn-i-Dāwar* (or Dar or Darwāzah), i.e. the 'land of entrance.'[116] But the 'frontier' could not remain fixed at Ghaznī. The hilly parts between Ghaznī on the one side and Bannū and Gomal plains on the other have changed lines several times and the line of advance has converged on the Indus. As Qandhār or Ghaznī played a historical role before Kābul came into prominence, this direction of movement has been of great importance. Across the Indus on the east the movement could proceed south of the Salt range towards Multān or the Dīpālpūr. Hence during the mediaeval history these two places were heavily fortified and successively defended. The other direction has been over the Salt range towards Taxilā or modern Rāwalpindī into Pothwar plateau. This northern route joined the invading forces coming from the northern passes right through the Central Afghān massif. Such a route was adopted by Alexander the Great, the Kushāns, the Hūns, Sulṭān Maḥmūd of Ghaznī, Sulṭān Muḥammad bin Sām and Bābar.[117] In this northern line of march the 'frontier' could vacillate from the Hindū-Kush as it was in the time of the Mughals,[118] on the extreme north, to the bank of the Jhelum[119] on the south-east. In between the boundary could be fixed on the Margalla pass, the Ḥasan Abdāl gap, the Indus at Aṭṭock, or even the Khyber pass as it was in the time of the British.

In this northern route the place of the Salt range known as Koh-i-Jūd in the mediaeval age has been unique. It makes a circle enclosing a hilly upland, which is much cut up by glacial moraines and fluvial deposits of big boulders. The Salt range stands like great barriers with their worn-out cliffs and encloses many small valleys, which give shelter to small land or tribes. As the area is rain-fed, and not irrigable, the people are very hardy and warlike and have always chosen the military profession for their living. It is probably because of this character of the people and the nature of the land that the Salt range is remembered in mediaeval history as Koh-i-Jūd, i.e. the hill of Jūd. The significance of the last word is not clear. The only one who has used the similar word is Babar,[120] who talks of a tribe called Jodh. Babar relates them to the Janjū'ā tribe and speaks of their common ancestry. Unfortunately no other historical source records the tribe of Jodh. Everywhere we are told of *Qaba'il-i-Koh-i-Jūd* (قبائل کوہ جودر).[121] It seems that such a reference led Babar to speak of a tribe of Jodh or Jūd. And as Janjū'ā happened to be the chief tribe of the area, this particular tribe was conferred with it on a supposed basis of common ancestry.

However, two points are important. The first is the presence of the important Janjū'ā tribe, so clearly mentioned by Bābar and in all the subsequent Mughal accounts, and the second is the very name Koh-i-Jūd having several tribes ( قبائل). As these tribes are all war-like, it appears that the word Jūd is related to the Sanskrit word *Yuddha*, which means battle or war, and hence *Yudh* meaning 'a fighter, warrior, hero."[122] Yaudha[123] meaning 'warlike', material; and also *Yaudheya* meaning a warrior soldier." If such a connection is acceptable, it is possible to think of Koh-i-Jūd as meaning 'Hill of warriors'. Certainly such a title is suited to the war-like tribe of the Janjū'ā, which, some would like to equate with *Jang-jū*, meaning 'a warrior', though, of course the name, Janjū'ā, is not derived from the latter term.

As the plateau, enclosed in the Salt range, has been a rough country in the western frontier its control by the Sultans of Delhī has been precarious. West of Jhelum right upto Khyber pass there is hardly any fortified place made as an administrative headquarter, directly under the Sulṭāns of Delhī. The cities of Multān and Dīpālpūr played leading roles, both these places lying south of the Salt range. Hence the penetration of the foreign invaders had been through the southern route across Sind Sagar Doāb, which lies south of the Salt range in Mianwalī and Dera Ghazī Khān districts. The tribes, living with in the enclosed area of the Salt range, another side of the Indus river, had an edge over others in so far as they could use their military strength to bargain with both the invaders and the Sulṭāns of Delhī. Such a necessary role was played by these tribes, as will be made clear by the details adduced in the following chapters.

### Tribes of Koh-i-Jūd

Several tribes are known to have been living within this vast zone, the details of which are given elsewhere.[124] However, a comparative study is made here of three important tribes as far as their historical role in this period is concerned. Among them the Janjū'ās have been described least often by name unless we identify them as one of the *Qabā'il* ( قبائل ) of Koh-i-Jūd. As their main location has been in the Salt range all through known history,[125] and it was here that they were found by Babar, ['. . . the non-mention of their name could be construed to imply that they may have been considered politically insignificant as a consequence of their loss of military power early in this region']. A close study of the Janjū'ās and their close neighbours on the north, the Gakkhaṛs, reveals a survival of their traditional history that can be used to understand the background of the history of the Ghaznavids.[126] It is at this time that the Gakkhaṛs claim to have come and lent a helping hand in the Muslim conquest, and hence in line with the spirit of Persian renaissance, at this time they associated themselves with the Kiānis: On the other hand the Janjū'ās claim to be Rājpūts – a feudal oligarchy that appears to have suffered defeat at the hands of Sulṭān Maḥmūd of Ghaznī. The ruling clique, which had strong fortifications at Nandana on the Salt range – exactly the same place where the Janjū'as are known to have been living – is known in history as Hindū Shāhis or Turkī Shāhis.[127] But these terms are only titles, while Turk is only a general name of several peoples that fall within that category at this time. It is, therefore, reasonable to assume that the particular name of the tribe that fought against Sulṭān Maḥmūd of Ghaznī has not been recorded. The only exception is Mas'ūdi who calls the ruler of Gandhāra as J-hj ( جهج ), which comes closest to the word Janjū'ā.[128] If the geographical locaton is of any help, it will not be unreasonable to conclude that the Janjū'ā tribe, with all its association with the Salt range, with their claim to be Rājpūt and with their fate during the early Muslim rule suggests that they have a greater claim to be identified with the main tribe, hidden under the name of Hindū Shāhis, who put up a formidable resistance against the Ghaznavid Sulṭāns, but who ultimately suffered a defeat and fell into oblivion in this period of history. On the other hand the Gakkhars are known to have played a leading role in this period right from the time of Sulṭān Muḥammad bin Sām to the time of the Mughals. They have been the real rulers in the area north of the Salt range, and east of the Indus river.

The region to the west of the Indus was greatly disturbed after the overthrow of the Hindū Shāhis, and particularly after the weakening of the Ghaznavid authority. Still later when the area became practically 'No Man's Land' with the pressure of the Mongols from the west, it appears that there must have been several tribal movements in this hilly zone. Most probably they all belonged to the Pashtūn group. The Pashtūns, according to their tradition, had already received Islām prior to the conquest of Sulṭān Mahmūd of Ghaznī. From the unwritten accounts of the 'Arabs[129] it is known that the 'Arabs penetrated into this part quite early and continued to exert influence for long. It is because of this reason that the Pashtūns associate themselves neither with the Rajpūts nor with any of the Persian heroes, but trace their origin from the Semetic tradition. However, not much is known about these tribes in the Peshāwar valley, until much later the Yousafzai[130] tribe settled in Swāt, Dīr and Mardān districts. On the other hand, the Pashtūn tribes, which were settled in and around the region of Takht-i-Sulaimān,[131] were greatly disturbed by foreign invasions. It is these tribes who moved into the Punjāb and later into India. Among them the Lodis and Sūris became the ruling power in Delhī.

The frontier of the 'India of Old'[132] is an important historical study as it provides a key to the understanding of many ups and downs in the history of the subcontinent. This frontier is unique in the sense that it has acted as a geographic frontier between the people of the subcontinent and those that live outside. And yet the frontier has not remained a separating line like the Great Chinese Wall. The frontier has always remained a 'fluid phenomenon' giving rise to a wide borderland which helped establish relationship between the Indian peoples on the one hand and those that moved around its border. The history of the frontier is actually the history of this borderland, of shifting boundaries, changing loyalties, of an intermediary between the passing phase of Central and Western Asian influences and that which can be called the base of the Indian culture in the Gangetic valley. This is particularly the case with the western borderland which stands out boldly in the perspective of the great movements that characterised the history of Central Asia and caused ripples in the historic movements of Asia. These subsided only when their full pressure was felt on the western borderland. And hence this borderland, alongwith the geographic and cultural orbit of 'India of Old' lay far away to the western gates and within the cultural constraints of the west. In historical terminology the western borderland is really an extension of the heartland of Asia. It has a unique role in establishing historical relations between different cultural zones. But the question to what extent it developed its distinctive character is difficult to answer. In the changing history of man the borderland was influenced more by cultural forces deriving from areas lying to its west. Such influences were incorporated into its way of life and social norms. This constant social pressure rode roughshod over its character. Whenever it tried to consolidate its character by weaving together the cultural trends pressing from across the border, there rose new peoples, new cultures, new movements and new pressures to change the gains. And yet the whole of borderland was not fluid all the time. There have been movements of consolidation which can be understood either in the perspectives of the Central and Western Asia or of India. In this consolidation the local geography and the composition of the local population played a definite role; in what way they played this role is analysed here from the angle of the Delhī Sulṭanate. This, it may be added, is one of the most significant of human experiences in building a Muslim empire in mediaeval India.

## II

The present study is undertaken on the basis of the original sources.[133] They are of two kinds; in the first category are contemporary or near contemporary sources and in the second are indirect sources giving, though minor, but useful information. Their description is given below:

a) **Contemporary Sources**

1. *Tarikh-i-Hind.* Abū Raiḥān Muḥammad bin Aḥmad Al-Berūni Khwārizmī wrote this book in Arabic known as *Taḥqiq ma Li l-Ḥind.* He accompanied Maḥmūd of Ghaznī and lived for many years in South Asia studying the Sanskrit language. Sachau has translated it into English entitled *Al-Berūnī's India* while A.H. Dānī also edited it under the title of *Al-Berūnī's Indica.*[134] This work is useful for studying the geography and old cities of the subcontinent. The section on the Hindū Shāhī kings of Kābul is the original source for the history of the region on the eve of its annexation by the Ghaznavids, and has been much used to elucidate the history of the important Hindū Shāhī Dynasty. The study of Hindū Shāhī Dynasty provides us material on the tribes of Koh-i-Jūd, a gateway between Central Asia and South Asia.

2. *Ādāb Al-ḥarb Wa'sh-shuja'a.* This book was written by Fakhr al-Dīn Mubārak Shāh alias Fakhr-i Mudabbir. It is also called *Ādāb al-Mulūk wa Kifayat al-Mamlūk.* Fakhr-i-Mudabbir was a learned man of repute in the courts of Ghaznī and later of Delhī.[135] The author presented this work to Iltutmish, the Sulṭān of Delhī. The book supplies informative details about the government and military organisation of the newly established kingdom of Delhī. Thus we get a good deal of material relating to this thesis. Sir Denison Ross has edited it.

3. *Al-kāmil Fi't-tarīkh.* This is a general history in Arabic of Shaikh Abū al-Ḥasan bin 'Alī bin Abul Karam Muḥammad bin Ash-Shaibānī known as Ibn al-Aṣīr written in A.D. 1230.[136] This chronicle stands out pre-eminently for the history of Central Asia and the rise of the Shansabānī dynasty of Ghor. Hence it is a useful source of information relating to the Shansabanī conquest of India and the Mongol conquest of Central Asia which took place later. C.J. Tornberg has edited it.

4. *Tāj al Ma'aṣir.* Ḥasan Niẓāmī wrote it and it was partly translated into English by Elliot and Dowson. Ḥasan Niẓāmī was born in

Nīshāpūr.[137] Political turmoil in his native country of Khurāsān induced him to travel and seek asylum elsewhere. Hence he came to India soon after the conquest of Delhī and commenced writing this book in A.D. 1205/A.H. 602 during the reign of Sulṭān Aibak to whom the first part of the work was dedicated. This chronicle contains a narration of the chief military events of the reigns of Sulṭān Muhammad bin Sām and Quṭb al-Dīn Aibak.[138]

5. *Jawāmi Al-ḥikāyat.* Nūr al-Dīn 'Awfī wrote and dedicated it to Niẓām-al-Mulk Junaidī, a wazīr of Iltutmish.[139] The whole work is divided into four parts, each containing twentyfive chapters. It contains in its preface the military operations which Sulṭān Shams al-Dīn Iltutmish conducted against Nāṣir al-Dīn Qubāchah in A.D. 1227.[140]

6. *Ṭabaqāt-i-Nāṣirī.* This book, which was completed in A.D. 1260 and dedicated to Sulṭān Nāṣir al-Dīn Maḥmūd, was written by Minhāj al-Dīn Abū 'Umar bin Sirāj al-Dīn al-Juzjānī. The work discusses the main events of the Sulṭāns of Delhī in great detail.[141] Its great value is in giving first-hand account of the Shansabānī conquests in India and the subsequent history of the new kingdom of Delhī in which the author held very high position.[142] Although the author is known to have lived till the accession of Balban, it is unfortunate that he did not continue his history down to the death of Sulṭān Nāṣir al-Dīn Maḥmūd.[143] Consequently the history of the period from A.D. 1260 to A.D. 1265 is left unrecorded and no subsequent writer has made any attempt to fill this gap. However, this chronicle is of the primary sources providing major material for the present study.

7. *Tārīkh-i-Jahān Gushā.* This work was written by 'Alā al-Dīn Malik also known as Atā Malik Juvainī. The author, who held a very high position under Halākū Khān in Baghdād and hence was able to use the official documents of the Mongols,[144] completed it in A.D. 1260. It is the first detailed and authentic account of the Mongol conquests in Asia. It not only sheds light on the movements of the Mongols in Asia but also provides information about the activities of the fugitive prince Jalāl al-Dīn Khwārizm Shāh in South Asia.

8. *Tārīkh-i-Waṣṣāf.* Abdullah bin Faẓlullah Shīrāzī known as

Waṣṣāf wrote it in A.D. 1300.[145] It is a continuation of Juwainī's history of the Mongols in Asia and begins with the death of Mangū Khān and the accession of Qublai Khān. In the third and fourth volumes it gives some information about India and furnishes other useful material about the relations between Sultān Nāṣir al-Dīn Maḥmūd, the Sultān of Delhī, and Mangū Khān, the Mongol Khān. This information corroborates and supports the account of the official chronicles of Delhī. As a history of the Mongol dynasty, the work is held in the highest estimation. An edition of Waṣṣāf in lithograph was published at Bombay in A.D. 1853.

9. *Tarikh-i-Hind Wa Sind.* This work is also called *Chach Nāmah* which was written by Muḥammad Alī bin Ḥamid bin Abū Bakr. Elliot and Dowson conjecture that this work was translated from the original Arabic by Muḥammad 'Alī Kūfī in the time of Sultān Nāṣir al-Dīn Qubāchah.[146] It describes the usurpation of the Brahman Chach and the 'Arab conquest of Sind. The *Chach Nāmah* is the original source from which Niẓām al-Dīn, Firishta, Mīr Ma'sūm and others have borrowed their accounts of the conquest of Sind. This chronicle provides us information about the geography of various *iqtā's* of Sind.

10. *Rajatarangini.* This is a metrical chronicle of the kings of Kashmīr which was composed by Kalhana about A.H. 545/A.D. 1150.[147] It is the only Sanskrit work that contains some brief references to Sultān Maḥmūd of Ghaznī in the account of a battle fought between Sultān Maḥmūd and Rāja Trilochanpāl of the Hindū Shāhī dynasty. This source also describes the boundaries of the western frontier of the subcontinent adjoining Kashmīr. Sir Aurel Stein has edited and translated it into English.[148]

11. *Sīrat-i-Jalāl al-Dīn Mangbārnī.* It was written by Nūr al-Dīn Muḥammad Zaidārī also known as Shihāb al-Dīn Naṣawī, who was a friend and companion of the fugitive prince.[149] He completed it in A.D. 1240. It supplies valuable detail of the prince's activities in India.

12. *Futūḥ Us-Salāṭīn.* 'Isāmī wrote this work in A.D. 1348.[150] P. Hardy opines that 'Isāmī does his best to fulfil his declared intention of writing an Indo-Muslim work to emulate Firdausi's *Shāh Nāmā.*[151] Regarding the Mongol invasions in particular, he gives

many new facts, which makes his account of these invasions, perhaps, the most definitive available now. His vivid description of battles and sieges makes his book a source of great historical value.[152] 'Isāmī supports and supplements Baranī in many places.

13. *Tārīkh-i-Fīrūz Shāhī*. Zia al-Dīn Baranī[153] completed this work in A.D. 1359, which was dedicated to Sulṭān Fīrūz Shāh Tughlaq. The author claims to have resumed it from where Minhaj al-Sirāj left his account but his book opens with the first year of the reign of Sulṭān Balban. P. Hardy maintains that 'the *Tārīkh-i-Fīrūz Shāhī* shows what happened in the history of the Delhī Sulṭānate between Balban and Fīrūz Shāh Tughlaq when, according to Baranī, 'the content of that advice was regarded or disregarded'.[154] Hence, it covers a fairly long period. Later historians – Nizām al-Dīn Aḥmad, Badāūni and Firishtā–have greatly depended upon Baranī for information as well as inspiration. This book forms one of the main sources for the study of the frontier policy of the Sulṭāns of Delhī as it supplies considerable information especially on Balban's frontier policy as well as other relevant issues.

14. *Khazā'in al-Futūḥ*. Amīr Khusraū[155] wrote this prose history which comprises a detailed account of the victories of Sulṭān 'Alā al-Dīn. It gives some useful information about military organization, mode of warfare and weapons. This work, though it describes the Mongol invasions and Sulṭān 'Alā al-Dīn Khalji's military strategy towards the Mongols, still it is nevertheless also of great help in reconstructing the frontier policy of Sulṭan 'Alā al-Dīn Khaljī as well.

15. *Tārīkh-i-Bīnāgītī*. This work was written by Abū Sulaimān Dāūd bin Abul Fazal bin Muḥammad Fakhr Bīnāgītī in A.D. 1317, who dedicated it to Sulṭān Abū Sa'id, the ninth Mongol king of Persia.[156] Though it purports to be a general history of the world, in reality it is nothing more than an abridgement of Rashīd al-Dīn's *Jāmi'-ut-Tawārīkh*. However, it provides some material which has been found to be useful.

16. *Tārīkh-i-Guzīdā* This book was written by Ḥamdulla Musṭaufī, who completed it in A.H. 730/A.D. 1329.[157] The third and the fourth books deal with the account of the early attempts of the Arabs on the Indian frontier and the history of the Ghaznavids and

the Ghorids. It is also a useful source dealing with the Mongols of Persia and Transoxania.

17. *Jāmi-ut-Tawārikh* (Collection of Histories). This work was written by Rashīd al-Dīn who completed it in A.D. 1310.[158] He was appointed as Wazīr in A.H. 697/A.D. 1297 by Ghāzān Khān and after his death he was maintained in his office by Uljaitū, the successor of Ghāzān Khān. Being a courtier of the Mongols of Persia, Rashīd al-Dīn's history gives a reliable and direct account of the 13th century and the history of Central Asia. Its first part, called *Tārīkh-i-Ghāzānī*, helps to a great extent to understand Ghāzān Khān and his relations with the Delhī empire. Karl Yan edited and published it from London in A.D. 1940.[159]

18. *Tārikh-i-Fīruz Shāhī*. This book dealing with the reign of Sulṭan Firuz Shah Tughlaq was written by Shams al-Dīn bin Sirāj al-Dīn 'Afif.[160] In fact, it is a continuation of Baranī's *Tārīkh* and is carried down to A.D. 1388. It also throws light on the reign of Sulṭān 'Alā al-Dīn Khaljī, and also supplies some information regarding the Mongol invasions. P. Hardy concludes 'the most coherent account which can be given of the work, and probably of 'Afif's other work, is that he aimed to preserve the impression, in the Manāqib idiom, of a golden age for the Delhī Sulṭanate before the calamity of A.H. 801/A.D. 1398-99.[161]

19. *Kitāb al-Reḥla.* Ibn Baṭṭūṭah wrote his travel-account known as *Kitab al-Reḥla* after he had left India.[162] He started his travels in A.D. 1325[163] and reached Sind on the 12th of Sept. 1333. Sulṭān Muḥammad bin Tughlaq appointed him the Qāẓī of Delhī and later then he was sent by him to China as an ambassador in A.D. 1342.[164] This book is of great importance for the study of the history of the Tughlaqs.

20. *Masālik Al-abṣār Fi-Mamālik al-Amṣār*. Shihāb al-Dīn al-'Umarī wrote this book in Arabic. He was born in Damascus in A.D. 1301 and died in A.D. 1398.[165] He was a distinguished scholar of history and geography. The portion dealing with India consists of two parts. In the first part al-Umari describes different aspects of the Indian life and culture during the reign of Sulṭān Muḥammad bin Tughlaq (A.D. 1324-51). The second part is based on earlier works and provides information about the geography of certain

places in India. It is translated into English by I.H. Ṣiddīque and Muḥammad Aḥmad. Shaikh ʿAbdur Rashīd also translated. This work helps us to determine the boundaries and the frontier provinces of Sulṭān Muḥammad bin Tughlaq.

21. *Inshā-i-Māhrū*. It is actually a collection of letters. ʿAin al-Mulk Multānī[166] wrote these letters under the instructions of Sulṭān Fīrūz Shāh Tughlaq. These letters are very useful for the history of Sulṭān Muhammad bin Tughlaq and Sultān Fīrūz Shāh Tughlaq. Shaikh ʿAbdur Rashīd has edited it.[167]

22. *Ẓafar Nama*. Sharf al-Dīn Yazdī wrote it in A.D. 1424.[168] It is a useful book on the victories of Amīr Tīmūr. It provides us a lot of material about the invasion of Tīmūr on India and detail of the frontier *iqṭā'ṣ*[169] of the Delhī Sulṭānate.

23. *Malfūẓāt-i-Tīmūrī*. It is an autobiography of Tīmūr written originally in Turkish and, later translated into Persian by Abū Ṭālib Ḥusain in the 17th century who presented it to Shāh Jahān, the Mughal emperor of India.[170] It not only helps to understand Central Asian affairs but also reveals the political conditions prevailing then in India.

24. *Central Asian Works*. Among the contemporary chronicles of Central Asia, only those works have been consulted which have useful material for this study. Among these are: *Unus-i-Arba'ab-i-Chingizī* or *Shajrā tul-Aṭrāk*, which contains a detailed account of Chingiz Khān and his successors to the time of Timūr.[171] *Maṭlā Al-Sa'dain* or *Majmā Al-Bahrain* written by Kamāl al-Dīn Abdul Razzāq, which, being a history of Trans-Indus countries from A.D. 1334 to 1468, throws light on the story of Tarmānshīrīn[172] and the invasion of Tīmūr; *Raūzātus Safā* written in A.D. 1498 by Muḥammad bin Khwānd Shāh also called Mīr Khwānd, which contains in its fifth volume some valuable information about the Chaghatāis:[173] *Ḥabib us-Siyar* written by Ghiyās al-Dīn bin Hamām al-Dīn also known as Khwānd Mir in A.D. 1523 which is extremely useful for the history of the Mongols because it contains references to Tarmānshīrīn.[174]

### b. Later Works

Some later works, which are particularly useful, are:

25. *Tārikh-i-Mubārak Shāhi*. Yāḥyā bin Aḥmad bin Abdullah Sirhindi wrote this work in A.D. 1413.[175] It supplements Barani in many places and helps in the interpretation of material specially related to the military campaigns of the Sulṭāns of Delhī.

26. *Muntakhab al-Tawārikh*. 'Abdul Qādir Bādaūnī wrote this book in the time of Akbar, the Great.[176] It throws light on several aspects of Sulṭān Muḥammad bin Tughlaq. Though it is a general history, it does shed some light on the external expeditions of Sulṭan Muḥammad bin Tughlaq in particular and other such events in general. Ranking has translated it into English.[177]

27. *Tuzuk-i-Babri*. It is the autobiography of Bābar, founder of the Mughal empire in the subcontinent written originally in Turkish. It contains valuable material on the socio-political conditions of India at the time of his invasion and also provides information about the frontier *iqṭā's* of the Delhī Sulṭāns. During the reign of Akbar, in A.D. 1589, it was translated into Persian. Beveridge has translated it into English.[178]

28. *Tārikh-i-Firishtā*. It was written by Muḥammad Kāsim Hindū Shāh Astrabādi in A.D. 1606[179] and contains a detailed account of the period under review. It is also known as *Gulshan-i-Ibrāhimī* and its text was lithographed by Nawal Kishore Press, Lucknow in A.D. 1864.

29. *Tārikh-i-Sher Shāhī*. 'Abbās Sarwānī wrote it on the orders of Akbar, the Great.[180] Though it is primarily a source for the historical study of the Sūrs, it also gives some accounts of the Gakkhars of the Jūd hills.

30. *Tārikh-i-Dāūdi*. 'Abdullāh wrote it during the reign of Jahāngir.[181] It is a history of the Lodis and is full of ancedotes and praise of the Afghan rulers. It was edited by 'Abdur Rashid.[182]

31. *Kai' Gohar Nāma*. Rai'zāda Dunī Chand Brahman alias Belī wrote it in A.D. 1724. It is the only account of the Gakkhar tribe of the Jūd hills which helps us to understand the early political history of the Gakkhars and their relations with the Sulṭāns of Delhī. Bāqir has edited it [183]

Besides the particular works, there are other general works which deal with the Sulṭāns of Delhī, but do not furnish any major material on the subject under research. They are: *'Ain-i-Akbarī*.[184] *Ṭabaqāt-i-Akbarī*,[185] *Tārikh-i-Masūmi*,[186] *Tārikh-i-Rashidī*,[187] *Makhzan-i Afghānī*,[188] etc. These have, however, also been used to find out more about the frontier policy of the Sulṭāns of Delhī, to verify information obtained from the sources and to reinforce existing knowledge.

## c. Modern Works

In addition to the sources mentioned above, a large number of modern works have also been used. The most significant ones are: Barthold, *Turkestān down to the Mongols*;[189] Howorth, *History of the Mongols*;[190] Holdich. *Gates of India*;[191] Raverty, *Notes on Afghānistān and Baluchistān*;[192] Spate, *India and Pākistān*;[193] Olaf Caroe, *The Pathāns*,[194] etc. These sources provide us a detailed account of the western frontier of the subcontinent. Some of these authorities have served in India and travelled through the western borderland. Thus these modern sources help in understanding the various routes to South Asia. Other modern works have been given in the bibliography.

Various research articles have been consulted to collect more material on the subject under review. For example, U.N. Day, "The North West Frontier of the Sulṭanate during the 13th century", D. Pall, "Alā al-Dīn Khaljī's Mongol Policy", and I.H. Ṣiddique, "Qarlugh Kingdom in the North-Western India during the 13th century" have done relevant research which helps us to understand the western frontier policy of the Sulṭāns of Delhī. Similarly various other scholars in research journals have also discussed the different routes through which Central Asian forces moved towards the west of the subcontinent.

1. 'India of old' is designated here as South Asia. In the text, South Asia is used alternatively with the "subcontinent".
2. He was assassinated on 3rd Sha'ban 602 A.H. *T.N.* (Trans.), pp. 485-6.
3. Khaliq Ahmad Nizami, *Studies in Medieval Indian History*, 'Aligarh, 1956, pp. 243-86.
4. Wolsley Haig, *Cambridge History of India*, Cambridge, 1938, Vol. iv, pp. 345-89.
5. Sultan Muhammad bin Sam is better known as Sultan Shihab al-Din Muhammad Ghori.
6. W. Barthold, *Turkestan down to the Mongol Invasion*, London, 1958, p. 447.
7. Fakhr al-Din gives a list of sixty-four Turkish tribes in which he includes Turk, Ghuzz, Khalji, Tatar etc. *F.M.* (Text) p.47.
8. *T.J.G.*, (Trans.), p. 64.
9. *T.N.* (Trans.), p. 26.
10. *T.J.G.*, (Trans.), p. 61.
11. J.A. Boyle, *Cambridge History of Iran*, London, 1968, Vol. v, p. 369.
12. Boyle, *op. cit.*, p. 370; Peter Jackson, "Mongols in India, 1221-1351", Cambridge University, Ph.D. Thesis, 1976. p. 21.
13. *T.R.*, (Trans.), pp. 6-7.
14. *Ibid.*, p. 15.
15. *Ibid.*, pp. 19-21; *M.T.T.* (Trans.), p. 394.
16. *T.F.S.B.* (Trans.), Elliot, p. 362.
17. *Ibid.*, p. 378.
18. Timur gives reason of his attack against Hindustan that, "My great officers told me that the inhabitants of Hindustan were infidels and unbelievers. . . ." *M.T.T.*, (Trans.), pp. 394-95.
19. In Turkish language, Babar means "Tiger" and in Arabic Babar means "Lion".
20. It is now a small state in Russian Turkistan.
21. *T.B.* (Trans.), p. 190.
22. Sayyid Jamal bin Shirazi, *Tarkhan Nama* or *Arghun Nama* (Eng. tr.) Elliot, Vol. I, pp. 303-4.
23. *T.D.*, (Text), pp. 4-5.
24. K.S. Lal, *Twilight of the Sultanate*, London, 1963, p. 226.
25. Alastair Lamb, *Asian Frontier*, London, 1968, p. 4.
26. Mujtaba Rizvi, *The Frontier of Pakistan*, Karachi, 1970, p. 3.
27. Holdich, *Political Frontier and Boundary Making*, London, 1918, p. 57.
28. *Ibid.*
29. Adami, *National Frontier in Relations to Frontier*, Rome, 1919, p. 3.
30. Norman J.G. Pounds, *Political Geography*, New York, 1963, p. 57.
31. Davis C. Collin, *The Problems of the North West Frontier*, London, 1932, p. 3.
32. Patricia Kendall, *India and the British*, London, n.d., p. 18.
33. Holdich, *op. cit.*, p. 18.
34. O.H.K., Spate, *India and Pakistan*, New York, 1954, p. 467.
35. Patricia Kendall, *op. cit.*, p. 18.
36. Spate, *op. cit.*, p. xxix.
37. G. Gorgon East and O.H.K. Spate, (ed.), "India and Pakistan" in *The Changing Map of Asia*, London, 1950, p. 377.
38. Spate, *op. cit.*, p. 363.
39. Thomas Holdich, *The Gates of India*, Lahore, 1976, p. 6.

40. The hilly north western frontier consists of a singular mountain range, the Sulaimān, which stretches for nearly 300 miles between the Khyber pass in the north and the Bolān pass in the South. A Ṭayyab, *A Political Geography of Pākistān*, Toronto, 1966, p. 8.
41. Spate, *op. cit.*, p. 424.
42. *Ibid.*
43. *Ibid.*
44. Holdich, *op. cit.*, pp. 6-8.
45. Spate, *op. cit.*, p. 428.
46. K.U. Kureshy, *A Geography of Pākistān*, Karāchī, 1977, p. 145. It is situated at the links among Irān, Afghānistān and Baluchistān.
47. *Ibid.*, p. 146.
48. *Ibid.*
49. Ibn Haukal, *Kitāb Sūrat al-Arẓ*, quoted in Holdich, *op. cit.*, p. 6.
50. Holdich, *op. cit.*, pp. 6-7.
51. Spate, *op. cit.*, p. 426.
52. Kureshy, *op. cit.*, p. 145.
53. This name was probably given to the peak by the Mughals. According to one of the popular traditions Sulaimān married an Indian girl and as he was flying back with her he sat his bride on this peak for a moment so that she could look at her homeland. S.K. Karāmat, *op. cit.*, p. 59.
54. Spate, *op. cit.*, p. 425. South of the Gomal river, the Sulaimān mountains run southwards for a distance of about three hundred miles. Kāẓī, S. Aḥmad, *A Geography of Pākistān*, Karāchī, 1964, p. 19.
55. Spate, *op. cit.*, p. 425.
56. Kazi, *op.cit.*, p.40.
57 North of Kachhī, the plains of Sind are faced by a solid wall of rock called Kīrthar. Holdich, *op. cit.*, p. 10; The western boundary of the lower Indus plain is formed by the low Kirthar hills which are only about 7,000 feet. Kāẓī, *op. cit.*, p. 19.
58 Holdich, *op. cit.*, p. 7.
59. Spate, *op. cit.*, p. 425.
60. Karakoram means "black gravel" or a lens of black sand. It is probably much older than the Himalaya. Spate, *op. cit.*, p. 434 To the north of Himalayas in northern Kashmir and Gilgit lies Karakoram range, which is about 20,000 feet, high. Kāẓī, *op. cit.*, p. 15.
61. Spate, *op. cit.*, p. 434; The Hindū-Kush branches off from the Himālāyas at the Pamir Knot. Kureshy, *op. cit.*, p. 10; In the north west of Himalayas lies the Hindū-Kush range which runs from the high plateau of Pāmīr into Afghānistān. Kāẓī, *op. cit.*, p. 15; The name Hindū-Kush is generally used and will be used throughout this study to refer to the entire range of mountains which, starting from the water-parting of the rivers Hunzā and Gilgit, traverses Afghānistān for six hundred miles from east to west.
62 Spate, *op. cit.*, p. 434; It absorbs the drainage of the southern slopes of the Hindū-Kush. Holdich, *op. cit.*, p. 10.
63. Spate, *op. cit.*, p. 435.
64. Holdich, *op. cit.*, p. 10.
65. Spate, *op. cit.*, p. 436.
66. Kāẓī, *op. cit.*, p. 10.
67. It is a peak capped with perpetual snow and ice. *Ibid.*, p. 10.

68. South of the Kābul river is the Safed Koh range which runs east and west. The Safed Koh mountains have an average height of 12,000 feet, and are frequently covered with snow. Kāẓī, *op. cit.*, p. 10.
69. Spate, *op. cit.*, p. 436.
70. *Ibid.*, p. 436.
71. *Ibid.*
72. *Ibid.*
73. W.B. Cornish, *Modern Geography of Asia*, London, 1949, p. 74.
74. Spate, *op. cit.*, p. 449.
75. *Ibid.*, p. 450.
76. Pezū gap between the Bhittanī and Marwat ranges, which connects Tānk and Dera Ismā'il Khān in the south, and a gorge of Kurram near 'Isā Khel in the east. Kāẓī, *op. cit.*, p. 25.
77. North of the Salt range lies the Pothwār plateau, the height of which varies from 1,000 to 2,000 feet above the sea level. *Ibid.*, p. 21.
78. Spate, *op. cit.*, p. 450.
79. *Ibid.*, p. 447.
80. The Salt range starts in the Jogī Tilla and Bakrāla ridges near Jhelum and run southwest to the north of the river Jhelum for more distance before turning north-west to cross the Indus near Kālābāgh. Kāẓī, *op. cit.*, p. 20.
81. *Ibid.* Spate, *op. cit.*, p. 533
82. Explaining the word 'Hindū-Kush', Ibn Battūtah says, "The mountain is called Hindu-Kush because so many slaves, male and female, brought from India die or the passage of this mountain owing to the severe cold and quantity of snow." Ibn Battūtah as cited by Fraser Tytler, *op. cit.*, p. 4.
83. Thomas Holdich, *op. cit.*, p. 32.
84. See for detail, Tytler, *op. cit.*, p. 12.
85. Spate, *op. cit*, p. 439.
86. Holdich, *op. cit.*, p. 115.
87. *Ibid.*
88. Spate, *op. cit.*, p. 441.
89. Raverty, *Notes on Afghānistān and Balūchistān*, Quetta, 1976, p. 590.
90. Lyall, *The Rise of the British Dominion in India*, London, n.d., Vol. vii, p. 1.
91. P. Saran, *Studies in Medieval Indian History*, Delhi, 1952, p. 190.
92. Jamrūd, large village, founded, according to tradition, by Jamshed Bādshāh. The Jamrūd or Jām river or stream, which rises in the Khyber defile near Lāl Bāgh and received two smaller streams south of 'Alī Masjid, flows past the village and fort of Jamrūd, to which gives the name, towards the Nahr-i-Shāhi. Raverty, *op. cit.*, p. 37.
93. Dakka is a village on the south side of the river Kabul and also belonging to Tragzai Mohmands. *Ibid.*, p. 43.
94. A.H. Dānī, *Peshāwar: Historic City of the Frontier*, Peshāwar, 1969. p. 66.
95. G.B., Malleson, *History of Afghānistān*, London, 1978, p. 4.
96. Raverty, *op. cit.*, p.38; Jamrud is ten kos from Peshawar. Maulana Abdul Kadir Khān, "Memorandum of the Route between Delhi and Cābul; *The Punjāb: Past and Present*, April, 1978, p. 25.
97. Dānī, *op. cit.*, p. 67.

98. Its inhabitants are of the Tūrī tribe followers of Pīr-i-Roshan. Raverty, *op. cit.*, p. 81.
99. *Ibid.*, p. 38.
100. Holdich, *op. cit.*, p. 135.
101. The Chamkanī is a small tribe of the Ghevarī Khel. Raverty, *op. cit.*, p. 80.
102. It was the seat of government of the Kurram province during the rule of Muhammad bin Sām. *Ibid.*, *p.* 93.
103. *Ibid.*, Thal, the starting point for this route, is a village in Kohāt district sixty six miles south-west of the station of that name which again is thirty seven miles south of Peshāwar. Malleson, *op. cit.*, p. 556.
104. Holdich, *op. cit.*, p. 136.
105. Malleson, *op. cit.*, p. 37. The regional seat of the Waziris was in Birmal hills west of the Khost range. One of their prince had to take flight because of a blood fued, and settled in Ningrahar. About the close of 4th century they began to move east ward. Varma, B.C., "The Relations of the Mughals with the Tribes of North-west," *I.C.*, October, 1950, Hyderābād, Deccan, p. 251.
106. L.W. Lyde, *The Continent of Asia*, London, 1933, p. 344.
107. The Gomal river must be regarded as highways to Ghaznī. Holdich, *op. cit.*, p. 136.
108. "Route from Dera Ghāzī Khān to Kābul by Deraband and Ghaznee," *J.A.S.B.*, April, 1934, p. 77.
109. Malleson, *op. cit.*, p. 38.
110. Hughs and Buller, quoted by Niāz Ahmad, "The Bolān Pass: Political and Strategical Importance", M.A. Thesis, 1962, Punjāb University, Lāhore, p. 37; See also Raverty, p. 659.
111. For example the advance of Mahmūd of Ghaznī to Somnāth. C.E. Bosworth, *The Ghaznavids: Their Empire in Afghanistan and Easter Iran*, Beirut, 1973, pp.53, 78, 114.
112. R.E.M. Wheeler, *The Indus Civilization*, Cambridge, 1974, p. 38.
113. Ghirshman, *Irān*, Penguin, n.d., p. 258.
114. *Ibid.*
115. R.C. Majumdār, *The Arab Invasion of India*, Lāhore, 1974, p. 21.
116. G. Le Strange, *Land of the Eastern Caliphate*, Cambridge, 1905, p. 345.
117. Majumdār, *op. cit.*, p. 35.
118. Abul Fazl, *'A in-i-Akbari*, (Eng. tr.) Blochmann, p. 170.
119. The boundary between Rājā Porus and the king of Taxila.
120. *T.B.* (Trans.), p. 389.
121. *T.N.* (Text), p. 69.
122. Sir Monier Williams, *Sanskrit-English Dictionary*, Delhi, reprint, 1976, p. 855.
123. *Ibid.*, p. 859.
124. For details see in appendix "A".

*T.B.* (Trans.), p. 389; H.A. Rose, *A Glossary of the Tribes and Castes of the Punjab and North West Frontier Province*, Lāhore, 1978, vol. ii, pp. 353-6.

126. Nāzim, Muḥammad, *Life and Times of Sulṭān Maḥmūd of Ghaznī*, Cambridge, 1931, pp. 92-8.
127. 'Abdur Raḥmān, *The Last Two Dynasties of the Sāhīs*, Islāmābād, 1980, pp. 48, 49, 266.

128. Abul Ḥasan bin 'Alī Hussain bin 'Alī, Mas'ūdī, *Murūj al-Dhahab*, (ed.), 'Abdur Raḥmān, Muḥammad, Cairo, 1316 A.H., Paris, 1916, p. 103, cited by 'Abdur Raḥmān, *op. cit.*, p. 50. Raḥmān equates J-hj with Chhach, a geographical region on the east of the Indus and hence he assumes that the ruler was a Gakkhar. This is hardly possible. Mas'ūdī names the rulers, and not a region. On the other hand the Gakkhars are known to have ruled in Gandhāra. Therefore Mas'ūdī's evidence should be relied upon and the ruling tribe should be identified with Janjūas. Text runs as follow:

.... وبولدهفى هذاالوقت ملك الهند البلهزاملك القنوج من ملوك السند فروزة وهواسم بلد باسم ملوكهم وقد صارت اليوم فى حيزالاسلام وهى من اعمال الولتان ومن هذه المدينة يخرج احدالانهارالتى اذااجتمعت كان نهر (مهران السند' الذى زعم الجاحظ أنه من النيل وزعم غيره انه من جيحون خراسان وفروزة هذاالذى هوملك القنوج هوضدالبلهزاملك القندهار ومن ملوك السند وجبالها ويدعى جحج وهذاسمه الاعم ومن بلاده يخرج النهرالمعروف (بجايد ) وهوأحدالأنهارالخمسة التى منها مهران السند والقندهار سيلاد الدجبوط - ص ١٠٣ مروج الذهب

129. See *Ancient Pākistān*, vol. ii., p. 50.
130. See Raverty, *op. cit.*, p. 192-3.
131. The westernmost ridges, which can be plainly distinguished from Multān, a distance of over eighty miles on a clear day, and the highest of which is snow-capped in winter, are what is commonly known as the range of Mihtar Sulaimān, from its highest peak, called the Takht-i-Sulaimān. . . .'' Raverty, *op. cit.*, p. 5.
132. Various eminent experts have expressed different views regarding the extension of the term 'India' used in ancient times; These are: i) Holdich, who says, "the earliest recognisable term for India Bhāratvarsha (the land of the Bhāratas–a noble warrior tribe which came from the north) applied only to the basins of the Indus and the Ganges." Thomas Holdich, "Introduction" in *The Imperial Gazetteer of India*, vol. i., Oxford, 1901, p. 4; ii) Abdur Raḥmān who opines, "evidently 'Hind' is derived from the names of the river 'Indus' (Sind), the ancient Sindhūs, meaning river or ocean. 'Abdur Raḥmān, *op. cit.*, p. 4; iii) Spate and Basham describe, 'Persians and Greeks extended the name Sindhus – 'the river' – from the Indus, to which it belonged to cover such of the land as they know; and hence the Muslims named Hindustan, properly applied to the area of the most firmly based Islāmic power in north." Spate, *op. cit.*, p. xxvii; A.L. Basham, *The Wonder that was India*, Fontana, 1967, p. 1 fn.
133. It also includes narrative accounts and chronicles of the courtiers of Delhī Sultanate.
134. E. Sachau, *Al-Beruni's India*. London, 1910, vol. iii; A.H. Dani, *Al-Beruni's Indica*, Islāmābād, 1973.
135. I.H. Qureshī, *The Administration of the Sulṭanate of Delhī*, Lāhore, 1944, p. 12.
136. Elliot, *op. cit.*, p. 244.
137. *Ibid.*, p. 207.
138. Ḥabīb Ullah, *Foundation of Muslim Rule in India*, Lahore, 1945, p. 7.
139. Nāzim, *op. cit.*, p. 7.
140. Qureshī, *op. cit.*, p. 12.
141. Ḥabīb Ullah, *op. cit.*, p. 10.
142. *Ibid.*

143 The abrupt ending of his work and his lapsing may be due to his falling out with the powerful Balban. A suggestion to this effect is implied in a remark of Balban recorded in *Saroor-us-Ṣodūr*, a 13th century anonymous compilation of the conversation of a saint Farīd-al-Dīn Mahmūd, the son of a disciple of Mo'in al-Dīn Chishtī of Amjer Balban is reported to have observed that among the Qāzis he had Minhāj, who was one of those who feared neither him nor any others. . . ." Nāẕim, *op. cit.*, p. 144.

144. Ḥabīb Ullah, *op. cit.*, p. 6.

145 Nāẕim, *op. cit.*, p. 9.

146. Elliot, *op. cit.*, p. 131.

147. Ḥabib Ullah, *op. cit.*, p. 6; Nāẕim, *op. cit.*, p. 10.

148 Kalhana. *Rājataranginī*, (tr.) A. Stein, London, 1900.

149. Nāẕim, *op. cit.*, p. 10.

150 *F.S.* (Trans.), p. 618.

151 P. Hardy says that it is interesting to note that a contemporary of 'Isāmi' in Persia, Hamdallah Mustaufī, completed a *Ẓafar Nāma* in A.H. 735/A.D. 1334-5 written in the same mutaqarib metre as the *Shāh Nāmā*, intending it to be a sequel covering the history of Islam: P. Hardy, *Historians of Mediaeval India*, London, 1966, p.97.

152. Khwaja Abdullah Malik 'Isāmī was born in A.D. 1311, and his ancestor Fākhr Malik 'Isāmī had come to India from Baghdad in the time of Iltutmish. So his family had served under the various Sulṭāns of Delhi. 'Isāmī's grandfather was the chief huntsman of Balban.—K.S. Lal, *op. cit.*, p. 365; Dr. P. Hardy concludes that this work offers the students not critical history but historical evidence. P. Hardy, *op. cit.*, p. 110.

153. Barani's father Muaiyyid al-Mulk and his uncle 'Ala al-Mulk held official position under the Khaljis, *Ibid.*, p. 356.

154. P. Hardy, *op. cit.*, p. 25.

155. His original name was Abul Ḥasan who was born in A.D. 1253 (A.H. 651). P. Hardy, *op. cit.*, p. 68.

156. Nāẕim, *op. cit.*, p. 10.

157. Muḥammad 'Azīz Ahmad, *Political History and Institutions of the Early Turkish Empire*, Lahore, 1949, p.14; E.G. Browne (Text and abridged tr.), London, 1910.

158. Elliot, *op. cit.*, vol. iii, p.l. Fazl Ullāh Rashīd al-Dīn bin Imām al-Daulā 'Abul Khair bin Muwāfī al-Daulā, was born in A.D. 1247 (A.H. 645) in the city of Hamadān. His practice of medical art brought him into notice at the court of the Mongol Sulṭāns of Persia.

159. *Tārīkh-i-Ghāzānī*, (ed.,) Karl Yan, London, 1940.

160. 'Afif was born in A.D. 1350 and served under Sulṭān Fīrūz Shāh Tughlaq. Lal, *op. cit.*, p. 367.

161. 'Afif certainly wrote after the sack of Delhi by the forces of Amīr Timūr, but of his own life at the time, the *Tārīkh-i-Fīrūz Shāhī* reveals nothing but that he was an old man. P. Hardy, *op. cit.*, p. 40.

162. He was a native of Tangiers, Morocco. K.S. Lal, *History of the Khaljīs*, Allahabad, 1950, p. 365.

163 *Ibid.*

164 Gibb, *op. cit.*, p. 26.

165 Shihab al-Din al-'Umari, *A 14th C. Arab Account of India under Muhammad bin Tughlaq*, (ed.), I.H. Siddique and Q.M. Ahmad, 'Aligarh, 1971, p. 7; Shaikh 'Abdur Rashid *et al.*, (Eng. Tr.) Lahore, 1943.

166. He served under Sultan Muhammad bin Tughlaq and Firuz Shah. Lal, *op. cit.*, p. 371.

167. It was written in Persian. Agha Mahdi Husain, *op. cit.*, p. 584; *Insha-i-Mahru* (ed.), Shaikh 'Abdur Rashid, Lahore, 1967.

168. Agha Mahdi Husain, *op. cit.*, p. 584. It was written in Persian.

169. See Glossary.

170. Husain, *op. cit.*, p. 581.

171 It was written in the middle of 15th century and literally the genealogical tree of the Turks. Habib Ullah, *op. cit.*, p. 16.

172 Abdur Razzaq was also known as Samarqandi. Nazim, *op. cit.*, p. 10.

173 *Ibid.*

174. *Ibid.*

175. Lal, *op. cit.*, p. 369. Manuscript of the *Tarikh-i-Mubarakshahi*. belonged to Sir Jadunath Sarkar.

176. Agha Mahdi Husain, *op. cit.*, p. 580.

177. *M.T.B.* (Trans.)., p. 140.

178. *T.B.* (Trans.), p. 80.

179. Agha Mahdi Husain, *op. cit.*, p. 581; *T.F.* (Trans.).

180. Elliot, *op. cit.*, p. 10.

181. Shaikh 'Abdur Rashid, (ed.), Aligarh, 1954.

182. *Ibid.*

183. *K.G.N.* (Text), Lahore, 1964.

184. Abul Fazl, *Ain-i-Akbari*, Calcutta, 1877.

185. Ahmad Nizam al-Din Bakhshi, *Tabaqat-i-Akbari*, Calcutta, 1913.

186. Mir Ma'sum, *Tarikh-i-Ma'sumi*, Poona, 1938.

187. Mirza Muhammad Haider Daughlat, *Tarikh-i-Rashidi*, London, 1885.

188. Niamat Ullah. *Tarikh-i-Jahani wa Makhzan-i-Afghani*, London. 1836.

189. W. Barthold, *Turkestan down to the Mongol Invasions*, London, 1958.

190. H. Howorth, *History of the Mongols*, London, 1886.

191. Thomas Holdich, *The Gates of India*, Quetta, 1977.

192. H.G. Raverty, *Notes on Afghanistan and Baluchistan*, Quetta, 1976.

193. O.H.K. Spate, *India and Pakistan*, London, 1954.

194. Olaf Caroe, *The Pathans*, London, 1958.

## Chapter II

# THE FRONTIER POLICY OF THE MAMLŪK–I
# (A.D. 1206 – 1236)

The western border of South Asia has been defined in the previous chapter. It has been shown that the position of the Indus river vis-a-vis India remained a bone of contention. However, in the time of the Ghaznavids and Ghorids the Indus became a part of their Central Asian empire.[1] The later Ghaznavids were confined to the Punjāb and had to face the advance of the Ghorids from the west.[2] As a result, Sulṭān Shihāb al-Dīn Ghorī led several expeditions to the subcontinent, and after successive victories he appointed his Turkish slaves as his deputies in various parts of his newly conquered territories. According to Minhāj, "the Sulṭān appointed his Turkish slaves Tāj al-Dīn Yaldūz at Karmān[3] and Sankūran;[4] Nāṣir al-Dīn Qubāchah at Uchh[5] and Multān; and Qutb al-Dīn Aibak at Delhī."[6] All these Maliks of Sulṭān-i-Ghāzī[7] were responsible to the Sulṭān for their action. Minhāj has recorded that. "On his [Sulṭān's] return from India to Ghaznī in A.H. 588/A.D. 1192, Sulṭān Shihāb al-Dīn Ghorī had urged on Aibak to deal with the Hindū Rājās and to make further conquests in India."[8] Thus Aibak established himself in Delhi early in A.H. 589/A.D. 1193, and made it a spring-board for further conquests. The Ghorid empire thus extended eastward to Delhī and beyond in the Gangetic valley. As long as the Indus frontier was within the Ghorid empire, which was strong enough to hold its position in Central Asia, Delhī was safe and its frontier was well protected. With this domination of the Ghorids over Delhī, its political position changed. It was now exposed to the variable political forces of Central Asia, which, later on, affected its fortune. During the life-time of Sulṭān Shihāb al-Dīn Ghorī, the political authority of the Ghorid Sulṭān was recognised by all his Maliks in Hind and Sind. His Turkish Maliks did not manifest any hostilities among themselves and maintained friendly relations through matrimonial alliances. As Minhāj has stated, "By the command of Sulṭān-i-Ghazī, a daughter of Yaldūz was given in marriage to Aibak, and another daughter was married to Malik Nāṣir al-Dīn Qubāchah."[9] When Sulṭān Shihāb al-Dīn died, his Turkish Maliks thought of increasing their individual power. Each one of them claimed his right to sovereignty in his possessed *iqṭā'*[10] Nay, each went ahead to challenge the other's power and possible claim to the throne, and thus rivalrly developed among them. Consequently, the unity of the Ghorid empire was jeopardised. In actual fact, these Maliks received letters of manumission from Sulṭān Mahmūd of Ghor[11] and they became defacto and dejure rulers in thier respective territories. Yaldūz[12] came to Ghaznī and occupied it, Aibak declared himself as sovereign over northern India's territories of his late master, and Qubāchah[13] became independent in Sind.[14] As a consequence of the break-up of the Ghorid empire after the death of Sulṭān Shihāb al-Dīn Ghorī, the frontier issue once again cropped up. The break-up occurred because the Sulṭān had no male child and his empire of Ghaznī and Hindustān consequently devolved upon his Turkish salves known as Mū'izzī Maliks on his death. Minhāj refers to a talk of a bold courtier with the Sulṭān:

> To a sovereign like you, sons are necessary to succeed your vast empire, "Other kings have only a few sons", the Sulṭān replied, "But I have several sons, namely my Turkish slaves, who will rule my kingdom in my name after I am dead and gone.[15]

## I

## The Frontier Policy of Sulṭān Quṭb al-Dīn Aibak (A.D. 1206–10)

Quṭb al-Dīn Aibak[16] was the most capable Turkish slave of Sulṭān Shihāb al-Dīn Ghorī who left Aibak as his representative in India when he returned to Ghaznī in A.H 588/A.D. 1192. After capturing the Indian forts and cities Aibak was in the good books of his master and his rank was raised as mentioned in *Tāj-ul-Mā'aṣir*, which records, "After capturing the Indian forts and strongholds Aibak reached the capital of Ghaznī, where he enjoyed the happiness of kissing hands and received other ranks of special favour before the great Throne and the degree of his rank was raised above all other chiefs of the world."[17] After the death of the Sulṭān, Aibak held supreme and undisputed power in the subcontinent from 17 Ziqa'da 602/17 Marc1206.[18] Later his defacto position was legalised when, as Hasan Niẓāmī records, "Sulṭān Maḥmūd, a successor of Sulṭān Shihāb al-Dīn Ghorī, sent all the insignia of royalty, a throne, a canopy, standards, drums, and the title of king to Aibak in A.H. 605/A.D. 1208.[19] This historical evidence confirms that Aibak's political power was established in the subcontinent.

This infant kingdom of Delhī faced many critical problems: Firstly, there was the internal power of strengthening the power of Delhī; Secondly there was the imminent danger of the forces that was pressing hard from Afghanistan and Central Asia to push down towards the Indo-Gangetic plain. Qutab al-Dīn Aibak devised his frontier policy to meet these challenges.

### a) A Policy of Hit and Advance

Quṭb al-Dīn Aibak followed a defensive policy but one which was bold enough to deal with the external menace which threatened the western frontier of his empire. He had to deal with Khwārizm Shāh who was forcing Yaldūz to advance eastwards against him.

i) AIBAK AND YALDŪZ. Tāj al-Dīn Yaldūz was one of the devoted Turkish slaves of Sulṭān Shihāb al-Dīn Ghorī. Minhāj says, "During the lifetime of the Sulṭān he attained authority and power, and the Sulṭān conferred upon him the government of the *iqṭā's* of Karmān and Sankūran. Every year the Sulṭān would make a halt in Karmān on his expedition into Hindustān."[20] This historical evidence also suggests that the Sulṭān always used this Kurram route on which Karmān near modern Pārāchanār was situated, when he advanced towards the subcontinent. Hence these *iqṭā's* held by Yaldūz were of great strategic importance. Minhāj further records:

> Towards the end of his reign and his last expedition to Hindustān in A.H. 602/ A.D. 1205, the Sulṭān Shihāb al-Din Ghori halted at Karmān. Yaldūz welcomed the Sulṭān in the usual manner by presenting a thousand suits for him, out of which one was selected by the Sulṭān himself. The Sulṭān was pleased to grant a special robe of honour and a black standard for his troops, thus signifying his wish to make him heir-apparent to the throne of Ghaznī.[21]

This evidence confirms that Yaldūz could be a ruler of Ghazni after the death of the Sulṭān. Hence Yaldūz occupied Ghazni soon after the passing away of his master. He also claimed his right over the Indian territories of his late master which probably annoyed Quṭb al-Dīn Aibak, his powerful rival in the subcontinent. This was understandable since it was intolerable for Aibak to acknowledge him as his master as he was an equal Turkish Malik during the lifetime of Sulṭān Shihāb al-Dīn Ghorī.

Further there arose hostility between Aibak and Yaldūz on account of Yaldūz's bad relationship with his benefactor, Sulṭān Maḥmūd, as mentioned by Alfi who records, "when Yaldūz gained a firm hold of his authority over Ghazni Sulṭān Maḥmūd sent him a message from Feroz Koh, requesting him to coin the money and read the *Khuṭbah* in his name. Yaldūz sent a reply saying, "That when Mahmūd should send him a deed of manumission, he would do so, otherwise, he would give his allegiance to whomsoever he chose. As Mahmūd was not safe from being assailed by Khwārizm Shāh, and fearing lest Yaldūz should go over to him, he sent the required deed of manumission to Yaldūz."[22]

This conditional recognition not only shook the confidence of Sulṭān Maḥmūd but also disillusioned Aibak. The latter had great respect for Sulṭān Mahmud, a successor of his late master Sulṭān Shihab al-Din Ghorī. It was his supreme position in Ghor that stood as a defence to his somewhat precarious position in the Gangetic valley. But Yaldūz's action created a new problem for him in his frontier. Hence it was but natural that Aibak should hold the authority of Sulṭān Maḥmūd and work for the continuation of the old order. The turn of events is explained in the action taken by Abī Dakūr,[23] a noble of Sulṭān Maḥmūd in Kābul by Alfī: "When Abī Dakūr reached Kābul after his desertion of Jalāl al-Dīn 'Ali, Quṭb al-Dīn Aibak's emissary reached him, which emissary he had first despatched to Tāj al-Dīn Yaldūz reproaching him for his conduct towards his benefactor, Sulṭān Maḥmūd, and exhorting him to discontinue it. This emissary was directed to ask Abī Ḍakūr to cooperate with him [Aibak] and in case Yaldūz did not hold his hand and repent for his acts, that Abī Dakūr should assemble his troops and assail Ghaznī and wrest it from Yaldūz."[24]

Thus Aibak took his first action against Yaldūz by joining hands with Abī Ḍakūr and trying to weaken the power of Yaldūz. In this way Aibak desired to secure his position in the frontier. But this act of Aibak annoyed Yaldūz as well as Khwārizm Shāh and his ally Jalāl al-Dīn, the Sulṭān of Bāmiān, whom Abī Dakūr had deserted. As a result, Aibak was brought face to face with Khwārizm Shāh.

ii) KHWĀRIZM SHĀH AND AIBAK. During the last decade of 12th century, the tension between Khwārizm Shāh and the Ghorids reached its height. The Shāh took advantage of the situation when Sulṭān Shihāb al-Dīn Ghorī died and as a result there was a contest for the throne between Sulṭān Mahmūd, son-in-law of the late Sulṭān, and Bahā al-Dīn Sām, his sister's son. According to Minhāj, "for the successor to the throne of the Ghorid empire, the Turkish troops were in favour of Sulṭān Maḥmūd, whereas Ghorid commanders stood for Bahā al-Dīn Sām of Bāmiān, and then after the latter's death, his two sons."[25] Ultimately Sulṭān Mahmūd succeeded to the throne. The new Sulṭān being weak in comparison to his predecessors, was never able to establish his direct control over the eastern fringes of the Ghorid empire. Relations between him and Yaldūz became strained. Ibn al-Asīr writes, "Yaldūz squashed the Bāmiān Ghorid's pretentions to rule in Ghaznī but only reluctantly and tardily did he recognise Sulṭān Maḥmūd. The Sulṭān dared not leave Ghor and march to Ghaznī, and hence in A.D. 1207 he called in the Shāh of Khwārizm and Ḥussain bin Kharmil, the governor of Herāt, to expel Yaldūz from Ghaznī and enforce his rights there."[26] Khwārizm Shāh, taking advantage of the weak position of Sulṭān Mahmūd in relation to Yaldūz, invaded Ghaznī. He occupied it after putting to death several of the Ghorid Amīrs. According to Minhāj, "Khwārizm Shāh made over his new acquisition to his son, Jalal al-Dīn Mangbarnī, and a Khwārizmian noble was installed there at Ghaznī as his governor and the Sulṭān himself returned to Khwārizm."[27]

Thus the Shāh established his own authority at Ghazni and for the first time Aibak now faced Khwārizm Shāh directly since he had now established himself close to Aibak's frontier. It was absolutely necessary that he should take some measures as a precaution to defend himself. This could be done by cementing the old friendly relations with Sulṭān Maḥmūd, who appears to have approached Aibak for throwing out the forces of the Shāh from Ghaznī. Aibak feared that after establishing his power at Ghaznī, the Shāh could march towards the frontier of the subcontinent, and his advance could occur at any moment. To make matters even worse for Aibak, Yaldūz invaded and occupied Lāhore after fleeing from Ghaznī. The situation in the north-west had, thus, forced Aibak to resist Yaldūz from acquiring a footing in Lāhore. Quṭb al-Dīn Aibak, soon after, marched against Yaldūz with all available troops of Hindustān, and a battle took place between them in the Punjāb,[28] in which Yaldūz was defeated and compelled to retire towards his former possessions of Karmān and Sankūran after a defeat.

The Map No. 3 shows that Aibak was determined to safeguard the western frontier of his empire from the onslaughts of the Central Asian powers. Consequently Yaldūz was forced to leave Lāhore where Aibak established himself and watched the movements on his western frontier.

Aibak now realised that it was imperative to forestall the Shāh and occupy Ghaznī. Minhāj states: "A party of its citizens also suddenly felt an affection for him and sent an invitation. Aibak then moved to Ghaznī and occupied it in A.D. 1208 after driving out the governor of Jalāl al-Dīn Mangbārnī."[29] Aibak's conquest of Ghaznī was, thus, in response to the request of the citizens of Ghazni who had leagued up together and wanted Aibak's help. Minhāj further tells us that, 'Aibak here at Ghaznī received a letter of manumission from Sulṭān Maḥmūd.'[30] This fact also suggests that Aibak's advance to Ghaznī was partly undertaken in league with Sulṭān Maḥmūd in order to drive out the Shāh's forces. The Sulṭān on his part might have joined in the venture with a view to rewarding Aibak's loyalty on the one hand and on the other hand, probably to enlist the sympathies of the citizens of Ghaznī in favour of Aibak. Anyhow, this advance of Aibak is a proof of his intrepid attitude to meet the challenge from Central Asia and to defend his territory by pushing himself forward to Ghazni and following a forward policy.

iii) YALDŪZ AND AIBAK. It has been shown earlier how Yaldūz was forced to come towards Lāhore and how Aibak defeated him in the Punjāb. After occupying Ghaznī, Aibak remained there only for a period of forty days. Then the citizens of Ghaznī developed a dislike for his rule. Various historians have ascribed this antipathy to different causes. Firishtah has stated that it was due to Aibak's indulging in wine and the bad reputation of his soldiers.[31] Habīb-ullah, a modern historian, has opined that the attacking of Ghaznī by Aibak was taken in haste and was militarily ill-supported [32] The opinion of Ḥabībullah seems to be nearer the truth as it has been found after re-examining these charges that Aibak had no direct association with the citizens of Ghaznī, who did not accept him as their ruler and did not support him later. Anyhow, the inhabitants of Ghaznī secretly contacted Yaldūz who was again restored to favour and requested to come back.[33] Yaldūz reoccupied Ghaznī and Aibak, thus, retreated to Lahore by way of 'Sang-i-Surkh'. Here it is essential that 'Sang-i-Surkh' must be identified. Raverty observes, "the lower and easternmost ranges of Sulaimān are styled as 'Koh-i-Surkh' due to a yellowish red colour. The Pushto and Tājik words for red are constantly occurring in these parts; namely *Sūr* in the former language, and *Surkh* in the latter. The Turkish equivalent of 'Koh-i-Surkh' would be *Kanzil Tāsh* or *Ulān Tāgh*, which is sometimes used. On the eastern or Indus side we have the addition of the Hindī names for both ranges, red being *ratta*, while farther south again, we have the same reference to the peculiar colour of red ranges."[34] It is clear that 'Koh-i-Surkh' or 'Sur Ghar' or 'Ulān Tāgh' runs most regularly outside the eastern and western slopes of the range of Mihtar Sulaimān. A.H. Dānī further adds that, "the 'Koh-i-Surkh' dies away towards the Indus in the plains of the Kuchchī while in the south-west direction in the neighbourhood of Qandhār, the 'Koh-i-Surkh' dies away in the red sandy tract towards the Arghandāb river and Hilmand."[35] This description of Koh-i-Surkh, a red mountain, proves that it was situated in the Gomal route. Hence Aibak must have used the Gomal route via

'Sang-i-Surkh' when he advanced to Ghaznī as well as on his return march to Hindustān. This route was the nearest and easiest from Ghaznī to Lāhore as compared to the Kurram route where his rival Yaldūz was already in possession of the strong *iqṭa's* of Karmān and Sankūrān. The route has been explained in Map No. 3.

This forward step taken by Aibak, though temporary, forced him to realise the gravity of the recurring threat from Central Asia to the north-western frontier of his empire. Soon after Aibak's retreat to Lāhore, Central Asian politics took a new turn. Ibn al-Asīr says, "The nobles of Khwārizm Shāh invaded and captured the dominions of Ghor from Sulṭān Mahmūd in A.D. 1208 "[36] Raverty further writes, "Sulṭān Mahmūd was forced to acknowledge the suzerainty of Sulṭān Muhammad, who accepted it and despatched valuable presents to the Sulṭān."[37] This acknowledgement of the superiority of the Sultān Mahmūd remained at Ghor as a mere vassal of Khwārizm Shāh till his assassination which, according to Minhāj, "took place in A.H. 607."[38] Later on, Yaldūz also made reconciliation with the Shāh.[39] This alliance of Yaldūz alarmed Aibak who decided to shift his head quarter from Delhī to Lāhore: Henceforth, according to Raverty, "Aibak remained at Lāhore until A.H. 607/A.D. 1210, when he met the accident which caused his death."[40] Aibak's stay at Lāhore suggests that he was determined to safeguard his western frontier from the Central Asian invaders.

## b) A Policy of Matrimonial Alliances

Another former slave of Shihāb al-Dīn Ghorī, Nāsir al-Dīn Qubāchah, the governor of the *iqṭās* of Uchh and Multan, "married a daughter of Yaldūz,"[41] on the orders of Ghorī. As Ghorī did not assign the *iqṭā's* of Lahore to any other slave during his lifetime, so after his death, it became a bone of contention between Yaldūz and Aibak. Soon Aibak laid his claim over this *iqṭā'* considering it a part of his own dominion. As this *iqṭā'* was situated on the north-east of Qubāchah's territory, so naturally he was, understandably, interested in it. Minhāj writes: "Qubāchah was the son-in-law of Aibak because of marrying his two daughters one after the other."[42] As a token of these matrimonial relations, Qubāchah was able to have close friendship with Aibak. Minhāj further records: "Yaldūz being driven out from Ghaznī by the Shāh, invaded Lāhore and defeated Qubāchah who was holding it nominally on the part of Aibak."[43] This evidence confirms that Aibak had already conferred upon Qubāchah the government of Lāhore. Though contemporary chronicles have not mentioned any reasons for this, it was presumably given to Qubāchah as a token of his family relations on the one hand, and on the other because Aibak was, at that time, engaged in establishing his power at Delhī. Yaldūz's attack on Lāhore certainly strained matrimonial relations between him and Qubachah. At the same time, as has already been mentioned, Aibak came forward and defeated Yaldūz in the Punjab. It cannot be said with certainty – since no contemporary source furnishes any information – whether Qubachah took part in this battle on the side of Aibak or not. However, it does not seem that Qubachah might have aided Aibak in the battle because it was fought in his territory and, moreover, it was waged in retaliation to Qubāchah's defeat. Thus Aibak was successful in wooing Qubāchah and consequently in maintaining a policy of friendship. But later Aibak himself remained at Lāhore[44] and most probably controlled it personally. Qubāchah lost his position in Lāhore.

In conclusion the frontier policy of Sulṭān Quṭb al-Dīn Aibak may be said to be bold and forward looking in response to the changes that were taking place in the western horizon. Firstly, the rivalry of Yaldūz, and, secondly, the occupation of Ghaznī by the Shāh of Khwārizm who had already swallowed the whole of Iran and Central Asia, and was now casting covetous glances at the subcontinent, were the determining factors. Aibak addressed himself to the task in all seriousness. To meet the danger from the north-west Aibak followed the advanced frontier policy. He not only smashed Yaldūz's hostile designs but also marched on Ghaznī. His advance, though, short-lived, was a powerful deterrent to any Central Asian force, to advance towards the north-west of the subcontinent. This threat from Central Asia also compelled Aibak to maintain friendly relations with Qubāchah, the ruler of Sind, on the one hand, and on the other to stay at Lāhore for the rest of his life.

II

## The Frontier Policy of Sulṭān Shams al-Dīn Iltutmish (A.D. 1210–36)

Shams al-Dīn Iltutmish occupied the throne of Delhī in A.H. 607/A.D. 1210.[45] At this time, Iltutmish had to confront very serious external and internal problems, which arose as a consequence of far-reaching changes in Central Asia and which affected directly the fortune of the Delhī empire. Sulṭān Maḥmūd, the ruler of Ghor, died in A.H. 607/A.D. 1210.[46] Tāj al-Dīn Yaldūz, the ruler of Ghaznī, though he acknowledged the suzerainty of Khwārizm Shāh, was forced into India in A.H. 612/A.D. 1215-6.[47] In the same year the Bāmiān line of Ghorids was extinguished, the whole of the Ghorid territory was annexed to the Khwārizmian empire. According to Juzjāni, "The countries of Herāt, Ghor, Gharchistān[48] and Sijistān[49] to the frontiers of India were now added to the Sulṭān's domains. . . and the Sulṭān's son Jalāl al-Dīn, was installed there as a governor."[50] Consequently, the territories of Khwārizmian empire extended up to the west of the Indus. But Khwārizm Shāh did not advance towards India, because in the words of Juvainī, "in the treasury at Ghaznī which had been set up by Sulṭān Shihāb al-Dīn Ghorī, there were discovered letters-patent from the Holy Seat of the Caliphate wherein the Ghorids were incited to attack the Sulṭān of Khwārizm. . . . The Sulṭān's anger with the Supreme Dīvān was increased hereby for he now knew that the hostility of the Ghorids had been largely due to the incitement of the Seat of Caliphate. [51] These remarks of Juvainī reveal that Khwārizm Shāh came to know about his real enemy and hence he returned to Samarqand instead of advancing towards India. Thus, Iltutmish was not disturbed for some time by the advance of Khwārizm Shāh. In the succeeding years A.D. 1218-21, there arose a conflict between Khwārizm Shāh, and the Mongols. Soon the Mongols under Chingiz Khān rolled up the vast Khwārizmian empire Khwarizm Shāh was driven to find shelter in the Caspian coast and his crown-prince, Jalāl al-Dīn, came to India for asylum. As a result, the Mongols captured and started ruling over vast areas of Central

Asia which also posed a grave danger for the defence of the Delhī empire. Thus, these political upheavals in Central Asia had serious consequences for Delhī, and externally Iltutmish now had to bear the brunt of three rival forces of Central Asia. The first of these forces was that of Yaldūz who had arrived into the Punjab after his flight from Ghaznī; second, one was that of Jalāl al-Dīn Mangbārnī who had sought refuge from the Mongols in the subcontinent; and the third was that of the Mongols who, led by the Chingīz Khān, had now appeared on the Indus in pursuit of Mangbārni.[52] On this side of the Indus, Iltutmish had to face the obstinate attitude of Qubāchah and the hostile designs of the tribes of Koh-i-Jūd. Thus, Iltutmish found himself in a critical situation which not only made his frontier insecure but also threatened the very existence of the Delhī kingdom. Being a wise diplomat, Iltutmish dealt with these difficult issues courageously, and, finally, emerged victorious.

i) ILTUTMISH AND YALDŪZ. The immediate frontier problem, which Iltutmish had to face, was created by the arrival of Yaldūz in the Punjāb. Describing the early relations between Iltutmish and Yaldūz, Minhāj records, "On the death of Aibak and dethronement of Ārām Shāh, Yaldūz reasserted his sovereignty of the entire Indian possessions of the Ghorids and their officers and sent a canopy of state and durbash to Iltutmish."[53] At this critical juncture, Iltutmish accepted the canopy of state—a symbol of conciliation—sent by Yaldūz. There could be two reasons for adopting such a policy. Firstly, Yaldūz was powerful, and secondly, such recognition would tend to make the Mu'izzī chiefs and Turks more compliant to his rule. In fact, during the initial years of his rule, Iltutmish intended to devote his attention towards the consolidation of the empire rather than to the power-struggle with Yaldūz. In the meantime, Khwārizm Shāh invaded and occupied Ghaznī, Bāmiān[54] and Khurāsān.[55] Soon after this Shāh despatched an agent to Yaldūz, intimating that, "if he would acknowledge his suzerainty, and stamp the coins with his name and pay him a yearly tribute, he would be left in quiet possession of Ghaznī, otherwise he must be prepared to meet his troops."[56] This historical evidence shows that Khwārizm Shāh had warned Yaldūz giving him the alternatives of either accepting his suzerainty or war with the Shāh. This was a matter of great concern and, according to Minhāj, "Yaldūz called a council of his Amīrs to consider this demand of the Shāh. Qutlugh Tigīn, *Amīr al-Umarā* and one of the late Sulṭān Ghori's slaves, advised that the Sulṭān's demands should be acceded to, as it was impossible for them to resist Sulṭān Muḥammad Shāh of Khwārizm."[57] Yaldūz accepted the advice and dispatched befitting presents for the Shāh as an appeasement gesture signifying his acceptance of the Shāh's terms.[58] Yaldūz was, thus, able to continue his hold over Ghaznī. "But soon", according to Raverty, "there arose a conflict between Yaldūz and his *Amīr-i-Shikār,* Malik Nāṣir al-Dīn, when Yaldūz was on his return to Ghaznī from Sīstān. Malik Nāṣir al-Dīn was overthrown and he retired towards Khwārizm."[59] Relations between Yaldūz and Khwārizm Shāh were once again strained. Minhāj records, "after a period of forty days Sulṭān Khwārizm Shāh marched with an army from the side of Tukhāristan,[60] and advanced towards Ghazni, and his troops suddenly and unexpectedly seized the frontier route leading into Hindustān, towards Gardez[61] and Karāhah[62] Daṛah (کراهه دره). Sulṭān Yaldūz took the route towards Hindustān by way of 'Sang-i-Surkh',[63] and reached Lāhore."[64] Consequently, Khwārizm Shāh occupied Ghaznī. Using the Gomal route via 'Sang-i-Surkh', Yaldūz reached the neighbourhood of Lahore and fought a battle with Qubāchah, the ruler of Sind, and defeated him. Taking possession of Lāhore, Yaldūz soon made some demands upon Iltutmish which the latter was unwilling to accept. According to 'Isāmi, these demands were: 'Yaldūz sent to the renowned Iltutmish a parasol set with pearls, and wrote him a charming letter saying:

> O wise and enlightened man! you should rule over Hindustān and capture it to the liking of your friends. Our frontier stretches to the region of Lahore where we have numerous troops. You must not bring your army to this side; make a capital on that side. You can march your army upto the rough sea and may forcibly seize the whole Hindu country.[65]

This statement of 'Isāmī reveals many issues relating to the frontier of Iltutmish's kingdom. Firstly, Yaldūz suggested to Iltutmish that he should rule over the whole of India. Secondly, Yaldūz demarcated his frontier line stretching up to the region of Lahore. Thirdly, he intimated that his forces were strong enough to deter his enemies in the frontier region. Above all, Yaldūz intended to have control over the north-western frontier of the Delhī kingdom after making Lāhore his capital. The choice of this city was strategically apt since expeditions against Khwārizm Shāh to recapture Ghazni could be mounted easily from here. Though none of the contemporary as well as modern writers have commented on this issue, it can be conjectured that Iltutmish understood the situation. If Yalduz's demands had been accepted, they might have led to a decisive clash between Yalduz and Khwārizm Shāh in the north-western frontier of the subcontinent which may have resulted in the probable advance of the Shāh towards India after the equally probable defeat of Yaldūz. Hence the security of the Delhī kingdom was at stake. Now it was time for Sulṭān Iltutmish to deal effectively with Yaldūz whose political power was now insecure because of his strained relations with Khwārizm Shāh and Nāṣir al-Dīn Qubāchah. Iltutmish marched against Yaldūz and inflicted upon him a crushing defeat on the field of Tarā'in.[66] This event, as narrated by Minhāj, poses the question as to how Yaldūz had reached Tarā'in which lies on the way to Delhī, while he was staying at Lāhore, as already mentioned. Raverty quotes *Tāj al-Ma'āsir* whose author has explained this event in detail saying, "Yaldūz, who had possessed himself of the Punjāb, advanced as far as Thānisar, . . . and was moving upon Dihlī, when Iltutmish, now sufficiently powerful to resist them, resolved to oppose him, and advanced to Samnad (Samanah?), and the troops of the two kingdoms encountered each other near Tarā'in on the 3rd of Shawwāl, 612/A.D. 1215."[67] Iltutmish defeated him and sent him as a captive to Badāūn where he died in A.D. 1215.[68] After the end of Yaldūz, Iltutmish's authority ultimately extended all over the Punjāb and now he directly came to face Khwārizm Shāh on the one hand, and Nāsir al-Dīn Qubāchah on the other.

ii) ILTUTMISH AND JALĀL AL-DĪN MANGBARNĪ. Jalāl al-Dīn Mangbarnī[69] offered a stiff resistance to the Mongols, who were determined to destroy the whole of the Khwārizmian empire. Describing the enmity between Khwārizm Shāh and the Mongols, 'Aṭā Malik Juvainī says, "Sultān 'Alā al-Dīn Khwārizm Shāh having provoked the wrath of Chingiz Khan, the mighty Mongol, by putting to death his envoy invited his own doom."[70] In A.D. 1219, the Mongols compelled Sulṭān 'Alā al-Dīn to take shelter in the Caspian region.[71] His son Jalāl al-Dīn Mangbarnī resisted for a time but eventually vanished and reached Ghaznī on the 17th Zil' Hijjah, 617 A.H. Amīn Malik, the governor of Ghaznī, came out to receive the Prince.[72] Juvainī records, "As soon as the news of his arrival spread abroad, chieftains and troops began to flock to his standard from all around, and among them was Saif al-Dīn Ighrāq with 40,000 men of Kankūlīs, Khaljīs and Turkmāns, and the Āmīrs of Ghor also joined him from the parts adjacent."[73] Chingīz Khān himself came in pursuit of Mangbarnī by way of Andarāb,[74] Kābul and Bamīān. Jalāl al-Dīn advanced against the Mongol army as far as the limits of Barwān, five or six stages north of Ghaznī, and overthrew the Mongols.[75] Minhāj records, "On the news of these successes of his reaching Chingīz Khān, he, being at Tālkān of Khurāsān,marched his armies towards Ghaznī. Jalāl al-Dīn was unable to offer resistance to these forces and retired towards Barshūr, modern Peshāwar, and, on the banks of Indus, an encounter took place between them."[76] Juvainī says that, "The Mongols blocked the escape routes, and consequently, Mangbarnī put his family in a boat and sent them over to be drowned in the Indus water, flung his horse into the river and crossed over to India."[77] Here it would be interesting to identify the place where Prince Jalāl al-Dīn crossed the Indus because the authorities have devoted little attention to this issue. The *Madan-i-Akhbār-i-Ahmadī*, one of the medieval chronicles, is the only source which provides a clue which may help in identifying this place. He records the place as Chual Jalāliā.[78] Raverty mentions that the Prince entered the Chual, an uncultivated or desert tract, of Jarūk, called to this day, the Chual-i-Jalāliā[79] Referring Alfī, Husain Khān writes, 'a battle took place between the Shāh and the Mongols in the vicinity of Lāhor, which was a town of Swābi, modern district Mardān, and was situated at a distance of four and a half miles in the north-west of the historic town of Hund. Chual-i-Jalāliā is situated on the eastern bank in the area called Chach, and in the tract Chach, six miles to the south-east of Hund, and one and a half miles from the eastern bank of the Indus, is situated a populous village called Jalāliā.'[80] Looking at the topography of the Chach tract, where Jalāliā stands, and the Swābī Tehsīl where Lāhor and Hund are situated, Jalāliā appears to be Chual Jalāliā of the *Madan-i-Akhbār-i-Ahmadi*. Thus, the statement of Boyle that Chingīz Khān overtook the Sultan on the very banks of the river Indus, probably at Dinkot near modern Kālābāgh,[81] does not appear to be correct. However, Mangbarnī made his way into the Sind-Sāgar with fifty or hundred men, as Raverty has mentioned.[82] He attacked a town, where there was a considerable force of Hindūs, defeated them and captured the place.[83] Shortly after, some other of his men, who had escaped from the banks of the Indus, also joined him. He sent a force of five hundred horsemen against another place in that vicinity, and again defeated the people of those parts. By degrees his forces increased from 4000 to 5000 men, and Chingīz Khān who was still in the vicinity of the Indus, on hearing of it, and measuring the strength of Jalāl al-Dīn, dispatched a force against him under a leader named Tūrtae. The Sulṭān, not being strong enough to oppose the Mongols, retired through a part of the Punjāb towards the frontier of the Delhī kingdom.[84] For Iltutmish this was a potential danger as it was possible that the Mongols might invade India and ravage it in pursuit of Mangbarnī. Meanwhile, Mangbarnī having arrived within two or three days journey from Delhī, sent a man whom he had given the title of 'Ain al-Mulk with a message to Sulṭān Iltutmish, captioned "The noble have a place for the noble."[85] The text of the message reads as under:

> The vicissitudes of fortune have established my right to approach thy presence, and guests of my sort arrive but rarely. If, therefore, the drinking-place of friendship be purified upon either side and the cups of fraternity filled to the brim, and we bind ourselves to aid and assist one another in weal and woe, then shall all aims and objects be attained, and when our opponents realise the concord, that exists between us, the teeth of their resistance will be blunted.[86]

Jalāl al-Dīn Mangbārnī suggested that the combined forces of Islām should get together and fight against the infidels, but Sulṭān Iltutmish rejected the request on the plea of the uncongenial climate of the country.[87] But there seem to be other reasons for the rejection of Mangbārnī's request: Firstly, Iltutmish was much too astute a strategist to take the risk of having a brave warrior with a large army of more than 10,000 men camped upon his frontier. Secondly, he was apprehensive about the Kokar (Gakkhar) – Mangbārnī alliance which had already come into existence, and which showed signs of developing into a triple alliance between Mangbārnī, Kokar (Gakkhaṛ) and Qubachah.[88] Lastly, Sulṭān Iltutmish being both cautious and far-sighted, was not prepared to take the risk of offending the terrible Chingīz Khān by offering shelter to his enemy. In this predicament Iltutmish acted with remarkable astuteness and thus saved the kingdom from what might have been a terrible calamity. He sent a diplomatic refusal to Mangbarnī. According to the author of *Tārīkh-i-Jahān Gushā* Iltutmish sent the message to Mangbarnī:

> . . . with offerings of a food worthy of such a guest but excused himself from providing a place of abode on the grounds that nowhere in that region was there a suitable climate or any locality such as would be fit for a king.[89]

This historical evidence confirms the diplomatic refusal of Sultān Iltutmish. But Nizāmi, a modern historian, calls it a policy of appeasement. He argues that Iltutmish at the same time received an envoy from Chingīz Khān for entering into a non-aggression pact according to which no enemy could be given asylum by the Sulṭān of Delhī and in return the territorial integrity of the Delhī empire was to be respected by the Mongols.[90] This argument of Nizāmī is also supported by Raverty. But Nizāmi's view of an appeasement policy may be better described as the defensive policy of Iltutmish. Actually, Iltutmish acted upon a policy of non-involvement keeping in view the mighty power of the Mongols and avoided involvement in the politics of Central Asia. This refusal was naturally resented by Mangbārnī, who, after turning back, went to the region of Balālā and Nikāla near Lahore where all his followes joined him in due course.[91] He now sent general Malik Jalāl al-Dīn with an army to the mountain of Jūd which they ravaged.[92] After this, the prince sought the hand of the daughter of Kokar Sankin, a chief of the Kokars,[93] (i.e. Gakkhaṛs) of Koh-i-Jūd in marraige. Accordingly, a messenger with the marriage proposal was despatched to Kokar Sankin who agreed to the match.[94] The marriage took place and helped to strengthen Jalāl al-Dīn's power. But here the question as to why Mangbārnī thought it essential to establish matrimonial alliance with a tribe of Koh-i-Jūd arises. None of the contemporary works have thrown any light on it but it seems that Mangbārnī wanted to ally himself to the local tribes in order to deter the possible aggression of the Mongols. However, on getting news of this matrimonial alliance Chingiz Khān despatched another army against him, and the prince, thereupon, moved towards lower Sind. On his arrival in Multan, he attacked Qubachah, a ruler of Multan and Sind, and weakened his power by extorting an enormous tribute from him."[95]

It was Mangbārnī's presence in the subcontinent and his pursuit by Chingiz Khān right to the bank of the Indus, which created a new frontier problem for the Delhī empire. D'Ohsson calls this new development in the frontier one of the most baffling problems of international politics which resembles rather than a phenomenon of human history.[96] Nizāmī also talks of the Mongol barbarity: "Wherever they went, a crimson streak marked their trail, and the cultural centres of mediaeval 'Ajam[97] were practically wiped out of existence."[98] Thus the fear of the Mongols reinforced by Mangbārnī's presence in the subcontinent were a challenge to Iltutmish because he found himself in a dilemma. Iltutmish preferred acting pragmatically rather than ideologically because he realised that his kindgom could be saved only by following an external policy of a dignified non-involvement in Central Asian affairs. It was the result of this policy that after the flight of Mangbārnī from the subcontinent Chingiz Khān departed from India without ravaging the kingdom of Iltutmish.

iii) ILTUTMISH AND NĀSIR AL-DĪN QUBACHAH. Iltutmish now defeated Yaldūz who had captured Lahore from Nāṣir al-Dīn Qubachah and restored it to Qubachah instead of annexing it for himself.[99] This step won Iltutmish the friendship of Qubachah. However, this action was motivated by the fact that the zone towards the west of Lahore was a sort of a buffer state between Delhī and Ghazni, and at this time Iltutmish was less interested establishing direct control over this buffer zone for two reasons: firstly, Iltutmish intended to avoid any direct clash with Khwārizm Shāh; and secondly, he was inclined to devote his full attention to the consolidation of his empire. But these measures of safety, although, astutely created by Iltutmish, were not destined to last long. The safety of the frontier was threatened first by the unsatiated ambitions of Qubāchah and then by the overwhelming Mongol storm that arose in Central Asia. Contemporary writers have different views regarding the tussle between Iltutmish and Qubāchah. Ḥasan Niẓāmī, for instance, points out that there was an agreement between both rulers whose alleged breach in A.D. 1217 furnished Iltutmish with a *causus belli* to make war and wrest the territory of Qubāchah.[100] But Minhāj writes: "Iltutmish attacked Qubāchah because the Khalji[101] fugitives after their defeat by Qubāchah threw themselves upon Iltutmish's protection."[102] These statements of Nizāmi and Minhāj show that the relations between Iltutmish and Qubāchah were strained and consequently a clash took place between them. At this time, Lāhore was in the possession of Qubāchah when Delhī forces marched out. "As they crossed", according to Nizāmi, "Qubāchah fled to Uch and Iltutmish occupied Lāhore, and he appointed his elder son, Nāsir al-Dīn Mahmūd as *muqti* of Lāhore."[103] But Qubāchah reoccupied Lāhore as argued by Ḥabibullah and K.A. Nizāmi, after the departure of Iltutmish from Lāhore to Delhī.[104] This is also confirmed by the accounts of Juvainī and Nasāvī that Lāhore was included in the dominions of Qubāchah when Prince Jalāl al-Dīn entered India in A.D. 1221.[105] Thus there arises the question why Iltutmish did not take precaution to thwart Qubāchah's designs on Lāhore. It may be that Iltutmish wanted only to punish Qubāchah on account of his pride and arrogance. It can also be that Iltutmish wanted this buffer state to remain in the hands of Qubāchah so that he could avoid any direct clash with the Mongols. This was perhaps the reason why Iltutmish did not press his claim over Lāhore till A.D. 1224. At this time, Lāhore occupied a strategic position and could easily destroy the flanks of any army marching towards Multān. Moreover, it also formed a suitable base for any expedition in the unregulated tract of Koh-i-Jūd. Keeping these strategic considerations in mind, Sulṭān Nāṣir al-Dīn Qubāchah held Lāhore. Anyhow, Qubāchah remained confined to Multān, Lāhore and Sind bearing the brunt of the attacks of the Mongols and the Khwārizmian fugitives. In A.D. 1224, the Mongol army under the command of Torbāe Toqshin came to the north-western frontier of the subcontinent in pursuit of Mangbarnī. They invaded Multān and laid siege to the city which was occupied by Qubāchah. The people of Multān gave stiff resistance and forced the Mongols to raise the siege and go back. At the same time, Jalāl al-Dīn Mangbarnī and his nobles after their refuge in Sind-Sāgar created trouble for Qubāchah. Iltutmish had, thus, the satisfaction of seeing Qubāchah nearly crushed by these events. Considering the weak position of Qubāchah, Iltutmish prepared to make his final attack on Multān in A.D. 1228/A.H. 625, and marched his forces to Uchh [106] Juvainī records, "Unable to offer resistance at the frontier, Qubāchah left the garrison in the town and himself fled to the fortress of Bakar on the lower Indus."[107] Uchh was capitulated after three months of brave resistance and defence. Nizām al-Mulk, the minister of Iltutmish, pursued Qūbāchah and besieged him in the fort. In desperation Qūbāchah sent his son, 'Alā al-Dīn Bahrām Shāh, to Iltutmish for his unconditional surrender, which was refused. When the citadel was assaulted, Qubāchah threw himself into the river Indus and was drowned.[108] Thus, Iltutmish's policy of cautiously advancing and taking action against Qubāchah at a time when he found his military power strong and that of his adversary at its weakest because of the onslaughts of Mangbarni and the Mongols, proved successful. After the death of Nāṣir al-Dīn Qubāchah, the frontier *iqṭās* of Lāhore and Multān came under direct control of Iltutmish, whereas the lower Sind was conferred on Malik Sinān al-Dīn Chatisar of the Sūmrā line, who became a vassal of the Sulṭān. As a result, Iltutmish now directly faced the Mongol forces who were in possession of the territory west of the Indus.

iv) ILTUTMISH AND THE MONGOLS. The Mongol cataclysm and the asylum of Mangbārnī in India, which were to develop into the most formidable frontier problem of all for Iltutmish, followed within three years (A.D. 1219-21) after putting to death of the Mongol envoy by the Shāh. Prince Jalal al-Din, though, offered stiff resistance to the Mongols, had eventually to fly across the Indus and took shelter in the Doab between the Indus and Jhelum.[109] Chingīz Khān watched the princes's escape to the opposite bank of Indus and stopped the pursuers of Mangbarnī from chasing him. Juvainī records: "As Mangbarnī climbed ashore safe and sound, still grasping his sword, lance and shield, Chingīz Khān pointed out to his sons with expressions of amazement and admiration."[110] However the flight of the prince to India marked the virtual end of the Mongols' campaigns in the west and it paved the way for 'their movements in the subcontinent. According to Juvainī: "After the refuge of Mangbarnī in Sind-Sāgar, Chingīz Khān followed the Indus some distance upstream and then turned off into the valley of the upper Kurram."[111] Here Chingīz Khān was informed that Jalāl al-Dīn had recrossed the river and buried his dead. The Khān left Chaghatāe in Karmān, who not finding Jalāl al-Dīn, still continued the pursuit. But when Chaghatāe returned without having found the prince, the Khān despatched Torbāe Toqshin with two *tūmāns* (twenty thousand troopers) to cross the Indus in his pursuit.[112] Mangbarnī set out in the direction of Delhī as already discussed. The Mongols, for their part, upon hearing the news of his flight, turned back and laid waste the district of Malikfūr.[113] Torbāe then went to the region of Nandanā and took the fortress of Nandanā and wrought great slaughter. He also ravaged the *iqṭā's* of Multān and Lāhore and finally returned and recrossed the Indus as mentioned by Juvaini.[114] These movements of the Mongol forces in the western frontier of the subcontinent were, of course, a source of great apprehension for the Sulṭān of Delhī who was fully aware of the Mongol strength. Consequently, Iltutmish dealt with Mangbarnī diplomatically and refused him asylum as mentioned earlier. The Khān set his winter quarters in a region probably to be identified with the Swāt valley. From this area Chingiz Khān started his home-return marches because of Tangut's revolt. Juvainī writes: "When the army had recovered its health, the Khān conceived the idea of returning home by a route through India to the land of Tangut."[115] Rashīd al-Dīn also records, "He [The Khan] advanced several stages, but as there was no road, he turned back."[116] According to Juvaini, "The Khān had, from his encampment in the Gibarī or Girī[117] area, dispatched envoys to Iltutmish in Delhi seeking permission to return through India, and he was still in that encampment in the Gibarī, when the news arrived of the Tangut's rebellion ... and the Khān decided to return through Farshāvar, modern Peshāwar, to his original home."[118] The contemporary works are silent about the arrival of the Khān's envoy in Delhī and the reply of Iltutmish. But it seems that before the arrival of his envoys in Delhī, Chingiz Khān had already decided to return home through modern Peshāwar so that he could squash the Tanguts. Iltutmish had faced the Mongol storm boldly, and his policy of non-involvement had also succeeded. This is how Iltutmish succeeded in warding off the Mongol menace, and saving himself from getting involved into the problematic developments of Central Asian politics.

v) ILTUTMISH AND KHWĀRIZMIAN NOBLES. Although Mangbarnī went back, his marriage with a Gakkhar girl and a number of men that he left behind in the frontier region continued to create trouble for Delhi. The author of *Sirat-i-Mangbarnī* records: "Before his departure for Persia in A.D. 1224, Mangbarnī held a council of his army generals and consulted them on the course of his action, whether he should leave India or not."[119] Hasan Qarlugh[120] and a few other nobles were of the view that India should be preferred to Persia for permanent stay as it was a vast country full of resources. But the prince accepted the views of others who were in favour of returning to Persia.[121] Mangbarnī divided his subjugated Indian territories among his generals. Hasan Qarlugh was entrusted with the administration of the territory west of the Indus, such as Ningrahār,[122] Karmān, Furshor (modern Peshāwar) and the northern part of Banīān[123] which still lay outside the Mongol control. Another general, Ozbek Tāi was posted at Nandanā in the Koh-i-Jūd to control the area including Banīān. Malik Khalj Khān, was left in the town of Manṣurah, a sub-division in the *iqṭa'* of Siwistan,[124] which was destroyed by Nāṣir al-Dīn Qubāchah in A.D. 1226 as already mentioned. The territories of these Khwārizmian nobles as shown in Map No. 4, were of importance from the point of view of military strategy and overland trade with the foreign lands. The route from Ghaznī through the Tochī pass follows the Tochī river to its junction with the Kurram, the latter flowing through Bannū valley reaching the Indus. For this reason the possession of Karmān and Banīān was considered necessary for maintaining links between Ghaznī and India. With the occupation of Central Asia by the Mongols, the route through Banīān acquired further importance. Besides the merchant's caravans, the Mongol armies also penetrated into the Indian border through it. Consequently its possession was eagerly sought after by both the Mongol Chiefs of Central Asia and the Sultāns of Delhī.

Sulṭān Iltutmish marched against the Khwārizmian nobles in Koh-i-Jūd and the Banīān territories.[125] One of them, called Ozbek Tāe[126] was driven away from India,[127] but the other, called Ḥasan Qarlugh was not only spared but also allowed to govern Banian on condition that he should bear allegiance to Iltutmish.[128] Through entry of Qarlugh in the service of Iltutmish, the Sulṭān was able to extend his influence in the north-western frontier spreading upto the boundaries of Ningrahar, Karmān and Ghaznī. But soon in A.D. 1235, the situation changed when Qarlugh was threatened by the appearance of a large army headed by the Mongol general Hoqūtār.[129] In an attempt to save himself from destruction, Qarlugh acknowledged the suzerainty of the Mongol emperor Ogetāe and also pledged to pay annually a fixed tribute from the revenue of Banīān.[130] This development aroused Iltutmish into action against Qarlugh. He marched at the head of a formidable army towards Banīān but fell seriously ill on his way and was brought back to his capital in a litter. Shortly afterwards, Iltutmish died in A.D. 1236.[131]

vi) ILTUTMISH AND THE GAKKHARS. Iltutmish also faced another frontier problem which was created by the obstinate designs of the tribes of Koh-i-Jūd.[132] When refused asylum in India, Mangbārnī turned back and went to the region of Balālā and Nikālā as already mentioned.[133] From here, as mentioned by Juvainī, Malik Khalj, called Tāj al-Dīn, was sent to the hills of Jūd. They ravaged and carried off much booty. At this time, Chingiz Khān also sent an envoy to the Rānā of Jūd hills who at first accepted submission but soon went back on his word. Chingiz Khān, thereupon, sent an army which seized and slew him.[134] It is curious to note that Juvainī has not given any reason for this action of the Khān. However, his statement that 'Mangbārnī sent an envoy to Rāi Kokar Sankin, and sought his daughter in marriage[135] suggests that the punishment was motivated by the Rānā's matrimonial alliance with his enemy, Mangbārnī. Incidentally, this also confirms the surmise that this

Rānā was a Gakkhaṛ chief. It also helps us to understand how the tribes of Koh-i-Jūd[136] who made alliances with the Khwārizmian nobles.[137] were perceived as possible source of trouble by the Sulṭān of Delhī. Accordingly, Nasāwī informs us that after having destroyed Qubāchah and having consolidated his power in the Punjab and Sind, Iltutmish felt it essential to subdue the tribes of Koh-i-Jūd. Consequently, the *Muqṭīs* of Lahore and Multan, were instructed to gradually reduce the Jhelum and the Indus tracts.[138] The occupation of the stronghold of Nandana in Koh-i-Jūd which was placed under the charge of Altigīn, as recorded by Minhāj, could only have been the result of such operations.[139] Moreover, Iltutmish personally led an army towards Koh-i-Jūd to crush the Jūd hill tribes and the Khwārizmian nobles who had become their allies, but could not succeed in this venture because of his illness and final death.

To conclude, Iltutmish emerges as a great realist, steadfast soldier and far-sighted statesman. The western frontier of Iltutmish's empire was threatened both by internal and external dangers. In the beginning of his rule, Iltutmish inherited as insecure frontier on the north-west of his empire and consequently had to confront Yaldūz and Qubāchah. But on account of internal disturbance and instability during the early phase of his rule, Iltutmish made alliances with them acting upon the policy of compromise. He devoted his attention towards the consolidation of his empire. Soon after strengthening his power, Iltutmish turned to deal with Yaldūz and Qubāchah with stern hand and crushed them. But the crucial problem which Iltutmish faced was the presence of Mangbarnī and the arrival of Chingīz Khān on the banks of the Indus. Iltutmish wisely adopted a policy of dignified non-involvement in the Central Asian politics. Mediaeval India owed him not a little gratitude for helping her to escape from the Mongols' fury which had uprooted more powerful and far older empires. Soon after warding off the Mongol threat and the flight of Mangbarnī from the subcontinent to Persia, Iltutmish followed a policy of hit and advance. He crushed the tribes of Koh-i-Jūd on the one hand, and subdued the Khwārizmian nobles allied with the tribes of Jūd on the other. Thus Iltutmish followed various strategies: that of compromise, of non-involvement, and of advance: as parts of his overall policy in the north western frontier of his empire.

## FOOT NOTES

1. M. Nāzim, *op. cit.*, p. 90.
2. C.E. Bosworth, *The Later Ghaznavids*, New York, 1977, pp. 11-19.
3. At present this place is situated in Kurram Agency. This Karmān is in the Bangash country between Kabūl and Bannu. *T.F.S.B.* (Trans.), p. 221; The province which Tāj al-Dīn held, included the tract of country containing several Derhas or long valleys with hills on two sides and rivers running through them, extending from the southern slopes of Spinghar, the White Mountain in Pushto, and south-westerly slopes of the Salt range, and to the Indus on the east, a large tract of country, watered by the Kurram river and its tributaries. *T.N.* (Trans.), p. 498 fn. 7.
4. It is also pronounced as Shalūzān. See for detail, Muḥammad 'Azīz, *op. cit.*, p. 98.
5. The old town of Uchh is situated on the eastern bank of the Punjnad, 70 miles to the South-west of Multān and 45 miles to the north-east of the present confluence with the Indus at Mithunkot. See Cunningham, *The Ancient Geography of India*, London, 1871, Indian reprint, 1963, p. 204.
6. *T.N.* (Text), pp. 125-36, (Trans.); Raverty, pp. 469-70.
7. *Ibid.*, p. 138.
8. *Ibid* (Text), p. 140, (Trans.), p. 515.
9. *T.N.* (Text), p. 133, (Trans.), p. 500.
10. *Ibid.*, (Text), p. 140, (Trans.), pp. 502, 525, 533.
11. According to Minhāj, both Aibak and Yaldūz were manumitted together in about A.H. 605/A.D. 1208. *Ibid.*, (Text), p. 140.
12. Yaldūz is a Turkish word which has been spelt differently. In the different copies of *Ṭabaqāt-i-Nāṣirī*, it is written as above. But in other works like those of Yafā'i and Faṣḥ'i the word is written as I-yal-dūz. So we adopt here Yaldūz ( یلدز ) which was written by Minhāj. Its literal meaning in Turkish language, we get 'Yal' means brave or valiant, and 'Dūz' means flat or smooth, level.
13. Raverty argues that the name should really be pronounced as Kubāchah. *T.N.* (Trans.), p. 531 f.n. 8. But the above form is confirmed in Hindī script on one of his coins. *J.A.S.B.*, 1887, p. 17.
14. *T.N.* (Text), p. 132, (Trans.), p. 592.
15. *Ibid.*, (Text), p. 131.
16. Aibak in the Turkish language means finger only. In every contemporary work it is distinctly stated that he was called Aibak because one of his little finger was broken or injured.
17. *T.M.N.* (Trans.), pp. 220-1; *T.N.* (Text), p. 139.
18. *Ibid.*, (Text), p. 140, (Trans.), p. 525.
19. *T.M.N.* (Text), f. 202; *T.N.* (Text), p. 140, (Trans.), p. 525.
20. *T.N.* (Text), p. 132, (Trans.), p. 499.
21. *T.N.* (Text), p. 133.
22. Sulṭān Maḥmūd gave him manumission and conferred upon him the title of Malik-ul-Umrā (Chief of nobles). *T.N.* (Trans.), p. 502.
23. *Tārīkh-i-Alfī* as quoted by Raverty. *Ibid.*, p. 502.
24. *T.N.* (Text), p. 128, (Trans.), p. 502.
25. *Ibid.*, p. 128.
26. *I.A.* (Text), vol. xii, p. 146-9.
27. *T.N.* (Text), p. 134, (Trans.), p. 502.

28. *T.N.* (Text), p. 140, (Trans.), p. 526
29. *T.N.* (Text), p. 140, (Trans.), p. 503.
30. *Ibid.*, (Trans.), p. 502.
31. *T.F.* (Text), p. 64, (Trans.), p. 199.
32. Habibullāh, *op. cit.*, p. 90
33. *T.N.* (Trans.), p. 503.
34. Raverry pronounces it as *"Sang-i-Surakh"* which signifies 'perforated Rock or Stone'. Raverty, *op. cit.*, p. 441 fn. See also, Raverty, *Notes on Afghānistān and Baluchistān*, Quetta, 1976, pp. 458-60. Hodivala records that a Surkh-Sang Pass, N.W. of Ghaznī, is shown in Constable 22 Cc and 24 Ba. Hodivala, *op. cit.*, p. 201. What Elphinstone in his work and map calls the district of "Hallataugh" is nothing more than the hilly region of Ulān Tāgh (Bābur Bādsha's Uls Tāgh), the Turkish interpretation of Tajzil, "Koh-i-Surkh" and Afghān "Sūr Ghar" where the two ranges mixed up.
35. A.H. Dānī, *Ancient Pākistān*, Peshāwar, 1973, p. 5.
36. *T.A.* (Text), p. 149.
37. *T.N.* (Trans.), p. 402.
38. *T.N.* (Text), p. 55, (Trans.), p. 504.
39. *Ibid.*
40. *Ibid.*, (Trans.), p. 527.
41 *Ibid.*, p. 132.
42. *T.N.* (Text), p. 132.
43. *Ibid.*, (Text), p. 143.
44. *T.N.* (Trans.), p. 527.
45. Soon after the demise of Sulṭān Quṭb al-Dīn Aibak, a struggle to possess the throne of Delhī ensued between Ārām Shāh and Iltutmish the son and son-in-law of the late Sulṭān. Iltutmish emerged successful and occupied the throne: *T.N.* (Text), p. 170, (Trans.), p. 606.
46. *Ibid.*, (Text), p. 171.
47. *T.N.* (Text), p. 171.
48. To the east of Badghīs, at the head-waters of the Murghāb river, is the mountainous region known to the earlier 'Arab geographers and Gharj-ash-Shar. The prince of these mountains had the title of Shār, and Gharj, according to Mukaddasī, meant 'mountain' in the local dialect, so that Gharj-ash-Shar was equivalent to the 'mountains of the Shar'. In the later middle ages this region came to be more generally known as Gharchistan. . . Le Strange, *op. cit.*, p. 415.
49. Sīstān, which the earlier 'Arabs called Sījistān from the Persian Sāgistān, is the lowland country lying round, and to the eastward of, the Zarah Lake, which more especially includes the deltas of the Helmund and other rivers which drain into this inland sea. *Ibid.*, p. 334.
50. *T.J.G.* (Text), p. 86, (Trans.), p. 354.
51. *Ibid.*, p. 353.
52. Mangbarnī is a word of non-descript origin meaning one equal to one thousand men in strength. Its Persian equivalent is Hazār Mardāh. *E.I.*, 2nd edition, p. 121.
53. *T.N.* (Text), p. 170.
54. The city of Bāmīan was the capital of a great district of the same name which formed the eastern part of Ghor. Le Strange, *op. cit.*, p. 418.

55. In old Persian Khurasan means 'the Eastern Land', and in the earlier middle-ages the name was applied, generally, so as to include all the Muslim provinces east of the Great Desert, as far as the frontier of the Indian mountains. See for detail, Le Strange, pp. 382-483.
56. *Tarikh-i-Alfi* as quoted by Raverty, *T.N.* (Trans.), p. 504.
57. *T.N.* (Text), p. 133, (Trans.), p. 506.
58. *Ibid.*, (Trans.), p. 622.
59. *Ibid.*, (Trans.), p. 630.
60. The great district of Tukharistan lay to the eastward of Balkh, stretching along the south side of the Oxus as far as the frontiers of Badakhshan and bounded on the south by the mountain ranges north of Bamian and Punj-shir. See for detail, Le Strange, *op. cit.*, pp. 426-7.
61. It is sixty five miles south-east of Kabul. According to Raverty, 'in 251 A.H./865 A.D. Gardez was the chief place of an independent Muslim territory, the ruler of which was the Amir, Abu Mansur-i-Atlaj. He was made tributary by Ya'ku b-i-Lais, the Suffari, ruler of Sijistan. Raverty, *op. cit.*, p. 686.
62. It is one of the passes on the route from Ghazni towards Lahore, the name of which has been changed with the change of the inhabitants of those parts. *Ibid.*, p. 505. It is probably Kurram pass. See pp. 62-63.
63. *T.N.* (Text), p. 135.
64. *Ibid.*, (Text), p. 135.
65. *F.S.* (Text), p. 110, (Trans.), p. 216.
66. *T.N.* (Text), p. 171. Badauni and *Tabaqat-i-Akbari* suggest that Tarain was then known as Serai Talwari.
67. *T.M.N.* (Text), quoted by Raverty. *T.N.* (Trans.), p. 608
68. *Ibid.*, (Trans.), vol. ii, p. 195.
69. He was the son of Sultan Muhammad Khwarizm Shah and heirapparent of Khwarizmian Empire.
70. *T.J.G.* (Text), p. 99, (Trans.), p. 369.
71. Barthold, *op. cit.*, p. 404.
72. *T.J.G.* (Text), p. 135, (Trans.), p. 405.
73. *Ibid.*, (Text), p. 135.
74. It was a village near Merv in the then province of Tukharistan.
75. *T.J.G.*, (Text), p. 136, (Trans.), p. 287.
76. *T.N.* (Text), p. 290.
77. *T.J.G.* (Text), p. 141.
78. Kanbu, *Maaan-i-Akhbar-i-Ahmadi*, as quoted by Husain Khan, "The identification of place where Sultan Khwarizm Shah crossed the Sind", *J.A.S.P.*, April, 1970, p. 13.
79. Reverty, *op. cit.*, p. 293.
80. *Tarikh-i-Alfi* as quoted by Husain Khan. Husain Khan, *op. cit.*, p. 15.
81. Boyle, *op. cit.*, p. 320.
82. Raverty, *op. cit.*, p. 293.
83. *Ibid.*
84. *T.J.G.* Text), p. 144.

*Ibid.*, (Text), p. 144.

86. *T.J.G.* (Text), p. 145, (Trans.), p. 413.

87. *Ibid.*

88. K.A. Nizami, *op. cit.*, p. 330.

89. *T.J.G.* (Trans.), p. 414.

90. Nizāmī, *op. cit.*, p. 330.

91. *T.J.G.*, p. 146. It is also written as Balālā and Mankālā in *Ṭabaqāt-i-Nāṣirī*. *T.N.* (Trans.) Elliot and Dowson, p. 394. See for details in Appendix "A".

92 *T.N.* (Trans.), p. 295.

93 Kokar hence be written as Gakkhar. See for details Appendix "A".

94 *T.N.* (Trans.), p. 295.

95 *T.J.G.* (Text), vol. ii, p. 147.

96 *D'ohssen, C., Historie des Mongols*, Paris, 1824, p. 387.

97 'Ajam or 'Ajamī is the name originally applied by the 'Arabs to a foreigner or non-'Arab. Since the Persians were the first foreigners with whom the 'Arabs came into contact 'Ajam or 'Ajamī soon became specialised to mean the Persian foreigner, and as the equivalent of Persian is in use at present time. Le Strange, *op. cit.*, p. 185. The Muslim or Saracenic expansion outside 'Arabia came in two great swells or pushes, the first under the Pious Caliph, Omar I (A.D. 634–44), and the second under the Ummayad Caliph, Walid bin Abdul Malik (A.D. 705–15). . . . The 'Abbāsid Caliphate, thereafter, was left with its eastern lands along the lands of the Persians and the Turks, conveniently designated as 'Ajam. Muḥammad Ḥabīb, *Politics and Society During the Early Medieaval Period*, (ed.) K.A. Niẓāmī, 'Alīgarh Muslim University, 'Aligarh, n.d., vol. i., p. 37.

98. K.A. Niẓāmī, *op. cit.*, p. 330.

99. Habībullah, *op. cit.*, p. 90.

100 Ḥasan Niẓāmī, *op. cit.*, p. 241.

101 Raverty narrates that eighteen months after the appearance of the Mongols on the Indus, and the investment of Multān by Tūrtae in A.H. 623, a chief named Malik Khān with his followers and the Khalj tribe. . . arrived on the north-west frontier of Sind. Qubāchah moved against them and defeated them. *T.N.* (Trans.), p. 540.

102. *Ibid.*

103. Nizāmī, *op. cit.*, p. 223.

104. *Ibid.*

105. Ḥabībullah, *op. cit.*, p. 84; Niẓāmī, *op. cit.*, pp. 214-5.

106. *T.N.* (Text), p. 173.

107 Juvaini describes that the Akar and Bakar are the two fortress on an island. *T.J.G.* (١٤٨), p.١٩٥.

108. U.N. Day, *Studies in Medieval History*, Delhi, n.d. p. 202.

109. *T.J.G.* (Trans.), p. 411.

110. *Ibid.*

111 *Ibid.*, p. 414.

112. *T.J.G.* (Trans.), pp. 141,413. Chingīz Khān had commanded Bala to pursue Mangbarnī, the ruler of the Huei-huei, and Milik Wang across the Sin river into the land of Hindus. He (Bala) searched for Jalāl al-Dīn everywhere but failed to find him;

On his way back he seized all the camels and goats of the people in the Hindū frontier cities. Yuan-Chao Pī Shī, *The Secret History of the Mongol Dynasty*, (Eng. tr.) Weī Kwei Sun, 'Aligarh, 1957, p. 171.

113. It is in the Rāwalpindī district. In ancient times, Malikfūr was the residence of the Provincial Governors, which lies in the direct route from the Nandanā on the Jhelum to the locality in which Chingīz had pitched his camps. *T.N.* (Trans.), p. 537.

114. *T.J.G.* (Trans.), p. 142.

115. The Tanguts for two centuries had been a powerful people in the border area between Tibet and China. *T.J.* (Text), pp. 233-35.

116. *Ibid.*, p. 225.

117. Raverty locates the fortress of Gibarī in Bajaur. *T.N.* (Trans.), p. 1043. Juvainī suggests that it is possible to read Girī instead of Gibarī and identify it with the fortress in which Mas'ūd, the Ghaznavid (A.D. 1030-40) was imprisoned and put to death, and which was situated close to the Indus, in the neighbourhood of Taxilā. *T.J.G.* (Trans.), p. 136 f.n. But this is not possible as Chingīz Khān did not cross the Indus.

118. *T.J.G.* (Trans.), p. 137 f.n.

119. *S.M.* (Text), p. 121.

120. The Qurlughs were of Turkish origin. In the early works of the 'Arab geographers they were mentioned as Kharlukh and in Chinese sources they are called Kol-lū. They are reported to have attained some political importance in the second half of the 8th century A.D. Jabghuy, chief of the tribe adopted Islām in A.D. 779, but the conversion of the entire tribe seems to have taken a long time. They were, however, influenced by the Persian culture in course of time, with the result that they became different in their physical features from the usual type. W. Barthold, *The Encyclopaedia of Islām*, p. 766; *Ḥudūd al-'Alam*, (tr.) V. Minorsky, London, 1937, p. 287; In the 13th century, the Qarlughs were divided into groups. Hasan Qarlugh, the founder of the Qarlugh's kingdom in the western India, remained loyal to Khwārizm Shāh. W. Barthold, *op. cit.*, p. 443.

121. *S.M.* (Text), p. 121.

122. It is also pronounced as Nagarahara (ننگرهار), which was the old name of a town and district near modern Jalālābād in Afghānistān. Hodivala, *op. cit.*, p. 195.

123. There is a controversy about the name of Banīān. Sir Henry Elliot reads it as Binbān while Raverty writes it as Banīān and identifies it with modern Bannū. According to him, the town was situated somewhere between Kurramān and Jhelum near Koh-i-Jūd. *T.N.* (Trans.), p. 541. However, it may be Bannā or Bannū.

124. Siwistān is identified with Sehwan, which was situated on the main stream of the Indus during the mediaeval age. According to Cunningham, the native historians of Sind mentioned it as one of the towns captured by Muḥammad bin Qāsim in A.D. 711. It was again captured by Maḥmūd of Ghaznī in the beginning of the 11th century. Under the Muḥammadan rule it would appear to have become one of the most flourishing places in Sind. Cunningham, *op. cit.*, p. 225.

125. *T.N.* (Trans.), p. 179.

126. Nasawī says that Jahān Pehlwān being the premier noble of the prince Jalāl al-Dīn was always honoured with the command of the advance guard of forces in the Sub-continent. In A.D. 1229, he was driven away to Irān by Iltutmish. *S.M.* (Text), p. 122.

127. *S.M.* (Text), p. 237.
128. *Ibid.*
129. *T.J.G.* (Trans.), p. 146.
130. *Ibid*, (Trans.), p. 146.
131. *Ibid.*; *T.N.* (Text), p. 180.
132. See for details in Appendix "A".
133. See page 82 fn.
134. Raverty speaks of a Rānā of the Jūd hills. *T.N.* (Trans.), p. 815.
135. *T.J.G.* (Trans.), pp. 145-46.
136. See in Appendix "A".
137. *T.N.* (Trans.), p. 730.
138. *Ibid.*, (Trans.), p. 539.
139. *Ibid.*, (Text), p. 179.

Chapter III

# THE FRONTIER POLICY OF THE MAMLŪKS–II (A.D. 1236-46)

Soon after the death of Sulṭān Shams al-Dīn Iltutmish in A.D. 1236,[1] the Delhī throne was occupied by four successors of Iltutmish, one after the other, within a short span of ten years (A.D. 1236-46).[2] They were Sulṭān Rukn al-Dīn Fīrūz Shāh (A.D. 1236-38), Sulṭānā Razia (A.D. 1238-40), Sulṭān Mu'izz al-Dīn Bahrām Shāh (A.D. 1240-42), and Sulṭān 'Alā al-Dīn Mas'ūd Shāh (A.D. 1242-46). During their reigns, the frontier of the Delhī empire faced serious turmoil on account of the political changes, both external and internal. Externally, it saw a political upheaval in Central Asia. Chingīz Khān died in A.D. 1227[3] while the western campaigns were still in progress.[4] Ogetāe, who succeeded his father, Chingīz Khān,[5] continued the western campaigns which lasted for seven years (A.D. 1236-42).[6] Sulṭān Jalāl al-Dīn, son of the Shāh of Khwārizm boldly fought against the Mongols but was murdered in A.D. 1231 by his own soldiers.[7] The Mongols overran and occupied western and central Asia after the complete extinction of the Khwarizmian empire. Ogetāe died in A.D. 1241 and his son, Guyūk, was elected as the Great Khān in A.D. 1246.[8] These historical facts suggest that the Mongols left the subcontinent alone except for two raids (A.D. 1241, 1245) in the frontier region of the Delhī Sulṭānate between the years A.D. 1236-46 because they were engaged in the subjugation of western and central Asia.[9]

I

## The Frontier Policy of Sulṭān Rukn al-Dīn Fīrūz Shāh (A.D. 1236-38)

After the death of Iltutmish, the throne passed to his eldest son, Rukn al-Dīn Fīrūz Shāh.[10] At this time, the Qarlūghs were around the Indus territory[11] and the Kokar tribe (i.e. Gakkhar) was dominant along the Jūd hills (i.e. Salt range).[12] These tribes of Koh-i-Jūd had transferred their loyalty to the Mongols towards the close of the reign of Iltutmish. Another development which occurred in the frontier region was that Kābil Khān, *muqṭī*' of the frontier *iqṭā*' of Multān, declared himself independent and made a bid to asset himself against the Qarlūghs.[13] Moreover, the Mongols too came forward to impose their own authority in this region.

The Delhī administration under Sulṭān Rukn al-Dīn Fīrūz Shāh realised the dangerous situation prevailing in the frontier region and *muqtī's* were appointed in the frontier *iqṭā's*. Malik 'Alā al-Dīn Jānī was made the *muqṭī*' of Lāhore. Malik 'Izz al-Dīn Kabīr, Khān-i-Ayāz, who was the *muqṭī*' of Multān, was removed from Multān and later the fief of Sunam was conferred on him.[14] Malik Saif al-Dīn Aibak, who was assigned the fief of Uchh by Iltutmish, remained at Uchh as a fief-holder because after the death of Iltutmish he had become powerful.[15] These arrangements were made to reassert the rights of the Delhī Sulṭān in the frontier *Iqṭā's* of Multān, Uchh, and Lāhore, and to meet the challenge of the Mongols. Ugetāe Khān, not the Great Khān, gave order to his forces to proceed towards Ghor and Ghaznī under the command of Bahādur Ṭā'ir.[16] This resulted in a series of fresh raids on the territories contiguous to the Delhī frontier. Earleir in A.H. 633/A.D. 1235, the principality of Sīstān in Western Afghānistān had been made to acknowledge the Mongol authority.[17] When the Mongol forces marching from Sīstān entered Kirman, *Nuin* Anban and *Nuin* Nikudar marched with their forces, which were in the territories of Ghor and Khurasān, towards Ghaznī.[18] According to Juvainī: "Ghaznī was under the sway of Malik Hasan Qarlūgh, who, in the meanwhile, had shaken off the yoke of the Mongols."[19] Ultimately Ghaznī was taken from Hasan Qarlūgh, who retired towards Baniān and where also he was threatened by the appearance of a large army headed by the Mongol General, Hoqūtar, who had already plundered Kashmīr and made a large number of people captives.[20] When Ḥasan Qarlūgh saw that he could not resist the power of the Mongols, he acknowledged the suzerainty of the Mongol emperor, Ogetāe Khān, and also pledged to pay annually a fixed tribute from the revenue of Baniān.[21] The author of *Tārīkh Alfī* records, "In A.H. 633/A.D. 1236, Ogetāe Khān dispatched armies to various directions including an army under a leader named Makānū ( ماکانو ) towards Hindustān and Kashmīr."[22] In the same year (A.H. 633/A.D. 1236), the Mongols suddenly attacked Malik Ḥasan, who according to Minhāj, "fled discomfited from Karmān, Ghaznī and Baniān towards Multān."[23] This surprise raid of the Mongols was due to an unexplained estrangement between the Mongols and Malik Ḥasan. Al-Juzjānī says: "The Mongols ... left Ḥasan Qarlūgh untouched in Baniān on condition that he would pay the annual tribute regularly, but they attacked him all of a sudden in A.D. 1238."[24] On the other hand, the political situation in Delhī, as described by Minhāj, might have encouraged Qarlūgh to invade Multān. Hence he made his way from the direction of Baniān with a large army and reached the fortress of Uchh, but Malik Saif al-Dīn, the *muqṭi'* of Uchh, marched out of the fortress with a well organised force to meet the challenge.[25] Hasan Qarlūgh was defeated and his forces were routed without gaining their objective.[26]

Thus in his brief rule of two years, Sulṭān Fīrūz Shāh did not directly face the Mongols but rather made necessary administrative changes to guard his frontier against the possible Mongol raids. His *muqṭis*, it may be added, helped him to meet the challenge successfully.

## II

## The Frontier Policy of Sulṭānā Raẓīā (A.D. 1238-40)

At the time of Sulṭānā Raẓīā's accesson to the throne of Delhī after the dethronement of Sulṭān Rukn al-Dīn Fīrūz Shāh in A.D. 1238,[27] the internal situation became all the more precarious because the majority of the Maliks of the Sulṭanate, including Niẓām al-Mulk Muḥammad Junaidī, the Wazīr of Kingdom, did not acknowledge her sovereignty.[28] At this critical juncture, however, the Delhī kingdom fortunately remained safe from the direct onslaughts of the Mongols because they were engaged in the subjugation of Western Asia.[29] It is also possible that the Mongols could not directly disturb the affairs of the Delhī empire because of the existence of Qarlūgh's buffer state of Baniān between themselves and the Delhī kingdom.

The internal crisis also affected the frontier *iqṭā's* of the empire. Kabīr Khān, the *muqṭī'* of Lāhore, rebelled against Raẓia. Minhāj remarks; "In the year 637 A.H./A.D. 1238, Malik 'Izz al-Dīn Kabīr Khān, who was the feudatory of Lāhore, began to show a rebellious spirit."[30] It was essential for Sulṭānā Raẓīā to cope with the rebel *muqṭī'* with an iron hand and maintain peace in the frontier. Consequently, Sulṭānā Raẓīā led an army against him from Delhī.[31] The rebel *muqṭī'* of Lāhore retired before her towards the Indus until he reached the neighbourhood of Sodhrā.[32] Had the rebel *muqṭī'* gone any further to the west he could have fallen into the hostile hands of the Gakkhaṛs. He, therefore, stayed near Sodhra and when the royal forces crossed the Rāvī, submitted to them. However, he was removed from the fiefdom of Lāhore but later made the *muqṭī'* of Multān.[33] Malik Qarāqāsh, the then *muqṭī'* of Multān, was transferred to Lāhore. These changes of the *muqṭī's* in the frontier indicate that the Sulṭānā was determined to ensure the stability of the frontier *iqṭā's* and keep them under her direct control.

While Sulṭānā Raẓīā was still engaged in settling the affairs of

Lāhore, Ḥasan Qarlūgh being hard pressed by the Mongols, had to abandon his territory and retire towards Multān. Taking advantage of Raẓiā's presence in Lāhore, Ḥasan Qarlugh sent his eldest son Muḥammad to her court where she recieved him with honour, and confirmed the fiefdom of Baran,[34] east of Delhī, upon him.[35] The arrival of Ḥasan Qarlugh's son at the court of Raẓia shows that Ḥasan Qarlugh was compelled circumstances to maintain friendly relations with the Sulṭān of Delhī. The contemporary works are silent on this issue but it is reasonable to assume that Ḥasan Qarlugh was interested in concluding a friendly alliance with the Sulṭān of Delhī so that his forces reinforced by those of Delhī would jointly deter the advance of the Mongols. Minhāj says: "Soon after, without the cause being known, the disappointed prince fled secretly and rejoined his father who was still able to hold Banian."[36] His flight from Baran could have been the result of his inability to gain support from Raẓia in his war against the Mongols. Raẓia Sulṭāna's policy of refraining from direct confrontation with the Mongols was similar to that of her father when confronted by Chingīz Khān and Khwārizm Shāh.

Sulṭānā Raẓiā also tried to maintain good relations with the Gakkhaṛs and the Jāts. According to Minhāj; "In a battle against the Turk Amīrs, Raẓiā managed to raise a considerable force of Gakkhaṛs, Jāts and other tribes about Tabarhinda and from the adjoining fiefs."[37] Thus Raẓiā was the first among the Delhī Sulṭāns who tried to be on good terms with the Gakkhaṛs who were living along the frontier of her empire.

To sum up, Raẓia adopted a defensive policy during her short reign of four years. She did not involve herself in the dispute between the Mongols and the Qarlūghs. She suppressed the rebellion of the *muqtī'* of Lāhore, a frontier *iqṭā'*, and maintained good relations with the Gakkhaṛs. All these measures of Raẓiā confirm that she desired to maintain peace in the frontier and defend her territory from the raids of the Mongols.

## III

## The Frontier Policy of Sulṭān Mu'izz al-Dīn Bahrām Shāh (A.D. 1240-42)

Sulṭān Mu'izz al-Dīn Bahrām Shāh occupied the throne of Delhī in A.H. 637/A.D. 1240.[38] At this time, the empire faced serious internal crises because of severe dissensions among the groups of Turkish Amīrs.[39] We learn from Minhāj that "Malik Kabīr Khān, the *Muqṭi'* of Multān, assumed a canopy of state and possessed him self of Uchh."[40] It was at this time that the forces of the Mongols were directed against him. According to Minhāj: "In the year A.H. 639, when the Mongol forces and troops of Ghor were directed to advance to Lāhore, the *Bahādur* Ṭā'ir; a Mongol Commander of Herāt and Badghīs,[41] along with other *Nū'ins* incharge of Ghaznī, Garmsīr[42] and Tukhāristān[43] arrived in Sind."[44] The Mongols first of all invaded Multān. Malik Kabīr Khān assembled troops to fight against them.[45] Finding it difficult to capture Multān, the Mongols raised the siege and turned towards Lāhore. When the Mongols appeared before the gate of that city, the *hissār*[46] of Lahore was unprepared to resist the enemy and the people of Lāhore were not united. This state of unpreparedness was partly due to the reason that most of the inhabitants of the city were merchants and traders who had undertaken journeys into the upper parts of Khurāsān and Turkistān during the time of the Mongols and one of them had obtained a pass from them for a safe conduct. Hence in defending and fighting for the safety of *hiṣṣār* of Lāhore,[47] the inhabitants of the city used not to act in unison with Malik Qarāqāsh.[48] To make matters worse, the army too could not speedily set out from Delhī to defend Lāhore because the Turks and Ghorī Maliks were distrustful of Sulṭān Bahrām Shāh.[49] Instead, the troops of Delhī did not even assemble together in time. On account of these factors, there was considerable delay in relieving Lahore. In spite of all the disadvantages Malik Qarāqāsh, the *muqṭi'* of Lāhore, did manage to defend the city for a few days. Minhāj writes: "For some time fighting went on before the gate of the city of Lāhore and the Mongol army planted a great number of catapults[50] round about the fortifications of that city, and destroyed the walls, and, to such a degree as Malik Qarāqāsh was able, he remained and resisted the infidels."[51] However, Malik Qarāqāsh did realise that his position was weak, firstly because of the disunion and discordance among the citizens and secondly, because of the misconduct of the Qāẓī and Chief personages who were reluctant to keep guard on the walls of the city. As a result, Malik Qarāqāsh knew that the upshot of the affairs would be disastrous, and the defence of the city was beyond his power and capacity. He, therefore, came out with the troops and his followers under the pretext of a night attack and made a dash upon the camp of the Mongols. According to Minhāj: "In one charge he broke through the ranks of the Mongol army, and set out for Delhi."[52] This event shows that Malik Qarāqāsh was able to save himself from the cruel hands of the Mongols. Minhāj further says:

> In that charge, some of the principal females of his *Ḥaram* and of his retinue got separated from him. A number of his people were slain and made martyrs and some, in the darkness of night and in the tumult, threw themselves off the backs of the horses and hid themselves among the ruins and graveyards. During that tumult, likewise, the female members of the Malik's *Ḥaram* managed to conceal themselves somewhere.[53]

It was but natural that the flight of Malik Qarāqāsh horrified the remaining strength of Qarāqāsh army. Minhāj has mentioned that "The following day, when the inhabitants of the city and the fortress of Lāhore, and the Mongol forces, became aware of Malik Qarāqāsh's evacuation of the place, and of his flight, the hearts of the former were entirely broken and the Mongols became still more bold; and they captured the city."[54] Consequently, the Mongol forces entered the fortress and the conflicts arose in every quarter. The Muslims fought continuously with the infidels, and, in the words of Minhāj: ". . . two bands of Musalmāns, in that disaster, girded up their lives like their waists, and firmly grasped the sword, and, up to the latest moment that a single pulsation remained in their dear bodies and they could move, they continued to wield the sword and to send Mongols to hell, until the time when both bodies, after fighting gallantly for a long period against the infidels, attained the felicity of martyrdom."[55] The Mongols captured the city of Lāhore. Now, for the first time, the Delhi administrative frontier was sacked by the Mongols and it was a great challenge for the security of the frontier of the kingdom. So it was essential for the Sulṭān to take serious action in the matter so as to stop further advance of the Mongols towards Delhī. Minhāj writes, "When the dreadful intelligence of this calamity reached the capital, Sulṭān Bahrām Shāh assembled the people of the city of Delhī and he gave a command to deliver a discourse, and the people pledged their fealty to the Sulṭān."[56] In order to repel the Mongols, the Sulṭān nominated Malik Quṭb al-Dīn Ḥussain, the Ghorī, alongwith the Wazīr named Muhazzab al-Dīn and several Maliks, with the forces of Hindūstān to advance towards Lāhore for the purpose of guarding the frontier."[57] Minhāj reports; "When the forces assembled on the bank of the Beāh, the Khwāja Muhazzab al-Dīn, the Wazīr, in order to take the vengeance upon the Sulṭān so that by some means or other he might oust him from the throne, indicted a representation secretly to the Sulṭān from the camp, saying: "These Amirs and Maliks will never become obedient. It is advisable that an edict should be issued by His Majesty, that, I and Quṭb al-Dīn Ḥussain, should destoy all the Amīrs and the Turks, by such means as may be attainable, in order that the country may be cleared of them."[58] When that representation reached the Sulṭān, he commanded that an edict of the desired form be written and dispatched to the camp.[59] As soon as the edict reached the camp, the Wazīr showed the very edict itself to the Amīrs and the Turks saying: "The Sulṭān writes and commands respecting you on this subject."[60] In the words of Minhāj: "All of them became excessively incensed against the Sulṭān and, at the suggestion of the Wazīr, they pledged themselves to effect the expulsion and dethronement of the Sulṭān."[61] This sorrowful incident shows that because of the intrigue of the nobles against the Sulṭān, the Delhī forces could not reach Lāhore in time to help Malik Qarāqāsh and enable him to put up a strong defence of Lāhore against the Mongols. Consequently, the Mongols captured the city on 16th Jamādī al-Akhir, A.H. 639/A.D. 1241.[62] Minhāj has fully described the atrocity of the Mongols: "The Mongols martyred all the inhabitants or made captive of them; but such a number of Mongols went to hell as cannot be computed or numbered–about 30,000 or 40,000 Mongol horsemen, with 80,000 horses, indeed more than that. There was not a person among the infidel army that did not bear the wound of arrow, sword or *nawak*...The great number of the Mongol *Nū'ins* and *Bahādurs* also departed to hell, and among them was the *Bahādur* Ṭā'ir, who had encountered *Ak-Sunkar,* lance to lance, and they had wounded each other with those weapons. Ṭā'ir, the *Bahādur,* went to hell, and *Ak-Sunkar,* the lion-hearted, passed into paradise."[63] Two troops of the Muslims headed by *Ak-Sunkar* boldly fought the Mongols but at the end the Mongols succeeded and destroyed Lāhore. After the retirement of the Mongols, Malik Qaraqash, as mentioned by Minhaj, "returned again towards the city from the vicinity of the river Beāh, for on the night of his flight from thence, his *Jamādārs* (Wardrobe Keepers) had abandoned property of great value consisting of pure gold and other valuables; and they marked the spot, he returned to reach for and recover the property. On reaching Lāhore, he recovered it, for it had not fallen into the hands of the Mongols on the departure of the Mongols."[64] Malik Qarāqās͟h was now in a position to crush the allies of the Mongols after the discovery of his property. Describing the allies of the Mongols, Raverty records, "On the departure of the Mongols, the Hindū Kokars and Gabar[65] wretches had come to Lāhore, and were committing destruction. Malik Qarāqās͟h discovered them, dispatched the whole of them to hell and afterwards reached the Court of Delhī in safety."[66] But if Malik Qarās qās͟h was able to crush the allies of the Mongols, what prevented him from taking possession of Lāhore again? It seems reasonable to conclude that, in fact, Malik Qarāqās͟h could not oust the Gakkhars from Lāhore and consequently returned to Delhī. It is also clear that the local tribes living along the frontier sided with the Mongols and were, for this reason a source of trouble for the Sulṭāns of Delhī. Ḥasan Qarlūg͟h, a K͟hwārizmian noble seems also to have joined the Mongols in the sacking of Lāhore and after the departure of the Mongols from the Subcontinent, he marched towards Multān at the head of a large army because Kabīr, K͟hān-i-Ayāz, was dead and his son, Tāj al-Dīn Abū Bakr, had just succeeded his father. The young ruler of Multān rose to the occasion, and defeated the Qarlūgh army.[67] But this defeat did not dampen Qarlūg͟h's courage. According to Juvainī: "The Qarlūg͟h chief attacked Multān several times but every time he was defeated by Sulṭān Tāj al-Dīn Abū Bakr.'[68] Hence Qarlūgh could gain no advantage of the Mongols' sacking of Lāhore since he failed to capture Multān. The sacking of Lāhore by the Mongols reveals the degree to which the defensive policy of the Sulṭān of Delhī proved weak and ineffective. At the same time it also reveals the close alliance of the western tribes with the Mongols. It were these tribes who benefited by the sack of Lāhore.

## IV

### The Frontier Policy of Sulṭān 'Alā al-Dīn Mas'ūd Shāh (A.D. 1242-46)

Sultān 'Alā al-Dīn Mas'ūd Shāh, the son of Sultān Rukn al-Dīn Firūz Shāh, occupied the throne of Delhī in A.D. 1242.[69] At this time, the situation of the frontier region was very critical. The *iqṭā'* of Lāhore had been ruined by the Mongols, and, although under Sulṭān Mas'ūd, it is said to have been placed under Yuzbak-i-Tughral Khān but the city of Lāhore remained deserted.[70] Multān and Uchh had already declared independence under Kabīr Khān after where his death in A.H. 639/A.D. 1242, his son, Tāj al-Dīn Abū Bakr, became the ruler of the territory of Sind.[71] But after the death of the latter Uchh fell into the hands of Mughīs al-Dīn, a former slave of Tāj al-Dīn Abū Bakr's father's eunuch. Multan on the other hand, was captured by Malik Saif al-Dīn Ḥasan Qarlugh who, on account of the pressure of the Mongols, had been forced to leave his former territories.[72] In other words, both the two frontier *iqṭā's,* of Multān and Uchh, were outside the control of the Sulṭān of Delhi. At this critical juncture, several fundamental changes were also taking place in central Asia. Chaghatāe Khān died in A.D. 1241 and in the same year the death of the Great Khān, Ogetāe, also occurred at Karākoram.[73] Hence, two out of four chief divisions of the Mongol empire were suddenly deprived of their sovereign with the result that nearly all the successors of Chingiz Khān were set disputing the succession to the Mongol Khānate with each other.[74] Oliver writes in his summary of this period:

> Among the most violent as regards party spirit and warlike temper were some of the representatives of Chaghatae. For the time being it ended in Turakīna, Ogetāi widow, being appointed regent; but there were set up lasting disputes among the rival regent claimants, and the seeds of much future mischief were sown. For long after, the disputes regarding the succession to the throne of the Great Khān became inextricably mixed up with the affairs...[75]

Thus there arose mutual disputes among the successors of Chingīz Khān, which not only weakened the mighty position of the Mongols but also proved less favourable for making further military advances. The *Quriltāe* or assembly of the Mongol princes was summoned at which Guyūk, son of Ogetāe, was elected his successor as the Great Khān."[76] Minhāj records, "The Great Khān nominated armies to march into the different countries of Chīn, Irān, Hindustān, Khurāsān and 'Irāq. The *Nūin* Mangūtah ( منكوته نوين )[77] was made the leader of an army who entered into the land of Irān and made Tālikān of Kundūz[78] and Warwaliz his headquarters in A.H. 643/A.D. 1245. He then entered Sind and from there led an army towards Uchh and Multān."[79] Minhāj further says: "In A.H. 643/A.D. 1245, the throne of Hindustān was adorned with the splendour and elegance of Sulṭān 'Alā al-Dīn Mas'ūd Shāh, and the city of Lāhore had become ruined. Malik Saif al-Dīn Hasan Qarlūgh held possession of Multān and Hindū Khān, the Khāzin, was the governor of the city and the fortress of Uchh."[80] This precarious situation prevailing in the frontier *iqṭā's* of the Delhī empire was favourable for the Mongol incursion as there was no adequate oppositon to check their raids. When Hasan Qarlūgh heard about the arrival of the Mongol army under Mangūtah on the banks of the river Sind,[81] he had to evacuate Multān and having abandoned the city to its fate, he fled in a boat to Debal and Siwistān.[82] Mangūtah advanced to the foot of the walls of the fortress of Uchh and invested it. During his attack, he destroyed the environs and neighbourhood of that city. The people of the fortress, however, put forth, with the utmost diligence and fortitude, a formidable defence.[83] Minhāj records: "Notwithstanding all the efforts of the Mongol troops and the infidel *Nūins* and *Bahādurs,* the holy warriors of the fortress continued to defend the head of the breach until one of the famous *Bahādurs* of the Mongols, who had gone away in some direction, when he returned to Mangūtah, began to reproach him saying: "What stronghold and fortification is this in the taking of which thou makest so much delay and hesitation? I would take it in a single assault."[84] Minhāj further says, "The following night he made preparations, and put a great number of the Mongols under arms; and suddenly and unexpectedly, in the third watch, which was the time the guards on the walls took repose, and the men of the fortress had gone to sleep, he appeared on the top of the breach."[85] "Because the grace of Almighty God," says Raverty, "was such that the people of the fortress had mixed up a vast quantity of water and clay in the rear of the breach, and had prepared a great pit and deep quagmire more than a spear's length in depth. When that Mongol *Bahādur* planted his foot within the breach under the supposition that it was firm ground, he fell into the quagmire and sank in it. The people of the fortress raised a shout and they brought out torches and armed themselves. Consequently, the Mongols retired."[86] This event encouraged the defenders and the Mongols had to request them to release one of their *Bahādur* who had fallen into their hands. Minhāj has described the event as follows:

> The next day the Mongols deputed persons requesting the defenders to give up the *Bahādur* who had been taken prisoner the previous night, in order that the army might raise the investment and depart. As that accursed one had gone to hell, and had sunk into the black water and slimy mud, to give up was impossible.[87]

On account of the great loss of the Mongols and the courageous resistance of the people of U<u>chh</u>, the Mongols, thus, decided to raise the siege of the fortress and retire towards their country. The Muslims of U<u>chh</u>, therefore, saved themselves from the tyrannical hands of the Mongols. Moreover, this victory of the Muslims made them bold. They were encouraged by the timely assistance of the Delhī forces about which Minhāj says: . . .

> When the Mongol army appeared before the gate of U<u>chh</u>, the Muslims of that fort sent an account of it to the Court, at Delhi, imploring assistance in repelling them and Sultān Mas'ūd, animated and inspired through the efforts and exertions of Ulu<u>gh</u> <u>Kh</u>ān,[88] assembled the hosts of Hindustān, and moved towards the upper province for the purpose of driving off the Mongol invaders. When the royal forces reached the banks of the river Beāh, the army moved along its banks towards U<u>chh</u>. On the Mongol forces becoming aware of the advance of the forces of Islām, and the vanguard of the warriors of the faith having reached within a short distance of the territory of Multān and U<u>chh</u>, they did not possess the power of withstanding

> them. They retired disappointedly from before the fortress of Uchh and went away; and that fortress, through the power of the sovereign of Islām, and the divine aid, remained safe from the wickedness of those accursed ones.[89]

These words of Minhāj confirm that the arrival of Delhī forces on the banks of Beāh was another factor, which forced the Mongols to realise their weak position and retire.

A close study of this second invasion of the Mongols during the reign of Sulṭān 'Alā al-Dīn Mas'ūd Shāh help to understand the motives of the Mongol raids; the state of the Delhī frontier; the absence of a definite frontier policy of the empire; and the routes of the invading Mongol armies while marching towards Hindūstān and Sind. It becomes clear that the real motive of the Mongol raid was the destruction of the power of Malik Ḥasan Qarlugh, a governor of their old enemy Khawarizm Shah, and to make him captive. In this mission they pursued him, and though fortunately he made his escape towards Debul, his territories were ruined by their onslaughts.[90] The other reason of the Mongol raid was that they, in common with other conquerors, also wanted to capture the wealth of Hindūstān. As has been mentioned, there was at this time acute mutual conflict among the successors of Chingīz Khān for the selection of the Great Khān after the death of Ogetāe Khān in A.D. 1241. The wealth of Hindūstān was seen as a factor which could influence this significant event most critically. Thus the *Nū'ins* and *Bahādurs* who were holding the commands of Ghor and Ghaznī turned their attention to procure this wealth.

The raids of the Mongols also show the route which they followed to reach Multān and Uchh. It seems strange when we look at the map[91] of the Punjāb and notice the present position of the rivers of the province, that all the invaders came the same way through the Sind-Sāgar-doāb from the direction of Koh-i-Jūd, immediately south of which lay the great road from Ghaznī into the subcontinent. Why they followed this route and why it was always either Uchh or Multān which bore the brunt of the attacks from the north-west can only be conjectured.

To conclude, it may be said that, although no definite policy was followed by Sulṭān Mas'ūd Shāh, he was not unmindful of the request made by the Muslims of Uchh for their rescue from the Mongols. He immediatley sent forces under the command of Ghiyāṣ al-Dīn Balban who found no opposition to his occupation of Uchh and Multān after the retirement of the Mongols. Leaving both the frontier *iqṭās* under the command of Kashlū Khān, the Sulṭān moved his forces to the north to chastise the hill tribes of Koh-i-Jūd for their late depredation on Lāhore and also for their assistance to the Mongols.[92] But this venture of the Sulṭān of Delhī, however, had to be postponed because of the political move at the Delhī Court designed to remove Sulṭān Mas'ūd Shāh from the throne of Delhī which required his immediate return.

1. *T.N.* (Text), p. 176 (Trans.), p. 623.
2. *Ibid.*, (Trans.), p. 623.
3. See for details, *J.T.* (Trans.), pp. 233-5.
4. *T.J.G.* (Trans.), pp. 247-55.
5. According to Juvainī, "When Chingīz Khān returned from the lands of the west to his old encampment in the east. . . he was overcome by an incurable disease arising from the insalubrity of the climate. He called to his sons. . . and addressed them as follows: 'The severity of my illness is greater than can be cured by treatment, and of a truth, one of you must defend the throne and power of the state and raise up that pedestal which has received so strong a foundation. . . . For if all my sons wish each of them to become Khān, and be the ruler, and not be subservient to one another, will it not be like the fable of the snake with one head and the snake with many heads. . .' Chingīz Khān then spoke as follows: 'If it is your wish to pass your lives in ease and luxury. . ., my advice, as I have lately given you to understand, is that Ogetae should ascend the throne of the Khānāte in my place'. . . " *T.J.G.* (Trans.), pp. 178-82.
6. Bartold Spuler, *History of the Mongols*, London, 1972, p. 52.
7. Boyle, *op. cit.*, p. 335.
8. *T.J.G.* (Trans.), p. 255. Boyle argues that it occurred in April, 1248. Boyle, p. 338.
9. *T.N.* (Text), pp. 103-108; (Trans.), pp. 596,718.
10. *Ibid.*, (Trans.), p. 232.
11. W. Barthold, *The Encyclopaedia of Islam*, p. 786; *Hudūd al-Alam*, (Trans.), Minorsky, p. 287.
12. According to Bābar, "This range is called and written as Koh-i-Jūd". *T.B.* (Trans.), p. 379. See for details in Appendix A.
13. *T.N.* (Trans.), p. 1133.
14. *Ibid.*, p. 633.
15. *Ibid.*, p. 730.
16. *T.N.* (Trans.), p. 1125.
17. *Tārīkh-i-Sīstān* as quoted by Raverty. Minhāj writes Sīstān as Sejistān. *Ibid.*, p. 397
18. *T.J.G.* (Trans.), p.148.
19. *Ibid.*, p. 149.
20. Since the days of Sir Henry Elliot, its name has been read by the scholars as Banīān, but I.H. Siddīque, a modern historian, argues that the actual name of the territory was Binbān. *I.C.* 1980, p. 77. In the text it is used as Banīān.
21. *J.T.* (Text), p. 55.
22. *Tārīkh-i-Alfī* as quoted by Raverty. *T.N.* (Trans.), p. 1108.
23. *Ibid.*, p. 1129.
24. *Ibid.*, p. 96. Our impression is confirmed by the fact that there was no conflict between the parties after A.D. 1238 and Hasan Qarlūgh and his son and his successors continued to rule over Banīān as Mongol vassals. Minhāj also says earlier that as Ḥasan Qarlūgh found himself not strong enough to resist the Mongols, he accepted the Shāhn'agān to reside in Banīān. *Ibid.*, (Trans.), p. 388.
25. *T.N.* (Trans.), p. 633.
26. *Ibid.*, p. 731.
27. Sulṭān Fīrūz Shāh was dethroned through the contumacy of Turkish Amīrs, and Sulṭāna Raziā, daughter of Sulṭān Iltutmish, was placed on the throne on 8th Rabī'al-Awwal, 634/9th Nov. 1238 *T.N.* (Text), p. 94.

28. Chief Amirs like Malik 'Ala al-Din Jani assembled from different parts before the gate of Delhi and commenced hostilities against Razia. *Ibid.* (Trans.), p. 638.
29. Bartold Spuler, *op. cit.*, p. 52.
30. *T.N.* (Trans.), p. 726.
31. *Ibid.*
32. *Ibid.* The river Sodhra, modern Chinab, is called from the old town of that name on its eastern bank. See for details, Hodivala, *op. cit.*, pp. 183-4.
33. *T.N.* (Trans.), p. 726.
34. Baran is now called Bulandshahr, situated to the east of Delhi.
35. *T.N.* (Trans.), p. 645.
36. In the meantime, Hasan Qarlugh accepted the condition that the Mongol Shahn-agan (Political agent) would reside at his court at Banian. *Ibid.*, p. 388.
37. This large tribe appears to have extended, at this period, a considerable distance east of the river Beah, and good horses obtained from the Talwandis of the Gakkhars, are often mentioned. *T.N.* (Trans.), p. 647.
38. Sultan Mu'izz al-Din Bahram Shah bin Sultan Shams al-Din Iltutmish was raised to the throne on Monday, 28th of the Ramzan, 637 A.H./A.D. 1240 *T.A.*, (Text), p. 100.
39. When Malik Ikhtiyar-ud-Din, Aitigin, became deputy, by virtue of his deputyship, he took the affairs of the kingdom into his own hands, and in conjunction with the Wazir. . . the Mustaufi assumed control over the disposal of state affairs. After a month or two had passed away, this fact began to press heavily upon the noble mind of the Sultan and his sister. . . the deputy assumed the triple *naubat*, and stationed an elephant at the entrance of his own residence and the grandeur of his affairs and the execution of his mandates lasted until the month of Muharram of the year 638, when, unexpectedly. . . by the command of the Sultan, a discourse was delivered within the *Kasr* named Safed. After the termination of the discourse, the Sultan dispatched two reckless Turks. . . . They martyred Malik Aitigin, . . . They inflicted wounds on the Wazir. . . but he escaped. *Ibid.*, (Trans.), p. 650.
40. *Ibid.*, p. 1133.
41. The district of Badghis occupied the whole stretch of country lying between the Herat river on the west and the upper waters of the Murghab on the east. . . . See for details, Le Strange, *op. cit.*, pp. 412-3.
42. The 'Arab geographers divide Fars between two regions, namely, the Hot Lands, and the Cold Lands. Garmsir is referred to as the Hot Lands. *Ibid.*, pp. 249.
43. See at page 71 fn. 2.
44. *T.N.* (Trans.), p. 1133.
45. *Ibid.*
46. A walled city with a castle or citadel.
47. Minhaj writes it as Luhawar ( لهاور ). *T.N.* (Text), p. 103.
48. He was very warlike, energetic, intrepid and fearless.
49. *T.N.* (Trans.), pp. 633, 1133.
50. It was a kind of mechanical sling for casting stones and fire against enemy.
51. *T.N.* (Trans.), p. 656.
52. *T.N.* (Trans.), p. 1134.
53. *Ibid.*
54. *Ibid.*

55. "One of the heroes was Ak-Sunkar ( اقسنقر ). He was a Turk. Sunkar in the Rumi (Turkish) dialect, is said to signify a black-eyed falcon, which lives to a great age. He was also called the *Senschal* of Lāhore, (Kotwal of Lāhore), who, with his dependents, in combat and in conflict, surpassed a thousand times, *Rustam-i-Dastān*. The other hero was Dīn Dār Muḥammad, the *Amīr-i-Ākhūr* of Lahore, who, alongwith his sons and dependents – on that day, waged holy war. . . and fought against the unbelievers in such manner as if the purified soul of 'Alī-i-Murtaẓa in concert with the whole of (sic) the prophets and apostles, were showering blessings upon him from the garden of paradise." *Ibid.*, pp. 394, 1134.

56. *T.N.* (Trans.), p. 1135.

57. *Ibid.*, p. 658.

58. *Ibid.*

59. *Ibid.*, (Text), p. 104, (Trans.), p. 658.

60. *Ibid.*

61. *Ibid.*, (Trans.), pp. 105,659.

62. *Ibid.*, p. 659. According to *Tārīkh-i-Alfī*, this happened in 628 A.H. . . *Tārīkh-i-Alfī* as cited by Raverty p. 1135.

63. *T.N.* (Trans.), p. 1135. An arrow discharged throwing a tube probably a cross-bow or balists, or something similar.

64. *Ibid.*, p. 1136.

65. It is not identified by any authority so far.

66. *T.N.* (Trans.), p. 1136.

67. *T.N.* (Trans.), p. 727.

68. *T.J.G.* (Trans.), p. 416.

69. Sulṭān 'Alā al-Dīn Mas'ūd Shāh ascended the throne on the 8th of Zī-Qad A.H. 639/A.D. 1242, after the dethronement of Sulṭān Bahrām Shāh. *T.N.* (Trans), p. 197.

70. *Ibid.*, p. 660.

71. This indicates that the Iqṭa' of Multān as well as Uchh was included in Sind in those days.

72. *T.N.* (Trans.), p. 668.

73. *T.R.* (Trans.), p. 33.

74. After the death of Chingīz Khān, his empire was divided amongst his four sons. Jujī, the eldest son of Chingīz Khān died before the death of his father and his son Bātū ruled his father's empire of Kipchaq. Chaghatāe, the second son of the Khān, was ruling Transoxaniā. Ogetāe, the third son, occupied the country of the original Mongols having his capital at Karākoram. Kublae Khān, the fourth son, ruled over China. Oliver, *op. cit.*, pp. 90-1.

75. Oliver, *op. cit.*, p. 91.

76. *T.J.G.* (Trans.), p. 247

77 He was an aged man, very tall with dog-like eyes. Elliot calls him Mangū Khān. T.F.S. (Trans.), p. 344.

78. Tālkān of Kunduz or more correctly Kuhandujz also called Tālīkān of Tukhāristān which was one of the most populous town in 10th century. See for details, Le Strange, *op. cit.*, p. 428.

79. *T.F.S.* (Trans.), p. 344.

80. He was incharge of Uchh and its dependencies in Raziā's reign, and he returned to the court of Delhi when Bahrām Shāh came to power who conferred upon him the fief of Jalandhar. *T.N.* (Trans.), p. 745.

81 At this period in question no river intervened between Sind and Multān. He, consequently, embarked on the combined rivers Jhelum, Chināb and Rāvī, which then ran east of Multān, and so, placing river between himself and the Mongols, was enabled to get down into Sind without molestation.

82. *T.N.* (Trans.), p. 399.

83. *T.N.* (Trans.), p. 400.

84. *Ibid.*

85. *Ibid.*, p. 1155.

86. *T.N.* (Trans.), p. 1156.

87 *Ibid.*

88. His name was Ghīyāṣ al-Dīn Balban, who later on became the Sultān of Delhī in A.D. 1266.

89. *T.N.* (Trans.), p. 1156.

90. *Ibid.*

91. See map No. 2 of the routes between Central Asia and South Asia.

92. *T.N.* (Trans.), p. 1154.

## Chapter IV

# THE FRONTIER POLICY OF THE MAMLŪKS–III (A.D. 1246-90)

## I

### The Frontier Policy of Sulṭān Nāsir al-Dīn Maḥmūd (A.D. 1246-66)

Nāṣir al-Dīn Mahmūd[1] ascended the throne of Delhī in A.D. 1246[2] after the overthrow of Sulṭān 'Alā al-Dīn Mas'ūd Shāh.[3] At this time, the politics of Central Asia entered a new phase. Guyūk, son of Ogetāe, was elected his successor as the Great Khān by the *Quriltāe.*[4] Soon Guyūk attacked Almāligh[5] in A.D. 1247 and Ebuskun was deprived of power.[6] Consequently, disorder prevailed throughout the *Khānate,* but Guyūk was able to set up one *Yāsū* Mangū who governed the country through the agency of a Muslim Wazīr called Bahā al-Dīn.[7] Guyūk died within three years of his accession and was succeeded as the Supreme Khān by Mangū, the eldest son of Tūlī, in July, 1251.[8] These changes in Central Asian politics alarmed the Sulṭān of Delhī who resolved to defend his frontier from the raids of the Mongol military commanders. This is confirmed by a representation of Balban[9] to the Sulṭān soon after his enthronement, as reproduced below:

> Since the *Khuṭbah* and the coin of the kingdom are adorned with the august Nāṣirī name, and, in the past year, the army of the accursed Mongols having fled before the forces of Islām, are gone towards the upper country, it may be advisable that the royal forces should march towards the upper parts.[10]

This counsel of Balban to the Sulṭān is the evidence that he was urged to advance towards the frontier of his empire in view of the situation prevailing beyond the Indus. Minhāj has explained the situation thus: "Mangū Khān, son of Ṭūlī Khān, son of Chingiz Khān, ascended the throne and under his orders, Rukn al-Dīn Kurt of Herāt exercised sway over the territories extending upto the river Indus and is even reported to have control of the highways as far as the frontier of Delhī."[11]

According to the author of *Tārīkh-i-Nāma-i-Herāt-*: "In A.D. 1246 Malik Shams al-Dīn and *Nūin Sāli* marched towards India. They laid siege to the city of Multān which was held by Jankar Khān, the slave of Sulṭān Iltutmish. On the fourteenth day, Jankar Khān sent Shaikh Bahā al-Dīn Zakariyā, a saint, to Malik Shams al-Dīn, so that the latter might persuade the Mongol chief to accept money and leave Multān. His visit had the desired effect. "On the persuation of Malik Shams al-Dīn the Mongol chief collected one hundred thousand dīnars and went to Lāhore where also Sālī extorted 30,000 dīnārs, thirty ass-loads of soft goods and one hundred captives."[12] These movements of the Mongols along the frontier of the Delhī empire were the real reasons which led Balban to counsel the Sulṭān as mentioned earlier. Following this counsel of Balban, the Sulṭān raised his Imperial standard in the year 644 A.H. and brought out his forces for the purpose of marching to the banks of the river Indus and Baniān in order to cause destruction of the infidels.[13] The Sulṭān crossed the river of Lāhore (Rāvī) on Sunday, the Ist of Zi-qaʿad A.H. 644 and issued a command to the forces of Islām to ravage the Jūd hills and the area around Nandanā.[14] Reaching the banks of Sodhrā, the Sulṭān himself encamped there and nominated Balban as the head of the army. Balban along with the other Amīrs and Maliks separated from the army on an expedition to the Jūd hills whose tribes had acted as guide to the Mongols.[15] Then, along with his forces he carried on incursions and ravaged the territory as far as the banks of the river Indus. He went even further and despoiled the land up to the domain of Rāe Jaspāl, a tribal chief, who fled away with his followers and dependents.[16]

According to Minhāj:

> The Delhī forces crossed the river Jhelum and carried its ravages as far as the banks of the river Sind, in such wise, that all women, families and dependents of the infidels who were in those parts, took to flight, and a body from the army of the infidel Mongols came to the ferries of the Jhelum, and beheld the lines of the Delhī troops serving under Ulugh Khān-i-A'zam, and fear fell upon their hearts, at the number of troops composing his army, the number of cavalry in defensive armour, and the great terror took possession of that gathering. That vigour, military organisation and overthrowing of enemies, in the assault of mountain heights, the gorges of mountain passes, and of ravines, the capturing of strong places and forts, and penetrating of forests, which Ulugh Khān-i-A'zam displayed, cannot be contained within the area of recital, and the fame of that holy warfare extended as far as the land of Turkistān.[17]

This action taken by Balban shows the determination of his army of Islām to follow an aggressive policy and push forward. Pointing out the impact of this action Minhāj says: "Since through the firmness of counsel and the justness of determination of Balban, the army of Turkistān and the Mongols had beheld those exploits and that military organisation, during the year A.H. 645, not a single man, from the parts stated above, came towards the territory of Sind."[18] This forward action of Balban created such an impact that the Mongols in the following years ceased to raid the borders of the Delhi empire. According to Minhāj: "After this triumphant victory Balban returned and presented himself at the court, and sublime standard moved to return again towards the capital of Delhī on Thursday, 25th Zī-qa'ad, 644."[19] At this time Malik Jalāl al-Dīn Mas'ūd Shāh, the Sulṭān's brother, presented himself to the Sulṭān in A.H. 646 and was granted the fief of Sanbhal and Badāūn. From Sanbhal and Badāūn, the prince proceeded towards Lāhore by way of Silmūr (i.e. Sirmūr).[20] Though contemporary works are silent about the actual reason of the prince proceeding to Lāhore, it seems that he did so because after his meeting with the Sulṭān he either became frightened or disaffected and thought it was best to fly to Lāhore after abandoning his fief. At this time, as mentioned by Minhāj, "The royal standard moved towards the upper provinces as far as the extreme confines, and the bank of the river Beāh, and from there returned again to the capital."[21] Though Minhāj has not given any reason for this movement of the Delhī forces it appears probable that this movement was connected in some way with the prince's flight, who is said to have gone to the Mongols from Lāhore.[22]

The internal situation also took a new turn. On account of meritorious services rendered by Balban, the Sulṭān appointed him as his deputy. According to Minhāj: "The status of Ulugh Khān was raised from the rank of Malik and Amīr Ḥājib to the dignity and eminent position of Khān, and on Tuesday, the 3rd Rajab, 647 A.H., a mandate was issued from the sublime court for conferring the deputy-ship of the kingdom and the leadership of the forces with the title and name of Ulugh Khān upon Balban."[23] This recognition was the result of Balban's sincere services to the Sulṭān and his courageous expedition against the Mongols. But Minhāj also gives another reason for his promotion – that the Sulṭān entered into a matrimonial alliance with the family of Balban after marrying his daughter who became the Malikah-i-Jahān.[24] The argument that this relationship with Balban was contributive to the latter's rise appears to be convincing. Anyhow, for whatever causes, Balban became the *Nā'ib* (deputy) of the Delhī empire in A.H. 647/A.D. 1249.[25]

## II

### The Frontier Policy of Sulṭān Ghiyāṣ al-Dīn Balban (A.D. 1249-86)

a) The Frontier Policy of Ghiyās al-Dīn as Deputy *(Nā'ib-us-Sultānat)* A.D. 1249-66.

Balban's reputation as the saviour of the frontier of the Delhī empire from the onslaughts of the Mongols now came to be firmly established and widely recognised. Soon after becoming deputy, he counselled the Sulṭān in matters of administrative appointments in the court and in the frontier *iqṭā's* of the empire. Consequently, with the counsel of Balban, the key posts of the state, especially those of the frontier region, went to his relations. Minhāj writes: "His brother Saif al-Dīn Kashlū Khān, who was *Amīr-i-Akhūr*, became *Amīr-i-Hājib;* Malik Tāj al-Dīn became deputy *Amīr-i-*

*Hājib,* and 'Alā al-Dīn became the deputy *Wakīl-i-Dār.* Balban's cousin, Sher Khān Sunkar, was entrusted with the government of the *iqṭā's* of Multān, Kuhrām, Sunam, Siwālik hills and Sirhind in addition to the charge of Lāhore and Bhatindah."[26] These administrative arrangements prove that Lāhore and Multān continued to be the westernmost *Iqṭā's* of the Delhī empire. Before Sher Khān took over the charge of Multān it was under Malik Kashlū Khān who was already engaged in a battle against Hasan Qarlūgh. According to Minhāj: "In retaliation to Ulugh Khān's incursion into Koh-i-Jūd and Baniān in A.D. 1246, Hasan Qarlūgh invaded Multān after full preparation in A.D. 1249."[27] Minhāj further records that: "When Hasan Qarlūgh besieged Multān, the *muqti* of Multān, Malik 'Izz al-Dīn Balban Kashlū Khān, rushed from Uchh to Multān. When the two armies stood face to face, a band of fifty warrior horsemen in Balban Kashlū Khān's contingent formed a ring and fell on the centre of the Qarlūgh's army and killed Hasan Qarlūgh but they were also encircled and killed. On the destruction of his heroic followers Balban Kashlū Khān shut himself inside the fortress. The Qarlūgh troops kept the death of their master concealed and continued to press the siege. At last, Balban Kashlū Khān sued for peace, surrendered the fortress and returned to Uchh."[28] Thus Multān came under the hold of the Qarlūghs in A.D. 1249. But the Qarlūghs could not retain their hold over Multān for long. According to Minhāj, "Soon after the occupation of Multān by the Qarlūghs, Sher Khān Sunkar advanced from Tabarhind and seized Multān from the Qarlūghs."[29] After the capture of Multān, Sher Khān[30] placed it under his *nā'ib,* Malik Kūrez.[31] Minhāj further says, "Sher Khān also snatched away Uchh from Kashlu Khān in A.D. 1250."[32] Thus the frontier *iqṭā's* of Multān, Uchh and Lāhore were captured and retained by Sher Khān Sunkar till the end of A.D. 1250. After these victories Sher Khān raised and disciplined a body of horses with which he marched forward upto Ghaznī and drove the Mongols out of Ghaznī and annexed it once more to the kingdom of Delhī."[33] Firishta points out that Sher Khān also struck coins in the name of Sulṭān Nāṣir al-Dīn Mahmūd and proclaimed him king of all the territories in that quarter.[34] This advance of Sher Khān upto Ghaznī was the second advance after Sulṭān Quṭb al-Dīn Aibak. It also shows that the "forward policy" reached a new climax.

In the following years, the power of Balban reached its zenith but in A.H. 651, a new development took place in the court. About this Minhāj says: "Balban's ascendancy to power led to the rise of a party headed by 'Imād al-Dīn Rayḥān against him and consequently Sulṭān Mahmūd dismissed Balban from the deputy-ship and fresh distribution of offices took place."[35] As a result, Sher Khān was also ousted from the *muqṭīship* of the frontier *iqṭā's* for sometime and, "His possessions in Sind were transferred to Arslān Khān in A.D. 1253."[36] Raverty has pointed out another reason for Sher Khān's ousting saying:

> "Unfortunatley, Sher Khān had been defeated by a body of insurgents from Sind and had lost several forts in Multān which furnished the favourities with an opportunity of disgracing him in the eyes of the Sulṭān and hence the Sulṭān was compelled by the situation to take the field in the direction of the Beāh and removed Sher Khān from government which was conferred on Arslān Khān.[37]

Though in this regard none of the contemporary works give us any clear indication of Sher Khān's ouster but it seems reasonable to infer that he had suffered due to Balban's downfall. However, Sher Khān retired to Turkistān and went to the court of the Mongol emperor, Mangū Khān, (Mongke Khān).[38] At the same time, the prince Jalāl al-Dīn Mas'ūd Shāh, brother of Sulṭān Maḥmūd, was already there, and according to Waṣṣāf, "The prince then proceeded, after his departure from Lāhore, to the court of Mangū Khān where his presence along with Qatlugh Khān and Sher Khān is also noticed by Binagiti."[39] Raverty refers to Rubrūquis, the contemporary European traveller, who corroborates this statement adding: "When the Great Khān of the Mongols held a great assembly at Karākoram on 15th June, 1254, at which a number of ambassadors attended, he noticed the ambassador from the Sulṭān of India."[40] As no contemporary work records that any ambassador had been sent by Sulṭān Nāsir al-Dīn Mahmūd to the court of the Mongol emperor, it seems reasonable to conclude that the persons mistakenly referred to as ambassador no other than Jalāl al-Dīn Mas'ūd Shāh and Sher Khān. The presence of Prince Mas'ūd Shāh and Sher Khān at the court of the Mongols deeply disturbed the authorities in Delhi. Sher Khān's ouster also made the defence of the Delhi frontier weaker. According to Rashīd al-Dīn Faẓlullāh, "Mangū Khān, the Mongol King, now treated Jalāl al-Dīn Mas'ūd Shāh with honour and ordered the Mongol *Nuin* named Sāli Bahādur to help Jalāl al-Dīn against his enemies. Thereupon, Sāli Bahādur accompanied the prince and taking Nāṣir al-Dīn Muḥammad Qarlūgh, son of Ḥasan Qarlūgh, from Baniān, entered Lāhore. They drove away the Delhī officers from the *iqtā's* of Lāhore and Jallandhar, and installed prince Mas'ūd Shāh there. The latter assumed the title of Sulṭān Jalāl al-Dīn Mas'ūd Shāh and ruled over the vast region of the Punjab comprising the trans-Sutlej region as a Mongol vassal.[41] The Mongols kept patronising Jalāl al-Dīn Mas'ūd Shāh after installing him as a vassal ruler over their trans-Indus possessions. Since this served their purpose.

Meanwhile Sher Khān Sunkar also returned with prince Mas'ūd and remained with him in Lāhore till A.D. 1254. In the same year the internal affairs of the Delhī empire took a new turn. On account of Rayḥān's nepotism and maladministration his opponents among the nobles forced the Sulṭān to dismiss him from his post and to transfer him to the province of Badāūn.[42] Balban was reappointed deputy while his kinsmen and supporters were all reinstated.

This political change in the capital brought the frontier problem, with which Balban had to deal to the fore. Kashlū Khān, the *muqṭi'* of Multān and Uchh, who belonged to Rayḥān's party, refused to acknoweldge the suzerainty of the Delhī emperor and declared himself independent. Prince Jalāl al-Dīn Mas'ūd Shāh had already transferred his loyalties to the Mongols and had become the independent ruler of Lāhore. The Qarlūghs of Baniān also accepted the vassalship of the Mongols. The frontier situation had further increased the possibility of the Mongol advance towards Delhī. Balban boldly faced the situation and watched vigilantly the movements arising among the frontier area of the Delhī empire.

BALBAN AND JALĀL AL-DĪN MAS'ŪD SHĀH. Jalāl al-Dīn Mas'ūd Shāh occupied the *iqtā'* of Lāhore in A.D. 1254 with the support of the Mongol Nū'in Sāli Bahādur. According to Raverty: "Jalāl al-Dīn assumed the title of Sulṭān and ruled over the vast region of Lāhore as a Mongol vassal.''[43] In A.D. 1254 Sulṭān Jalāl al-Dīn Mas'ūd Shāh alongwith Sher Khān marched from Lāhore to join Ulugh Khān against the faction of Qatlugh Khān and 'Imād al-Did Rayḥān who had got complete hold over Sulṭān Nāsir al-Dīn Maḥmūd Shāh.[44] When they moved in the direction of Delhī, Sulṭān Maḥmūd also came out with the Delhī army and met Ulugh Khān and his allies near Hānsī but the engagement was avoided by the intervention of certain nobles.[45] Thereafter, compromise was effected between Ulugh Khān and the Sultān. This annoyed Sulṭān Jalāl al-Dīn Mas'ūd Shāh because he felt deceived by Ulugh Khān and his cousin Sher Khān who had promised him the throne of Delhī. Sher Khān even won over a large number of Sulṭān Jalāl al-Dīn Mas'ūd Shāh's nobles to his side. Sulṭān Jalāl al-Dīn Mas'ūd Shāh, however, returned to Lāhore in disgust where he continued to reign till the close of Sulṭān Nāsir al-Dīn Maḥmūd's reign.[46] Balban tried to avoid any clash with Sulṭān Jalāl al-Dīn Mas'ūd Shāh, the ruler of Lāhore, and even Sher Khān was transferred from Tabarhindā to Gwālior in A.D. 1258 because Sher Khān was hostile to Sulṭān Jalāl al-Dīn Mas'ūd Shāh and wanted to occupy Lāhore.[47] Thus his presence in Tabarhindā could invite the Mongols to help their vassal. Balban was wise enough to understand this precarious position created in the western frontier of the empire, and consequently, Sher Khān was transferred from Tabarhindā as already mentioned. This action of Balban prevented a direct clash with Sulṭān Jalāl al-Dīn Mas'ūd Shāh who continued to rule Lāhore till the close of Sulṭān Nāṣir al-Dīn Mahmūd Shāh's reign.

BALBAN AND KASHLŪ KHĀN. The other Delhī noble who declared his independence and became the Mongol vassal was Malik 'Izz al-Dīn Balban Kashlū Khān, the *muqṭi'* of the *bilād* of Sind and Multān.[48] He belonged to the faction of Qatlugh Khān[49] and Imād al-Dīn Rayḥān. After the eclipse of his allies and the ascendancy of Balban at the royal court, he sent his officer Malik Shams al-Dīn Kurt Ghorī to Irān to negotiate with Halākū Khān for an alliance. His envoy was successful in effecting an understanding between his master and Halākū Khān. Thereafter, Kashlū Khān received a Mongol *Shāhna'gān* and sent one of his grandsons to Irān as his *wakil.*[50] It is clear that these nobles were in league with the Mongols and hence they were encouraged to move and raid the frontier of the Delhī empire. According to Minhāj: "In A.D. 1257 Kashlū Khān joined Sāli Bahādur, the Mongol *Nū'in,* who came from Ghaznī to India on a predatory expedition. The Mongols dismantled the defences of Multān and having plundered the *iqtā'* beyond the Sutlej river, returned to their base in Ghaznī."[51] At this time the Delhī forces could not move against the invaders as the forces of the Mongol allies in the frontier region of the Delhī empire had considerably added to the Mongol strength. Lāhore was under the sway of Sulṭān Jalāl al-Dīn Mas'ūd Shāh, and Multān, including the upper part of Sind, was ruled over by Kashlū Khān. At this period, therefore, the whole of the frontier zone was no longer under the control of the Delhī empire. Balban, who, at this time, had become the *de facto* ruler of the Delhī empire, decided to weaken the Mongol influence in the frontier region through diplomacy. He made a secret alliance with Sulṭān Nāsir al-Dīn Muḥammad Qarlūgh,[52] and with his help concluded a peace treaty with Halākū Khān in A.D. 1258.[53] After the death of Halākū Khān, Balban did not honour this treaty with Halākū's successors and invaded the *iqṭā's* of Lāhore and Multān. The pretext for doing so was provided by the following developments reported by 'Isāmī:

> There came a courtier from the confines of Multān. . . who said "O King! refuge of the faith: I have just arrived from Uchh and Multān from which area a clamour has shot up, its houses are ruined. The *Balban-i-Zār* whom your Majesty had personally appointed governor of Multān has revolted against you, and has created a tumult in that area.[54]

This evidence, however, helps us to know that great unrest was prevailing in Multān and that this demanded an immediate action against Kashlū Khān. Accordingly Balban marched towards Multān and achieved victory over the enemy. According to 'Isāmī:

> The following day Ulugh Khān marched towards Multān by the order of the king. He crossed the river Rāvī and reached the environs of the fortress with wind-like speed. Then he beat the drums confronting the fortress. But *Balban-i-Zār* was not in Multān at that time. The experienced man had gone to Punjab to bring that region under his control leaving behind his son Muḥammad at Multān. . . . Ulugh Khān captured Multān and Muḥammad saved his life and fled to his own father. . . and narrated to him the complete story.[55]

The same authority 'Isāmī further states that:

> When *Balban-i-Zār* became aware of the occurrences, he thought to himself: 'Ulugh Khān has brought a huge army from the capital. Now that the soldiers of Multān have also joined him and his troops have at any rate swelled enormously, with such small army as this, it will not be wise on my part to encounter him. I had better quit this place and go out of this area.[56]

At last, he gave up the idea of fighting, and, after a few days, left the Punjāb and rode at a stretch until he arrived at Baniān where he took up his residence. 'Isāmī further writes: "After this, on two occasions that accursed fellow brought the Mongols into Multān in the hope of siezing it and revenging himself on the Multānese, but his intention being evil, he was defeated on both occasions."[57] These sources reveal that Kashlū Khān was still in league with the Mongols and wanted to recapture Multān with their help. However, he failed in his venture and the *iqtā'* of Multān came under the control of the Delhī empire after two decades.

BALBAN AND THE QARLUGHS. After the death of Sulṭān Ḥasan Qarlūgh, his eldest son, Sulṭān Nāṣir al-Dīn Muḥammad succeeded as the ruler of Baniān and the Koh-i-Jūd region. With him a new phase of the history of the Qarlūgh rule in the north-western region began. He acted with patience and shrewdness in maintaining diplomatic ties with his Mongol suzerain and followed a pragmatic policy towards the Delhī Sulṭān, also an immediate neighbour. Al-Juzjani says, "Malik Nāṣir al-Dīn Muḥammad Qarlūgh developed a desire to cement his friendship with Ulugh Khān through a matrimonial alliance. The Qarlūgh ruler decided to give his daughter to Shāh, son of Ulugh Khān, in marriage. For this purpose he secretly directed one of his confidants in Delhī to enquire of his own whether Ulugh Khān would agree to the marriage of his son with the former's daughter. When the proposal was referred to Ulugh Khān, the latter could not turn it down."[58] This political marriage helped to establish good terms between Nāsir al-Dīn Muḥammad Qarlūgh and Balban. Once again contemporary works give no reasons for this marriage. However, it is not difficult to see that Balban desired it for two reasons: firstly, because Qarlugh was independent of the Delhī Sulṭāns and the marriage would seek to make this power an ally rather than an antagonist secondly, because Balban wanted to establish friendly relations with Halākū Khān and Qarlugh, in his capacity as the senior vassal of the Mongols, could help him to achieve his end.

The end, however, could not be achieved through the Qarlughs. For there arose a conflict between the Qarlūghs and Halākū Khān, which has been mentioned by Rashīd al-Dīn Fazlullah and Abu Sulaimān Dāud al-Binagiti: The last named who says:

> **The Qarlūgh ruler did not help the Mongol vassal against the aggression committed by the Delhī armies in the Trans-Sutlej region of the Punjab, which led Halākū Khān to issue *yarlugh* (counterpart of the Indian Nishān) to his officers of Ghaznī to inquire into the affairs of Qarlūgh. The officer, Malik Shams al-Dīn Kurt, who was not favourably disposed towards him declared him guilty of treachery and put him along with some of his officers and dependents to death.**[59]

After the removal of Qarlūgh, Baniān and Koh-i-Jūd tracts became part of the Chaghatāe's Khānate of Central Asia, which now extended to the territories west of the Indus[60] and was ruled by the Chaghatāe princes, and Qadū who had rebelled against Qublāe Khān (A.D. 1260-94) and occupied Ghazni and the territories of the Indian frontier. Thus Balban was now face to face with the Mongols.

BALBAN AND THE MONGOLS. Mangū Khān, the Mongol ruler, died in A.D. 1256 and the assembly of the Mongol princes elected Qublāe Khān as the Great Khan.[61] Halākū Khān was engaged in the conquests of western Asia and after his victories he laid the foundation of Il-Khānid dynasty of Persia. Halākū Khān sacked and captured Baghdād after the assassination of the Khalifah in A.D. 1258.[62] Balban realised fully the gravity of the situation that prevailed beyond the Indus, and hence he maintained diplomatic relations with Halākū Khān through Nāsir al-Dīn Muḥammad Qarlūgh, as already mentioned. The Qarlūgh ruler, Nāṣir al-Dīn Muḥammad, successfully completed his mission in effecting friendly relations between Balban and Halākū.[63] Being flattered, Halākū sent his emissaries along with Jamāl al-Dīn and also issued orders to the Mongol forces under the Nū'in Sālī: "If the hoof of a horse of your troops shall have entered the ground of the dominions of the Sulṭān of the Sulṭāns, Nāṣir al-Dīn Maḥmūd Shāh — the command upto you is this, that all four feet of such horse be lopped off."[64] This commanding statement of Halākū is of great significance and proves that a new trend in the frontier policy, that of the establishment of new diplomatic relations, had emerged.

In fact this event suggests that Sulṭān Nāṣir al-Dīn Muḥammad Qarlugh, had probably entered into a secret alliance with the Sulṭān of Delhī which is not explicitly mentioned by the contemporary sources. It is probable that the Qarlugh ruler might have realised the hidden antagonism of the Mongols against him for being a son of prince Mangbārnī's commander in the subcontinent. Hence he strengthened his relations through a matrimonial alliance with Balban. Balban too availed of this opportunity for estabishing a relationship with the Qarlugh ruler, and through him also maintained diplomatic relations with Hālāku Khān who had conquered Western Asia and murdered the Khalīfah.[65] But here one may argue why Balban should have established diplomatic relations with Halākū Khān who had sacked Baghdād, a seat of the Caliphate? The answer seems to be that the victories of Halākū Khān in Irān, and the independence of the westernmost frontier *iqṭā's* of Multān and Lāhore forced Balban to adopt a policy of expediency, and which necessitated the establishment of diplomatic relations with Il-Khānid Mongols. Balban, thus, gave preference to political considerations rather than religious ones, and welcomed the emissary of Halākū Khān in Delhī with great honour and ostentation. The impact of these new diplomatic alliances improved the situation and in the following years no Mongol raids occurred on the western frontier of the subcontinent. It is much to be regretted that Minhāj has not given us more information regarding these events, and particularly of the last six years of Sulṭān Nāṣir al-Dīn Mahmūd Shāh.

To sum up, Balban held the charge of *Nā'ib us-Salṭanat* at such a critical juncture that there was a possibility of the vast empire of Delhī being rolled up by Halākū Khān. Balban, being a wise and clever diplomat, soon realised the gravity of the situation prevailing beyond the Indus river. He did not take action against the rebel *muqṭī's* of Lāhore and Multān, following a policy of non-interference, because they had acknowledged the vassalship of the Mongols. He was fully aware of Halākū's victories in western Asia and also of the Caliph's assassination. Despite being a representative of the *Khalīfah*[66] in the subcontinent, he did not protest against this calamitous event because of the fear of Halākū Khān. Rather, he established diplomatic relations with Halākū Khān through the good efforts of Sulṭān Nāsir al-Dīn Muḥammad, the Qarlūgh, ruler of Banīān and the Koh-i-Jūd region, which reflects a new trend in the frontier policy of the Delhī empire. At the same time he also established matrimonial relations with Sulṭān Nāṣir al-Dīn Muḥammad Qarlūgh and made a secret pact with him. Being a far-sighted man, he avoided having a direct clash with the Mongols and hence saved the subcontinent from the barbarity of Halākū Khān. But as soon as the political situation in Central Asia took a new turn after the death of Halākū Khān in A.D. 1265, Balban gave up the policy of non-interference and followed a policy of advance. Consequently, the frontier *iqtā*'s of Lāhore and Multān were seized from the Mongol allies.

## III

## The Frontier Policy of Ghiyāṣ al-Dīn Balban as Sulṭān (A.D. 1266-86)

Ghiyāṣ al-Dīn Balban ascended the throne of Delhī in A.H. 664/A.D. 1266 after the death of Sulṭān Nāṣir al-Dīn Maḥmūd.[67] At the time of his ascendancy to the throne of Delhī, Balban had to face serious internal and external problems which directly affected the frontier security of the empire. Externally, the Sulṭān had to bear the brunt of the Mongol onslaughts as the Mongol empire now touched the border of the Delhī Sulṭanate and, internally, he faced the hostile activities of the tribes of Jūd hills. Halākū Khān was now dead and there started fratricidal warfare among the Mongols. Abaqa, the Il-Khānid's eldest son, came to power in Persia after the death of Halākū Khān on 9 March 1265.[68] During his tenure, there started a war between the Il-Khānid dynasty of Persia and the Chaghatāe princes of Transoxanīā.[69] Hostilities with the Golden Horde were also resumed at the very commencement of Abaqa's reign.[70] Thus the vast Mongol empire was divided into various factions and whenever, they found respite from their warfare in Central Asia, they launched invasions on India. They did not even respect Halākū's diplomatic agreement with the Delhī emperor. Hence, externally, the Mongol movements beyond the Indus river had alerted the Sulṭān of Delhī to keep close watch on their advance towards the subcontinent. It was also essential that the tribes of Jūd hills, the allies of the Mongols, would not be allowed to exist as an eyesore on the frontier of the Delhī empire. Baranī tells us about Balban's campaign in the Jūd hills as follows:

> He marched thither with suitable forces and inflicted chastisement upon the tribes of Jūd hills and the vicinity. The country was plundered and a large number of horses fell into the hands of the soldiers so that the price of a horse came to be forty tankas. . . .[71]

This is also confirmed by Firishta who says, "Balban marched his army towards the hills of Jud in A.H. 665/A.D. 1266, and was engaged for two years in taking forts and reducing the inhabitants to obedience. The country was famous for its breed of horses, many thousands of which were brought back to Delhī."[72] Thus Balban subjugated the tribes of Jūd hills which had proved to be a source of perpetual danger to the Delhī empire.

Pointing out Balban's frontier problems, Baranī writes that the intimate friends of the Sulṭān, such as 'Ādil Khān, Tābar Khān, and others of the Old Shamsī slaves, who, through the protection of the Sulṭān, still occupied exalted position, often said to him:

> Sovereigns like Quṭb al-Dīn Aibak and Shams al-Dīn Iltutmish, our former patrons, conquered Jhain, Mālwa, Ujjain, Gujrāt, and other distant countries, and carried off treasure and valuables and elephants and horses from the Rā'es and Rānās. How is it that with your well equipped and disciplined army, you do not undertake any distant campaign and never move out of your territory to conquer other regions.[73]

The Sulṭān replied:

> The thoughts which you have expressed have also been very active in my mind, but you have not considered the hordes of Chingīz Khān, and the evil they have brought upon the women and the children, the flocks and herds of my frontier.

> These Mongols have established themselves in Ghaznī, in Tirmūz, and in Māwārunnahr, Halākū Khān, the grandson of Chingīz Khān, with a vast horde, has subdued 'Irāq and occupied Baghdād. These accursed wretches have heard of the wealth and prosperity of Hindūstān, and have set their hearts upon conquering and plundering it. They have taken and plundered Lāhore within my territories and no year passes that they do not come here and plunder the villages. They watch the opportunity of my departure on a distant campaign to enter my cities and ravage the whole of the Doāb. They even talk about the conquest and sack of Delhi.[74]

This statement of the Sulṭān is of great importance because the Sulṭān has directly expressed his views about the frontier problems of his empire. From this it becomes clear that he realised the danger of the Mongol activities along the border of the empire, and the danger of the further atrocities being perpetuated by them on the population of his kingdom; secondly Balban was aware that the Mongols ruled over Ghaznī, Tirmūz[75]. and Mawarunnahr,[76] which were the bases from where they launched their raids on his Indian territories; thirdly, he knew the barbaric nature of the Mongol raids having heard news about the capture of Iraq and the sack of Baghdad and thought that the Mongol could move towards the south east to conquer the subcontinent. It was also thought that the Mongol desired to conquer Delhi and plunder its wealth, and since they had already captured and sacked Lāhore which was a frontier city of Balban's empire, the king was apprehensive of the looming peril of the Mongols.

Keeping in view the constant fear of the Mongol menace, the Sulṭān framed his frontier policy. He expressed his views thus:

> I have devoted all the revenues of my kingdom to the equipment of my army, and I hold all my forces ready and prepared to receive them. I never leave my kingdom nor will go to any distance from it. In the reigns of my patrons and predecessors, there was none of this difficulty of the Mongols; they could lead their armies where they pleased, subdue the dominions of the Hindūs, and carry off their gold and treasure, staying away from their capitals a year or two. If this anxiety, which admonishes me that I am the guardian and protector of Muslims, were removed, then I would not stay one day in my capital, but would lead forth my army to capture treasures and valuable elephants and horses, and would never allow the Ra'es and Ranās to repose in quiet at a distance. With the army that I possess I would take all the spirit out of the opponents and enemies of the Faith.[77]

This statement is important in so far as it throws light on Balban's frontier policy. He goes on to describe the various measures which had been taken for the defence of the country. The first important step taken by him was, it emerges from the statement, to reorganise his army by spending the greater part of the revenues of the empire on it and keeping the army alert so as to be ready at a short notice to fight the Mongols. The second measure which Balban took was to remain at the capital and not to give the Mongols an opportunity to invade India. Balban also understood well that the problem of direct Mongol invasion did not exist in the reigns of Aibak and Iltutmis͟h. During the reign of Aibak, this problem had not come into existence because the Mongols had not emerged as a military power then. During the time of Iltutmis͟h, though C͟hingiz K͟hān had reached the banks of the Indus while pursuing prince Mangbārnī,[78] he had manifested no desire to cross the Indus and invade the Sulṭānate. Consequently, Aibak and Iltutmis͟h launched expeditions on distant places and crushed the Hindus. Balban, however, could not do this because of the direct menace of the Mongols.

BALBAN'S MEASURES AND REALISTIC FRONTIER POLICY. The measures Balban took in order to forge out a viable policy in the frontier are explained here in detail:

i) **Reorganisation of the Army.** The army was accorded a highly significant position in that turbulent age. This is borne out by the following words of Barani: "In the first year after his accession, the ripe judgement and experience of Balban was directed in the first place to the reorganisation of his army, for the army is the source and means of the government."[79] Thus Balban turned his attention to improve the organisational efficiency of his army. The military personnel was greatly increased and officers of proved ability and loyalty were appointed to the commands. According to Baranī: "Balban enhanced the soldier's pay and gave some of them assignments of villages in lieu of cash salary."[80] Soon, however, he found out the disadvantages of this form of payment; and "It was brought to his notice that the old S͟hamsī military grantees of land were unfit and never went out campaigning."[81] Consequently, Balban ordered the muster-master to make out a list of them with full particulars and present it to the throne for instruction.[82] After conducting the inquiry, the muster-master reported to the king as follows:

> Thirty or forty years and even more had passed since the establishment of this body, many of the grantees were old and infirm, many more had died, and their sons had taken possession of the grant as an inheritance from their fathers, and had caused their names to be recorded in the records of the *Āṛẓ* (muster-master). Some who had no children sent their slaves as their representatives. All these holders of service lands called themselves proprietors, and possessed to have received the lands in free gifts from Sulṭān Shams al-Dīn. . . . Some of them went leisurely to perform their military duties but the greater part stayed at home making excuses, the acceptance of which they secured by presents and bribes of all sorts to the deputy muster-master and his officials.[83]

Finding these anomalies in his army, Balban took the following measures:

> Balban divided the grantees into three classes. The first consisted of the old and worn-out, upon whom the settled pensions of forty or fifty *tankas*, and resumed their villages. Second; those who were in the prime of life or were young, on whom an allowance proportionate to their service was settled; their villages were not to be taken from them, but the surplus revenues were to be collected by the government revenue officers. Third, the children and orphans, who held villages and sent deputies to perform their military service. The grants were to be taken from these orphans and widows, but a suitable allowance was to be made for their food and raiment.[84]

Besides, the Sulṭān also realised the importance of horses and elephants, and "frequently observed to his associates that elephants and horses were the strength of Hindustān, and one elephant was worth five hundred horsemen. . . in the first year of the reign, sixty three elephants were sent by Tātār Khān, son of Arslān Khān, from Lakhnautī to Delhi, which greatly pleased the people and was the occasion of great public rejoicing."[85] Thus Balban increased the strength of his army, reformed it, and made it into an efficient fighting force.

Balban not only made reforms in the army but also took measures to impart training to his soldiers and so maintained a disciplined army. According to Baranī, when reports of the hunting expeditions of the Sulṭān were carried to Halākū Khān at Baghdād, he said:

> Balban is a shrewd ruler and has had much experience in government. He goes out apparently to hunt. . . but really to exercise his men and horses, so that they may not be wanting when times of danger and war arrive. . . .[86]

These remarks of Halākū Khān show that the Mongols were aware of Balban's disciplined army which was ready in all odd hours to meet the forces of the enemies.

## ii) Rearrangement of the Frontier *Iqṭa's* and Appointment of the *Muqṭi's*

Balban rearranged his frontier *iqṭā's* and appointed *muqṭī*'s of experience and bravery to administer them. Since the days of Sulṭān Nāṣir al-Dīn Mahmūd, Sher Khān, the cousin of Balban, held charge of the districts of Sunam, Lāhore, Dipālpur and other territories in that direction exposed to the inroads of the Mongols.[87] According to Baranī: "He built a high tower at Bhatnīr and founded the city and fort of Bhatnīr. He had maintained several thousand horsemen and had many times routed the Mongols and completely overpowered them. He caused the *Khuṭbah* to be read in the name of Sulṭān Nāṣir al-Dīn Mahmūd at Ghaznī, and his terror, bravery greatness of his power and the strength of his army checked the Mongols from making assaults on the frontier of Hindūstān."[88] His presence on the frontier was a guarantee of security because he not only effectively resisted the Mongols but also thoroughly suppressed the Jāts, Kokars, Mandarīs[89] and Bhattīs living in these unregulated tracts. But unfortunately, Sher Khān died four or five years after Balban's accession[90] and thirty years after Iltutmish's death as mentioned by Baranī, and Tamar Khān[91] was appointed to the frontier *iqṭā's* of Sunam and Samānā.[92] Other possessions were granted to other noblemen. Sher Khān, as already mentioned, had brought under his subjugation all the tribes dwelling along the frontier and had successfully opposed and resisted the Mongols which no other noble or chief had accomplished.[93] Consequently the Mongols made headway against the appointees of Sulṭān Balban and ravaged *iqṭā's* on the frontiers. What Sher Khān accomplished in one decade, none of his successors could do. Hence, after firmly establishing himself, Sulṭān Balban appointed his own trust-worthy followers in place of Sher Khān. According to Barani, "Balban appointed prince Muhammad as *muqti'* of Sind and the other dependent frontier districts,[94] who bravely checked not only the advance of the Mongols towards the frontier *iqtā's* of Delhi empire, but he also led almost annual expeditions across the border capturing Tātār horses."[95] Barani further says:

> In the same year, the Sultān sent his younger son, Bughrā Khān, also entitled Nāsir al-Dīn,[96] to Samānā, having placed under his charge Samānā and Sunam with all their dependencies and neighbouring districts. . . . When the Sultān sent him to his government he commanded him to increase the allowances to the old soldiers and to enlist twice as many more new men. Balban also instructed him to promote the industrious and faithful officials, and to give them grants of land. He further directed him to be particularly careful in appointing officers for his army so that he might be ready to repel any advance of the Mongols.[97]

These remarks emphasise the importance of Samānā as an important post of the frontier regions but, since Barani is silent about Lāhore, it seems that perhaps this city might have lost its importance due to its destruction by the constant raids of the Mongols.

### iii) Building and Repairing of the Forts in the Frontier *Iqtā's*

Balban adopted a more sophiscated method of fortification in his frontier region which contributed to the effective defence of his empire. Barani comments as follows upon the matter: "Two years after the Sultān's return from the Jūd expedition, he marched to Lāhore and ordered the rebuilding of the fort of Lāhore which had been destroyed by the Mongols during the time of Iltutmish's successors. The town and villages of Lāhore, which the Mongols had devastated and laid waste, were repeopled, and architects and managers were appointed to superintend their restoration."[98] Thus, Lāhore was once again fortified although, as mentioned before, its position receded in importance. The other fortifications include that of Lāhore.

According to Barani. "It is Sher Khān, who had built a tower at Bhatnīr, founded the city and fort of Bhatnīr."[99] Amir Khusrāu also refers to the fortification of prince Muḥammad as the Afghan garrison on the outlying fortresses of the province where the prince, with whom the poet lived, used to spend some time during yearly campaigns against the Mongols.[100] Such Afghan garrisons must have been placed in the territory of the rulers of the frontier, in the neighbourhood of the Indus around Takht-i-Sulaimān. About one of them, Aḥmad Nabī Khān, quoting Baranī, says: "Sher Khān strengthened the fort of Dīpālpūr and maintained a well-equipped army of several thousand horsemen."[101] These were some of the developments in the fortification of the frontier of the Delhī empire. The state of fortification during the reign of Sulṭān Balban has been explained in the map No. 5.[102]

Thus, Balban's new and effective measures for the defence of the frontier consisted of: firstly, maintaining the forts on the routes of the invaders in perfect preparedness, fully garrisoned and equipped; secondly, building of new forts or watch-posts wherever necessary; thirdly, keeping vigilant watch on the routes; fourthly, appointing as wardens of marches, tried and experienced military hands; fifthly, reorganisation of the army, and sixthly chastisement of the frontier tribes. This realistic frontier policy did leave a lasting impact and during the first thirteen years of his rule, the Mongols did not dare invade the subcontinent. Afterwards they again tried to invade it twice. The first raid of the Mongols took place in A.D. 1279.

THE FIRST INVASION OF THE MONGOLS (A.D. 1279). There started a fratricidal war among the Mongol viceroys in Central Asia in A.D. 1278-9. According to Waṣṣāf: "In the winter of A.D. 1278, a force of Nigudaris invaded Kirmān[103] and Fārs[104] from their base in southern Afghānistān."[105] After their victorious return with prisoners and booty to the region of Sīstān, they were besieged by prince Arghūn in the summer of A.D. 1279. After this victory, Arghūn despatched his military troops to invade India. This event has been recorded by Barani as follows: "At this time, the Mongol horses crossed the Beāh,[106] and the Sulṭān sent against them prince Muḥammad from Multān, Bughrā Khān from Samānā, and Malik Barbak Bektars[107] from Delhī."[108] The same authority further mentions, "They marched to the Beāh, driving back the Mongols and obtaining many victories over them, so that the enemies were unable to advance beyond the Beāh. In each of these three armies there were about seventeen or eighteen thousand horses."[109] In the face of this evidence it may be said that the river Beah was the frontier defensive line on the one hand, and on the other Multān as well as Samānā were the frontier *iqṭā's*. The Delhī forces, also, repulsed their enemies not allowing them to cross the frontier line of Beāh.

THE SECOND INVASION OF THE MONGOLS (A.D. 1285). The political situation in Persia, however, changed in A.D. 1281 when Abaqa Khān died and his younger brother Tagudār occupied the throne bypassing Arghūn, the eldest son of Abaqa.[110] Consequently, Arghūn raised the standard of rebellion against his uncle, but was unsuccessful and found himself incarcerated though his life was spared. However, Tagudar converted to Islam and assumed the name of Aḥmad.[111] This was greatly resented by the Mongol generals who rescued Arghun Khan from the prison and revolted against Tagudar. In the general uprising that followed, Tagudar (Aḥmad) was overthrown and put to death in A.D. 1283.[112] The accession of Arghūn, however, did not bring peace and order at once in the Il-Khānid territory. This change in the situation of Mongol politics seriously affected the Indian frontier defence as the Mongols, in their efforts to replenish their resources, started raiding Indian territories. It was in this process that in A.D. 1285, Tamar Khan,[113] a Mongol military commander, came with a force towards the sub-continent.

According to Amīr Khusraū, "Prince Muḥammad,[114] the eldest son of the Sulṭān, and the Khān of Multān,[115] proceeded to Lāhore and Dipālpur to oppose Tamar Khān, the bravest dog of all the Chingiz Khānis."[116] The two armies, being drawn up in order of battle on the bank of the river Rāvī, engaged each other in an action in which both commanders greatly distinguished themselves. Baranī records: "At length, the Mongols surrendered and were hotly pursued by prince Muḥammad. Unfortunately, separated from the main body of his troops during the pursuit, the prince was halting on the bank of a stream three *farsangs* from Multan for offering his prayers, as a Mongol chief, who had concealed himself in an ambush in a neighbouring wood at the head of two thousand strong horses, suddenly fell upon Muḥammad's troops."[117] Baranī further says, "Prince Muḥammad fought heroically, waging a desparate struggle but an arrow from the famous Mongol bows struck him and he fell dead. It was a grievous disaster, that happened to the throne of Balban."[118] This calamity caused great and general mourning in the subcontinent. From that time, according to Barani, "The deceased prince was called the martyr prince."[119] When the news of this defeat and the death of the prince reached the Sulṭān, he was broken with sorrow,[120] and died in A.D. 1286.[121] Despite this disaster, the defence arrangements of Balban proved so strong that the Mongols could not penetrate any further and had to beat a retreat. After the death of the martyr prince, Balban gave the charge of Multān and the province of Sind to Kāi-Khusraū.[122] This second invasion of the Mongols shook the defence of the kingdom's frontier. It not only weakened the frontier defence but also caused the death of Sulṭān Ghiyāṣ al-Dīn Balban.

## IV

### The Frontier Policy of Balban's Successors (A.D. 1286-90)

Sulṭān Mu'izz al-Dīn Kaikubād ascended the throne of Delhi after the death of Sulṭān Ghiyās al-Dīn Balban in A.H. 685/ A.D. 1286.[123] Soon the Sulṭān faced a serious frontier problem because his cousin, Kai-Khusraū, who was holding the charge of the province of Sind and Multan, refused to acknowledge his suzerainty.[124] This event has, however, been given less attention than it deserves* by contemporary writers. Only one of them, Firishta hints at it in the following words:" That prince had gone to Ghaznī and endeavoured to induce Tamar Khan, the Mongol viceroy of the province, to aid him with troops, in deposing his cousin, Kai-Kubād."[125] Thus, it indicates that soon after Balban's death there started a tug-of-war between Kai-Kubād and Kai-Khusraū in order to capture the throne of Delhi. According to Firishta, Kai-Khusraū went to Ghaznī to the court of the Mongol military commander Tamar Khān, for help. However, "he failed in the attempt, and moreover, found that he had few friends in that quarter. He, therefore, petitioned the king to be allowed to retain Multān and the western provinces."[126] But Firishta's description seems to be incomplete because later events show that there was a secret alliance between the Mongols and Kai-Khusraū which must have ensured Mongol aid in favour of the latter. This, indeed, is confirmed by Barani who says: "The Sulṭān realised and took notice of Kai-Khusraū's obnoxious attitude and Malik Nizām al-Din, *Na'ib-i-Mumlikat*, was assigned to deal with Kai-Khusrau who prevailed on the prince to visit Delhī. Nizām al-Dīn hired assassins for the purpose of murdering Kai-Khusrau on his way to the capital at the village of Rohtak."[127] It was probably as a response to Kai-Khusraū's murder that the raid of the Mongols occurred. Firishta again says: "In this state of affairs, there came a report of the advent of a large army of the infidel Tatars under their leader Tamar."[128] Barani also records: "The Sulṭān appointed *Khān-i-Khānān*, Shaikh Barbak, at the head of three thousand cavalry to coerce the accursed insurgents. When the army of Islām reached near Lāhore, the accursed tribe took to their heels without any contest and were hotly pursued as far as the hill-skirts of Jūd."[129] Thus the Mongols did not succeed in their venture because the defensive measures of the late Sulṭān Balban's frontier policy proved effective enough to check their advance. This first raid of the Mongols, which took place during the reign of Kai-Kubād, was followed by another Mongol invasion.At this time Arghūn, the Mongol Khān of Il-Khānid dynasty, was engaged in a war against the Mamlūks. Moreover, he also became involved in a brief collision with the forces of the Golden horde.[130] It is possible that Arghūn had commanded his military general, Tamar Khān, to collect the booty and wealth of India so that they could replenish their resources and continue their war against the Mamlūks and the Golden Horde. This point has not been discussed by any contemporary authority. According to Amīr Khusraū: "On the eve of the king's departure to meet his father in Awadh, news came of another Mongol invasion. Tamar Khān had again overrun the territory from Multān to Lāhore and laid waste the whole country as far as Samānā."[131] The Sulṭān despatched Malik

Baktar to encounter the Mongols who easily routed them on the river Rāvī and took a great number of prisoners.[132] These two invasions of the Mongols which occurred within a short span of Kai-Kubād's reign, had threatened the defence of the empire and made insecure the frontier. The Sulṭān realised this danger and appointed Malik Shāhik, entitled Ajbar Khān, as the *muqṭi'* of Multān and Fīrūz Khaljī as the *muqṭi'* of Samānā.[133] Fīrūz Khaljī showed his mettle as a soldier and warden of the marches when he was posted on the frontier. He remained sometimes at Samānā and at other times at Sunam and controlled Dipālpur. Later on Fīrūz Yaghrash Khaljī became the *Arẓ-i-Mumālik* and obtained the title of *Shā'istā Khān* as mentioned by Sirhindī.[134] But soon after this the Maliks conspired against the Sulṭān who was deposed in A.H. 689/A.D. 1290.[135] This change also affected the frontier policy of the empire because it caused the negligence of the defence of the kingdom. The new Sulṭān Shams al-Dīn Kai-Kā'us [136] who was set on the throne in A.D. 1290, did not reign long and after three months his *nāib*, Jalāl al-Dīn Fīrūz Khaljī, made the Sulṭān prisoner and captured the throne of Delhi.[137]

## FOOTNOTES

1. The birth of Sulṭān-i-Mu'azzam, Naṣir al-Dīn Mahmud Shāh took place at the Kaṣr Bāgh of Delhī in A.H. 626. *T.N.* (Text). p. 201.
2. Sulṭān Nāṣir al-Dīn Maḥmūd ascended the throne of Delhī on Sunday 23rd Muḥarram, 664 A.H. (A.D. 1246). *Ibid.* (Text), p. 208.
3. Reverty says, "A number of very worthless persons in that army had clandestinely gained access to the presence of Sultān 'Alā al-Dīn Mas'ud Shāh, and used to influence him in the committal of unworthy acts and habits, so much so that killing and seizing of his Maliks was gaining a place in his nature, and he was steadfast in resolve. All his good qualities turned away from the laudable path and inclined towards sensuality, pleasure, drinking and chase, to such a degree of excess that disaffection began to spread through the country, and the affairs of the kingdom to be neglected. The Maliks and Amīrs agreed together and despatched letters secretly to Nāsir al-Dīn Maḥmūd and prayed for the appearance of his auspicious retinue. . . ." *Ibid.* (Trans.), p. 669.
4. It was an assembly of the Mongol princes.
5. It was the Mongol capital under Chaghatāe, the son of Chingīz Khān, and was built near the site of Old Kuljāh on the river Ilih. Le Strange, *op. cit.*, p. 487.
6. *T.R.* (Trans.), p. 33.
7. *Ibid.*, p. 33. He was the father of the historian Rashīd al-Dīn Juvainī. Boyle, *op. cit.*, p. 336.
8. *T.N.* (Trans.), p. 677. Boyle, *op. cit.*, p. 339.

9. Balban held the office of *Amīr-i-Hājib*. According to U.N Day, *Amīr-i-Ḥājib* was master of the court ceremonies. In all court ceremonies, the *Amīr-i-Hājib* made the necessary arrangements for proper places of the nobles according to their ranks. U.N. Day, *op. cit.*, p. 62.
10. *T.N.* (Trans.), p. 77.
11. *Ibid.*, p. 676.
12. Saif bin Muḥammad bin Ya'qūb Haravi, *Tārīkh-i-Nāma-i-Herāt*, (ed.), M. Z. Siddiqūe, Calcutta, 1944, pp. 157-8.
13. *T.N.* (Trans.), p. 677.
14. It is an important fortress situated in Jūd hills. See Col. K.A. Rashid, *Historical Dissertations*, Karāchī, 1962, pp. 58, 92.
15. *T.N.* (Trans.), p. 678.
16. *T.N.* (Trans.), p. 815.
17. *Ibid.*
18. *T.N.* (Trans.), p. 816. From the parts means the lands of Turkistān.
19. *Ibid.*
20. It was, in ancient time, a hilly range and presently may be identified with Siwālik hills. *Ibid.*, p. 839.
21. *T.N.* (Trans.), p. 818.
22. *J.T.* (ed.), p. 72; *T.N.* (Trans.), p. 699.
23. *Ibid.*, p. 820.
24. *T.N.* (Trans.), p. 820.
25. *Ibid.* Upto this date his correct title was Malik Ghiyās al-Dīn Balban.
26. *T.N.* (Trans.), p. 820.
27. *Ibid.*, p. 781.
28. Although the horsemen of Balban Kashlū Khān killed Hasan Qarlūgh, yet none of them was able to return to his master. *T.N.* (Trans.), p. 792.
29. *Ibid.*
30. According to Firishtah "Sher Khān was the viceroy of Lāhore and Multān. He was the most celebrated man of his age for his wisdom, valour and every princely quality. *T.F.* (Trans.), p. 114.
31. *T.N.* (Trans.), p. 277.
32. *Ibid.*
33. *T.F.* (Trans.), p. 239.
34. *Ibid.*
35. *Ibid.*, p. 694.
36. *Ibid.*
37. *Ibid.*, p. 694
38. Boyle, *op. cit.*, p. 339. He was the eldest son of Tulī and ruled from A.D. 1251 to 1259.
39. *Tārīkh-i-Wassāf* as quoted by Raverty, p. 1224; *Tārīkh-i-Binagiti*, as cited by Raverty. *T.N.* (Trans.), p. 1125.
40. *Ibid.* p. 1225.
41. *J.T.* (Text), p. f. 38a; *T.N.* (Trans.), p. 699.
42. According to Minhaj: "The Maliks of Hindūstān. . . prayed Ulugh Khān to return to the capital. . . . The majority of the Turkish Amirs posted in the *iqta*'s around the capital joined their forces and in Ramzān 652 A.H./A.D. 1254, marched towards the capital to impose their will on the king. . . . Balban's party offered to submit on condition of Rayhān's dismissal. *T.N.* (Trans.), p. 830.

43. *T.N.* (Trans.), p. 700. For the assumption of the title of Sulṭān Jalāl al-Dīn Mas'ūd Shāh by prince Jalāl Khān.
44. *Ibid.*
45. *ibid.*, p. 298.
46. *T.N.* (Trans.), p. 700. Minhāj does not seem to be correct in his statement that Lāhore was assigned to Jalāl al-Dīn Mas'ūd Shāh by Sulṭān Nāsir al-Dīn Maḥmūd at this time. He distorts the fact and he passes over the visit of Jalāl al-Dīn to the Mongol court in Karākoram. Ṣiddique, *op. cit.*, p. 90.
47. *T.N.* (Trans.), p. 794.
48. *Ibid.*
49. Qatlugh Khān to whom the mother of the Sulṭān was married in A.D. 1256, was given the fief of Oudn and shortly afterwards removed to Beraikh. He being dissatisfied with this arrangement, prepared for rebellion and after joining with Kashlū Khān revolted. *Ibid.*, p. 313.
50. *Ibid.*, *Wakil* means agent.
51. *T.N.* (Text), pp. 169-70.
52. He was the eldest son of Sulṭān Ḥasan Qarlūgh and succeeded after his father's death, as the ruler of Banīān and Koh-i-Jūd region.
53. *T.N.* (Trans.), p. 861.
54. *F.S.* (Trans.), p. 278; (Text), p.152.
55. *Ibid.*,(Text), p. 153.
56. *Ibid.*
57. *Ibid.*, (Trans.), p. 280; (Text), p. 155.
58. The envoy of Delhī mentioned the ruler of Banīān as Sulṭān Nāsir al-Dīn Muḥammad, but there is Malik instead of Sulṭān in Raverty's translation. *T.N.* (Trans.), p. 861.
59. *J.T.* (Text) f. 385 b; al-Binagitī, *Rauzatul Aulil Albāb fī Twārikh-i-Akhbār fil Ansāb*, London, add. 762, ff. 116-7. One of his officers Malik Fīrūz Khaljī, later known as Sulṭān Jalāl al-Dīn Khaljī, fled to India and joined the services of the son of Balban.
60. *J.T.* (Trans.), pp. 122-3.
61. *Ibid.*, p. 350; Walther Heissag, *A Lost Civilization: The Mongols Rediscovered*, London, 1966, p. 50.
62. *T.N.* (Trans.), p. 317.
63. Narrating the process of this diplomatic pact, Al-Juzjanī records, "That the envoy set out from Delhī to Banīān with slaves, money, and gifts. Whenever he met the toll collectors on the highway who took him to be a merchant and demanded established tolls and fixed cesses, he avoided them saying: 'I am an agent, and therefore, exempt from them.' As he crossed the frontier of the Delhī Sulṭanate and entered the territories of Kashlū Khān, it became known to all that he was proceeding on a diplomatic mission to some country. Thereupon Kashlū Khān ordered the envoy to be arrested and presented before him. When Jamāl al-Dīn Khaljī came to Kashlū Khān, he was interrogated about the nature, import and contents of the documents that he was carrying as well as his destination. When the envoy denied his mission, Kashlū Khān treated him with severity and thus forced him to show the documents; he confessed in the presence of the Mongol Shahna'gān: "I am an emissary and I am going upwards." After it Kashlū Khān considered it impolitic to interrogate him any further. He simply said to the envoy: "It is necessary for thee to proceed so that I may have thee taken to thy place of destination." In reply to him, Jamāl al-Dīn Khaljī said: "My orders are that I should proceed to the presence of

Sulṭān Nāṣir al-Dīn Muḥammad Qarlūgh." Hearing the name of Nāṣir al-Dīn Muḥammad Qarlūgh, Kashlū Khān at once allowed him to proceed on his mission. . . See for details, *T N.* (Trans.), pp. 861-3.

64. *Ibid.*

65. *Ibid.*

66. Caliph was considered a spiritual head amongst the Muslim *bilads* at that time.

67. Three days after the observance of the funeral rites consequent on the death of Sulṭān Nāṣir al-Dīn Maḥmūd, the Amirs and Maliks placed Sulṭān Ghiyās al-Dīn Balban on the Imperial throne in the white castle on the 13th Jamadi-ul-Awwal, 664 A.H./Saturday the 20th February, 1266 A.D. *T.B.S.* (Trans.), p. 37.

68. Boyle, *op. cit.*, p. 351-7.

69. *Ibid.*

70. *Ibid.*

71. *T.F.S.B.* (Text), pp. 58-9.

72. *T.F.* (Trans.), p. 256.

73. *T.F.S.B.* (Trans.), p. 102. The text follows as under:

گر پادشاه همچو سلطان قطب الدین ایبک و سلطان شمس الدین، که خداوندگاران ما بودند بجانب مالوه و اجین و گجرات و دور دست ها
نهب کردند و از رایان و رایگان خزاین و دفاین و پیلان و اسپان آوردند، نمی آوردند و با چندین لشکرهای آراسته و مستعد که دارد عزم لشکر کشی
دور دست نمی کند، و از ممالک خود بیرون نمی آید و در اقالیم دیگر نمی آویزد۔ ص،

74. *T.F.S.B.* (Text), p. 60. The text follows as under:

گر آنچه در کارهای جهانگیری شما می گوید در دل من بیش از آن است، اما شما نمی شنوید که تو منهای مغل چنگیزخانی با
در بناگوش مملکت من سفته است و در غزنین و ترمذ و ماوراءالنهر ساکن شده، و هلاکو نبیره چنگیزخان با چندین تمن
گرفته است و در بغداد متمکن گشته و آن ملاعین بسیار مال و منال هندوستان شنیده اند، و نهب و تاراج
دل دارند و برلاهور که سر حد مملکت ما است زده اند و خراب کرده۔ ص، ۵۹

75. It is situated north of the passage of the Oxus coming from Balkh. Le Strange, *op. cit.*, p. 440.

76. The provinces beyond the Oxus were known to 'Arabs as Māwārunnahr *Ibid.*, p. 433.

77. *T.F.S.B.* (Text), p. 60. The text follows as under:

و من تمامی محصول بلاد ممالک خود را در وجه حشم نهاده ام، و حشم را مستعد و مرتب کرده می دارم و منتظر در آمدن ایشان می
باشم، و از مملکت خود بیرون نمی آیم و در دهد و مز تر نمی روم۔ و لیکن در عهد و عصر مخدومان ما مغل مزاحم نمی شد۔ ایشان بفراغ
خاطر لشکرهای کشیدند و اقالیم و عرصات هندوان را نهب و تاراج می کردند، و زرها و اسپها می آوردند و می توانستند که یکان دو کان
سال از دارالملک دهلی غیبت کنند۔ و اگر مرا اندیشه مذکور که متعلق پاسبانی مسلمانان و شهرهای مسلمانان است دامن نگیرد من یک روز
در دارالملک و حوالی دارالملک نباشم، و لشکر کشیها کنم و خزائن و دفائن و پیلان و اسپان برایان و رایگان در دست نگذارم، و از
چنین حشمی مستعد و مرتب، که دارم، دمار از مخالفان دین و دشمنان دین برآرم و نهب و تاراج کنم۔ ص۔ ۶۰ تاریخ فیروزشاهی

78. *T.J.G.* (Trans.), p. 106.

79. *T.F.S.B.*, p. 100. The cavalry and infantry, both old and new, were placed under the command of Maliks of experience, of chiefs, who hold the first rank in their profession, and were brave, dignified and faithful . . ."

80. *T.F.S.B.* (Trans.), p. 29.

*Ibid.* p. 109.

82 *Ibid.*, p. 107.

83 *T.F.S.B.*, p. 107. The text runs as follows:

84 *Ibid.*, (Trans.), p. 103. The text runs as follows:

و چون سی چهل سال، بلکه بیشتر از استقامت آن حشم برآمد، بسیاری از آن سواران پیر و فرتوت شدند، و بیشتری نقل کردند،
و فرزندان ایشان به میراث پدران آن دهها را فرو گرفتند و نامهای خود در دیوان عرض ثبت رسانیدند، و آنان که از پدران
طفلان مانده بودند غلامان را بجائے ایشان مجری می داشتند، و آن اقطاع داران و فرزندان ایشان خود را ملک و انعامی تصور
کردندی و گفتندی که سلطان شمس الدین ما را این دهها به انعام داده بود . . . و بیشتری عذرها انگیختندی،
و در خانه و دههای خود نشستندی و نائب عرض ممالک را و دفتر داران صاحب عهده را به اندازه مدد بیست خود شراب
و گوسپند و مرغ و کبوتر و روغن و غله از دههای خود رسانیدندی . ص، ص ۸۲، ۸۳
سلطان بلبن اقطاع داران را بر سه قسم حکم کرد، قسمی که پیر و فرتوت و بجای مانده شده بودند، و از کار غزوه برگی بازمانده،
ایشان را از چهل تا پنجاه تنکه ادرار فرمود، و دههای ایشان را بر خالصه باز آوردند و از ایشان بکشید. و قسمی که کهل و جوان
بودند مواجب ایشان باندازه استعداد ایشان تعیین فرمود و فرمان داد تا فاضلات حاصل دههای قسم دوم هر سال دیوان
طلب نمایند و ده از ایشان نگشند. و قسمی که اطفال و ایتام بودند و دههای بردند غلامان را با اسپان و سلاحی
که می توانستند، در دیوان عرض می گذرانیدند، در باب ایشان حکم فرمود تا ایتام و بیوگان را هم از آن دهها
بقدر کفاف قوت و لبس بدهند . ص، ۸٤

85. *T.F.S.B.* (Trans.), p. 103.

86 *T.F.S.B.*, (Text), pp. 65-6. The text runs as follows:

با مقربان خود گفتی که آراستگی ملک هندوستان از پیل و اسپ است و هر پیلی در ملک هندوستان موازی پانصد سوار است..
و هم در سال اثنی و ستین و ستمایه که جلوس سلطان بلبن بود شصت و سه زنجیر پیل فرستاده تترخان پسر ارسلان خان از
ملک لکهنوتی در دهلی رسید. ص، ۶۳

87. *Ibid.*. (Text), p. 76.

88. *T.F.S.B.* (Trans.), p. 76. According to Ahmad Nabi, Sher Khān strengthened the fort of Dipālpur and maintained a well-equipped army of several thousand horsemen. Ahmad Nabī Khān, "Dipalpur through the Ages", *J.R.S.P.*, vol. ii, No. 1, January 1970, p. 70.

89 According to A.H. Dānī the correct name of the tribe is Madra and city of the Madra people was Madrapur. For their correct home we should look at the Central region in between the Ravi and the Chinab. It was a well-known ancient tribe with a record of maintaining its identity for nearly two thousand years. A.H. Dānī, "Al-Berunī and the city of Lāhore", *J.C.A.* vol. i, No. 2, December 1978, p. 33.

90 *T.F.S.B.* (Trans.), p. 76. Sultān Balban, though the Khān was his cousin, caused him to be poisoned. For details see at page seventy six of *T.F.S.B.*

91. He was one of the forty Shamsī slaves. *Ibid.*, p. 76.

92. *Ibid.*

93. *T.F.S.B.* (Trans.), p. 76.

94. *Ibid.* The date of his assuming charge of Multān has not been mentioned, but he was appointed to succeed Sher Khān who died four or five years after Balban's accession in A.D. 1266. It could therefore be conjectured that prince might have assumed charge in A.D. 1271. Before his appointment as *muqṭi'* of Sind, he was holding the territories of Ko'il and other neighbouring districts.

95 *Ibid.*, p. 109. Prince Muhammad, who had succeeded Sher Khān in charge of tho Multān province and the northern frontiers, kept the Mongols at bay on the line of Bias. A.M. Stow, "The Road between Delhī and Multān", *J.P.H.S.*, 1914, p.32.

96. The prince was also a refined and cultured man but in manners and qualities he could not be compared to his elder brother. *T.F.S.B.* (Trans.), p. 109.
97. *Ibid.*, p. 111.
98. *Ibid.*, p. 107.
99. *Ibid.*, p. 109.
100. *K.F.* (Trans.), p. 48.
101. *T.F.S.B.* (Trans.), as quoted by A.N. Khān. A.N. Khān, *op cit.*, p. 70.
102. See map No. 5 attached. He built a connected chain of forts on the route followed by these invaders. Bhatnīr, Abohar, Bhatindā and Sīrsā, situated at the angles of nearly square figure, with a side about 50 miles long, had each a fort on the same plan and of the same dimensions and thus formed a quardrilateral in the path of invaders from the north-west. Sita Ram Kohli and Hari Ram Gupta, *Students Historical Altas in India*, Lahore, 1936, p. 12.
103. East of Khuzistān, and bordering the Gulf, lay the great province of Fars, the ancient Persia and the cradle of the Persian monarchy. See for details, Le Strange, *op. cit.*, p. 6.
104. To the east of Fars lay the province of Kirman, far less fertile, almost lacking in rivers and bordering on the Great Desert. *Ibid.*, p. 6.
105. *T.W.* (Text), p.119.
106. Beāh at that time had a different bed from that of today. The name whenever it occurs in this thesis refers to the old bed.
107. Firishtah reads this name as Birlās. *T.F.* (Trans.), p. 458.
108. *T.F.S.B.* (Trans.), p. 112.
109. *Ibid.*
110. Boyle, *op. cit.*, p. 364.
111. *Ibid.*, p. 365 *T.T.* (Text), p. 111.
112. *Ibid.* At night, Arghūn was a prisoner and in the morning he was monarch of the face of the earth.
113. Baranī writes it as Tamar.
114. He was the heir-apparent of Sulṭān Balban. He was gifted with many virtues and personal qualities. *T.F.S.B.* (Trans.), p. 109.
115. He was the governor of Multān.
116. He held the provinces of Multān, Balkh, Badakhshān, Ghaznī, Ghor and Banian under the Mongol emperor Arghūn Khān, the grandson of Halākū Khān. Waḥid Mīrzā, *Amīr Khusraū*, Lucknow, 1943, p. 48.
117. *T.F.S.B.* (Trans.), p. 109. The prince chose as his battlefield, a place within the boundaries of *Bagh-i-Nayyir*, on the bank of the river Rāvī, so that he had in his neighbourhood the water of Dehandhī. He fortified the place strongly and made such dispositions that when the infidels came against him, both rivers should be in the rear of his army, so that no part of his troops would be able to take to flight *M.T.B.* (Text), p. 43.
118. *T.F.S.B.* (Trans.), p. 122. The author of *Ṭabaqāt-i-Akbarī* tells how the prince's sad end was supposed to be the result of the displeasure of the contemporary saint Ṣadr al-Dīn of Multān. In a fit of drunkenness the prince is reported to have divorced his wife, a daughter of the house of Sulṭān Iltutmish but subsequently he desired to take her back. The saint was persuaded to agree to taking her in marriage but later the lady refused to return to the prince and consequently, the saint refused to divorce her. The prince, thereupon, flew into a rage and swore to kill the saint Ṣadr

al-Dīn... but the Mongol invasion occurred to take him away to his fateful expedition before he had the time to execute his plan. *Ṭabaqāt-i-Akbarī*, (Trans.), p. 88.

119. *T.F.S.B.* (Trans.), p. 122.

120. Baranī gives a touching description of the king's grief, "The martyr prince was the son whom he had loved dearer than his life, and whom he had destined to be his successor. The Sulṭān was now more than eighty years old, and although he struggled hard against the effects of his bereavement, they day by day became more apparent. By day he held his court, and entered into public business as if to show that his loss had not affected him; but at night he poured forth his cries of grief, tore his garments and threw dust upon his head." *T.F.S.B.* (Trans.), p. 123.

121. Edward Thomas, *op. cit.*, p. 131. Baranī gives A.H. 685 but Khusrau writes A.H. 686.

122. He was the son of the martyr prince and was nominated by Balban as his heir-apparent.

123 He was the son of Bughrā Khān and grandson of Balban. *T.F.S.B.* (Trans.), p. 125.

124. "Three days before his death, Balban summoned to his presence *Malik ul-Umara*, Kotwāl of Delhi, Khwāja Ḥusain Baṣri, the Wazīr, and some others of his favourite servants, and said, "You are old and are versed in matters of government; you know how things go on when kings die, and I know that my end is near. .. . After I am gone, you must set upon the throne, Kai-Khusrau, son of my eldest son, the martyr prince, whom, after his father's death, I named as my successor, and who is worthy of throne. He is young and incapable of ruling as yet, but what can I do? Maḥmūd (Bughra Khan) has shrunk from his work, and people shut their eyes at him. He has gone to Lakhnautī, intent upon their views. The throne will not stand... Kai-Khusrau... . For a private reason... they had been unfriendly to the martyr prince, and they were apprehensive of danger if Kai-Khusrau succeeded... . They then took Kai-Kubād and placed him on the throne with the title of Mu'izz al-Dīn." *Ibid.* p. 124.

125. *T.F.* (Trans.), p. 275.

126. *Ibid.*

127. *T.F.S.B* (Trans.), p. 127.

128. *T.F.* (Trans.), p. 276.

129. *T.F.S.B.* (Trans.), p. 126. Badāunī also agrees with Baranī.

130. Boyle, *op. cit.*, p. 371.

131. *Q.S.* (Text), p. 49.

132. *T.B.S.* (Text), p. 56.

133. *Q.S.* (Text), p. 49.

134. *T.B.S.* (Trans.), p. 52. Badāunī records Fīrūz Khān bin Yaghrash Khaljī.

135. *T.F.S.B.* (Trans.), p. 135.

136. Shā'istā Khān known as Jalāl al-Dīn Fīrūz Khaljī placed prince Kai-Kāus, the son of Sulṭān Mu'izz al-Dīn on the throne on 19th Muḥarram, 689/Ist February, 1290. Shā'istā Khān became his deputy. *T.F.B.S.* (Trans.), p. 135.

137 *Ibid.*

## Chapter V

# THE FRONTIER POLICY OF THE KHALJĪS (A.D. 1290-1320)

## I

### The Frontier Policy of Sulṭān Jalāl al-Dīn Fīrūz Shāh Khaljī (A.D. 1290-6)

Jalāl al-Dīn Khaljī[1] had risen to the position of *Sar-i-Jandār*[2] during the reign of Balban.[3] He was appointed governor( نائب )[4] of Samānā by Sulṭān Kai-Kubād.[5] Jalāl al-Dīn was a very able soldier and, as a governor of the frontier post of Samānā,[6] had fought a number of battles against the Mongol invaders and repelled them. On the death of Malik Tuzākī,[7] he was brought from Samana and was promoted to the high office of *Ariẓ-i-Mumālik*[8] by Sultān Kai-Kubād. He was given the title of *Shā'ista Khān* and was also given the fief of Bārān.[9] The author of *Tārīkh-i-Mubārak Shāhī* writes: "When Sulṭān Mu'izz al-Dīn Kai-Kubād attained martyrdom, his son Sulṭān Shams al-Dīn Kai-Kā'us was raised to the throne in the year 689/A.D. 1290. Shā'ista Khān became his deputy and it was during the period of his deputyship that the country acquired stability in course of three months."[10] Soon the rival group of the Amīrs conspired against Jalāl al-Dīn (Shā'ista Khān) who easily suppressed them.[11] Moreover, Jalāl al-Dīn abducted Sultān Shams al-Dīn Kai-Kā'us and took him on horseback to the palace at Kīlugharī where, after a confinement of several years, Kai-Kā'us died.

Jalāl al-Dīn Khaljī now (in the year 689/A.D. 1290) ascended the throne of Delhī as the Sulṭān.[12] Immediately, the Sulṭān faced serious internal turmoil which created by the revolt of Malik Chajjū[13] in A.D. 1290. This internal development also affected the frontier affairs of the empire because the Sulṭān devoted his full attention to subduing this rebellion, and hence could concentrate little on strengthening the defence of his empire. However, the Sulṭān turned his attention to the affairs of the frontier after the suppression of Malik Chajjū. Baranī records: "Jalāl al-Dīn Khaljī appointed his eldest son, prince Arkalī Khān, as the *muqṭi* of Multan."[14] The appointment of Arkalī Khān confirms that Multan, upto this time, was the main frontier post. This is further supported by the statement of the Sulṭān, who, according to Baranī, said: "If I go to Multan, I will like Sher Khān to fight against, and give a good account of the Mongols, because they have invaded Muslim territory... ."[15] This evidence is further elaborated by the Sulṭān himself when he heard of the rebellion of Malik Chajjū. He says:

> Bravo! Is there any man in the world who dares to raise dust in my plain? What weakness has that wretch seen in me, that he dares to peer where my arrow can penetrate? If he has not seen the splendour of my sword, he must have heard its renown from afar. He must have heard how from Ghaznā, Kirmān, and Barghand, I have extended my conquests as far as Darband; how I have issued orders for the shedding of the blood of my enemies, who have become like worms, when they hear the whizzing of Kirmānī blade, how, at one time, from the heads of the Mughals, I have filled up my cup with blood, and stuck their inverted skulls upon the top of my standards; how, at another time, my spears have wounded the Afghāns, until the hills resounded with lamentations; how, at another time, I made the blood flow in Janjūa', so that a boat might have glided within the hills of Jūd. The Hindūs themselves cannot conceive how full I have made hell.[16]

These remarks of the Sulṭān are important in so far as they illustrate, both the strategic importance of Multān and the fact that the Mongol invasion was again imminent.

However, the invasions did not take place immediately. This happened as a result of developments in the political affairs of the Mongols in Central Asia. Arghūn Khān (A.D. 1248-91), the Il-Khānid ruler of Persia, resumed the war against the Mamlūks of Egypt on the one hand, and on the other he repelled an invasion launched by the ruler of the Golden Horde, Tole-Buqa, in A.D.

1291.[17] Soon Arghūn Khān appointed his son, Ghāzān Khān, as the governor of Khurāsān. After Arghūn's death, his brother, Geithau, the governor of Rūm,[18] was elected as the Great Khān in July 1291.[19] The Great Khān decided that Ghazān Khān should have control of 'Irāq-i-Ajam,[20] Khurāsān, Kūmis,[21] Mazandarān[22] and one of Fārs.[23] Soon Ghāzān Khān waged a war against Baidū, his cousin and the governor of Baghdād, on the one hand, and on the other he commanded an expedition against Davā Khān (A.D. 1272-1307) the ruler of the Chaghatāe dynasty of Transoxania.[24] Thus they started a fratricidal war among the Mongol princes which spared little time to them to invade India. As has been rightly pointed out by Ḥabīb: "This division of the Mongol power saved the kingdom of Delhī which could not have withstood a united attack of the Mongols."[25] However, the Mongol commanders posted in Khurāsān, especially at Ghaznī, launched their raids to capture the booty and wealth of India and to replenish their resources. " 'Abdullah, the grandson of the accursed Halākū Khān", according to Baranī, "invaded Hindustān with fifteen *tumāns* of the Mongols in A.H. 691/A.D. 1291. Sulṭān Jalāl al-Dīn Khaljī assembled his forces of Delhī and marched from Delhī to meet them with a large and splendid army. The Mongol advance guard had arrived in the boundaries of Barām[26] and the two armies were encamped opposite each other with a river[27] between them."[28] Explaining the battle scene fully Baranī further mentions:

> Some few days passed in arraying their forces, and the advanced parties of the opposing forces had several skirmishes in which the Mussalmāns were victorious, and took some prisoners, who were conducted to the Sultān. Shortly after, the Van of the Mongol army crossed the river. The Van of the Mussalmāns hastened to meet them and a sharp conflict ensued in which the Mussalmān forces were victorious. Many Mongols were put to sword, and one or two commanders of thousands and several centurians were made prisoners. Negotiations followed and it was agreed that war was a great evil, and that hostilities should cease.[29]

This historical evidence points to the conclusion that the Delhī forces were now more sound and capable of deterring the Mongols than they had been in the fort. The Mongol leader, therefore, found it impossible to stand against them and consequently sued for peace. Baranī reports on this matter as follows: "The Sulṭān and 'Abdullah had an interview. The Sulṭān called him son, and he addressed the Sulṭān as father. Presents were exchanged and after hostilities had ceased, buying and selling went on between the two armies.''[30] Not only peace was concluded but also matrimonial relations were established between the Mongol leader and the Sulṭān of Delhī. After this: " 'Abdullah departed with the Mongol army, but Ulghū, grandson of Chingīz Khān,[31] the accursed, with several nobles, commanders of thousand, decided to stay in the Sub-continent. They said the creed and became Mussalmāns, and a daughter of the Sulṭān was given in marriage to Ulghū."[32] Sulṭān Jalāl al-Dīn also extended numerous facilities to them. Barani writes: "The Mongols, who followed Ulghū, were brought into the city with their wives and children. Provision was made for their support and houses were provided for them in Kilūgharī and Indarpat.''[33] Their abodes were called Mughalpūrā. The Sulṭān continued their allowances for a year or two, but the climate and their city homes did not please them, so they departed with their families to their own country. Some of their principal men remained in India, and received allowances and villages. They mixed with and formed alliances with the Mussalmāns and were called "Neo-Mussalmān.''[34] This information is of great importance and needs further consideration. It does, indeed, appear inexplicable at first sight that the Sulṭān of Delhī should have established matrimonial relations and extended so many facilities to his old enemies, the Mongols. Moreover, no contemporary historian has made the causes of this amicable attitude of the Sulṭān quite clear. However, the causes are not far to seek. It is known that the Il-Khānid rulers of Persia were controlling the whole area beyond the Indus river and it was, therefore, important that friendly relations should be established with them. The Mongols were also aware of the bravery which Jalāl al-Dīn Khalji had shown as a warden of marches in the frontier region while he was posted at Samana. Jalāl al-Dīn's treatment of the Mongols could therefore be seen as an attempt to win over the hearts of his former enemies. It proved to be successful as the Il-Khānid rulers of Persia always respected their agreement with the Sulṭān of Delhī and desisted from raiding the territories of the latter. In conclusion Sulṭān Jalāl al-Din Khalji's policy can be termed as 'a policy of peace'.

## II

## The Frontier Policy of Sultan Ala al-Din Khalji (A.D. 1296-1316)

'Alā al-Dīn rose to the throne of Delhī in A.H. 695/A.D. 1296,[35] after the treacherous murder of his uncle Sulṭān Jalāl al-Dīn Khaljī.[36] At this time, 'Alā al-Dīn Khaljī internally faced a difficult situation because Multān, the bastion of the Delhī empire against the Mongol inroads, was threatened with a serious rebellion under Arkalī Khān.[37] Rukn al-Dīn Ibrāhīm, son of the late Sulṭān Jalāl al-Dīn Khaljī had also joined his elder brother Arkalī Khān at Multān after leaving Delhi.[38] There they lived in a state of independence in a far-off province and could any day become a source of danger by claiming the throne. 'Alā al-Dīn Khaljī, therefore, determined to put an end to this peril once for all. With this in mind he took the following action narrated by Baranī:

> Ulugh Khān and Ẓafar Khān, with other Maliks and Amīrs, were sent to Multān with thirty or forty thousand horses. They besieged that place for one or two months. The *Kotwāl* and the people of Multān turned against the sons of Jalāl al-Dīn, and some of the Amīrs came out of the city to Ulugh Khān and Ẓafar Khān. The sons of the late Sulṭān then sent *Shaikh al-Islām*, Rukn al-Dīn, to sue for safety from Ulugh Khān and received his assurance. The princes then went out with the Shaikh and their Amīrs to Ulugh Khān. He recieved them with great respect and quartered them near his own dwelling. . . Ulugh Khān and Ẓafar Khān returned triumphant towards Delhī carrying with them the two sons of the late Sulṭān.[39]

Thus the rebellion, which broke out in the winter of A.D. 1296-7 was brought under control.

Soon after this rebellion, Sulṭān Ala al-Dīn Khaljī made some administrative arrangements in the frontier region of his empire. The *iqṭā'* of Samānā was conferred upon Arslān Khān in A.D. 1296.[40] After the capture of Arkalī Khān, Malik Harnūmer, who was *Wakīldār*, received the *iqṭā'* of Multān; later on he was summoned from Multān and sent to Uchh.[41] The fief of Multān was bestowed upon Alp Khān, who was the Sulṭān's nephew.[42] Malik Tughlaq was made governor of Dipālpur early in the Sulṭān's reign because Baranī and Badāunī refer to him as fighting with the Sulṭān against the Mongols in A.D. 1298.[43] These appointments in the frontier region confirm that the Sulṭān took strong measures to guard the frontier against the Mongol raids.

By now the house of the Mongol was divided into four factions i.e., the Il-Khānid dynasty of Persia, the Chaghatāe dynasty of Transoxania, the Mongol Khāns of China and the Golden Horde.[44] Sulṭān 'Alā al-Dīn Khaljī's contemporaries among the Il-Khāns of Persia were Ghāzān Khān (A.D. 1294-1304), and his brother Al-Jaitū (A.D. 1304-16). In Transoxania his contemporaries were Dava Khan (A.D. 1272-1306) and his sons Kuyuk (A.D. 1306-8), Talikū (A.D. 1308-9), and Kubūk (A.D. 1309-10). In the mainland, the contemporaries of 'Alā al-Dīn were Al-Jaitū (A.D. 1294-1307) and Kubūk (A.D. 1307-11).[45] But here we are mostly concerned only with two branches of the Mongols; the Il-Khānids of Persia and the Chaghatāes of Transoxania because whenever they found respite from their fratricidal wars in Central Asia, they launched invasions upon India. The Mongol expeditions to India were sent either from Persia or from Transoxania. Davā Khān, the ruler of Transoxania, was a determined enemy of the Il-Khānids of Persia, who made allies with Naurūz, the son of Arghūn, who, as a military governor of Khurāsān, was the second-in-command of prince Ghāzān Khān.[46] Thus Davā Khān was successful in snatching Ghaznī from the Il-Khāns of Persia and made it a base of operations directed towards the subcontinent.[47] At this time the nature of these operations also changed, and they became, not border raids, but serious invasions designed to conquer the Delhī empire. Consequently, the full weight of the Mongol invasions was felt in the reign of Sulṭān 'Alā al-Dīn Khaljī. This occurred, according to Ḥabīb, because "Chaghatāe and Ogetāe princes of Transoxania were being hard pressed by the Khāqān in the west and by Il-Khān in the east, and this naturally made them anxious to carve out a principality for themselves elsewhere."[48] In the wake of the increased frequency and the greater strength of the Mongol incursions, the frontier policy of 'Alā al-Dīn Khaljī underwent significant changes. These changes were initiated at a meeting of the Sulṭān and his

Amīrs where this problem was discussed. According to Baranī, 'Alā al-Mulk, the wise Kotwāl, gave him the following advice:

> There are two important undertakings open to the King... one is the conquest and subjugation of all Hindustān... the second and more important undertaking is closing the road of Multan to the Mongols. The forts in that direction have to be repaired and the ditches dug, so that after being stored plentifully with provisions and arms, they may be entrusted to reliable Kotwāls; clever and skilled artisans have to be collected for the construction of *Manjanīqs* and *Arādās*. If, in addition to this, one general is stationed with a large army at Samānā, a second at Dipālpur, and a third at Multān, the path of the Mongols will be blocked. But the Mongols will not refrain from harassing Hindustān unless a very large army of trained soldiers is organised under experienced *Sar-jāndārs* and is provided with good horses and proper arms. After these two undertakings...and the establishment of experienced and reliable Amīrs in the direction of Mongol advance—have been fulfilled, the Sulṭān should stay in Delhī, the capital of the empire, and turn his attention to administrative affairs. The security of the empire or in the capital conduces to the maintenance of order in the provinces; after the realm has been put into order. The king (instead of wandering in search of conquest) should govern everything from his throne. He should send experienced generals with loyal Amīrs and large armies to plunder the distant provinces of Hind; all the horses, elephants and treasures of the Rā'is and Ranas must be seized and brought to the Sulṭān, but their territories are to be returned to them on the condition that they will send a tribute of money, elephants and horses to the city every year.[49]

These remarks highlight the frontier problems of the empire and their solution. As the inroads of the Mongols were the crucial problem, 'Alā al-Mulk offered several suggestions to the Sulṭān for solving this problem. He suggested the maintenance of a disciplined army; the appointment of faithful and brave Amīrs; the building of the forts; the storing of arms and grains in depots in the frontier *iqṭā's* of Multān and Samana. He also pointed out that the three important posts of the frontier were Multan, Samana and Dipālpūr and that they should be in capable hands. With these measures it was possible to check the Mongol advance. 'The Sulṭāṇ, as Baranī says "was pleased and commended the excellence of the advice which he had given, and promised to observe it."[50] Accordingly the Sulṭān adopted a frontier policy which could effectively counter the threat of Mongol invasion.

## WISE AND REALISTIC FRONTIER POLICY

It has been mentioned before that 'Alā al-Dīn Khaljī framed his frontier policy to face the advance of the Mongols in the frontier region of his empire. As Sirī enjoyed an eminent strategic position for the defence of the capital, 'The Sulṭān made Sirī, the capital of the empire, and built a fine palace there which rose to be flourishing city.'[51] Moreover a vigorous policy was pursued of repairing old forts and building new ones in places likely to be threatened by the Mongol hordes.[52] According to Baranī.

> The Sulṭān ordered the fort of Delhī to be repaired, and he also ordered the restoration of the old forts which lay in the tracks of the Mongols. Additional forts were directed to be raised wherever they were required. To these forts he appointed veteran and prudent commanders. Orders were given for the manufacture of the *Manjanīks* and *Arādās* (Balistas) for the employment of the skilful engines, for a supply arms of every kind and for laying in stores of grain and fodder.[53]

Baranī further mentions; that Samānā and Dipālpūr were ordered to be garrisoned with strong selected forces and to be kept in a state of defence; the fiefs in the tract of the Mongols were placed under Amīrs of experience, and the whole route was secured by the appointment of tried and vigilant generals.[54] The Sulṭān appointed Nuṣrat Khān[55] as governor of Sind after the defeat of Arkalī Khān. Similarly, Ẓafar Khān[56] was made the governor of Samānā, Lāhore and Multān.[57] The author of *Tārīkh-i-Mubārak Shāhī* records that Malik Tughlaq was the Amīr of Dipālpur.[58] The appointment of these officers in the frontier region had the effect of resisting the Mongol raids and also of keeping the tribes of the Koh-i-Jūd subdued. In fact these tribes did not rise against the Delhī empire for the first time and were, also for the first time, ravaged by the Mongols. This will, however, be discussed later.

The Sulṭān next turned his atention to the increase of his forces and discussed this issue with those who were said to be acknowledgeable in these matters. According to Barani: "After prolonged discussions with his ministers, 'Alā al-Dīn Khaljī carried out comprehensive reforms for the organisation of the army on a scientific basis.''[59] It was realised that the wild charge of the Mongol horse could not be checked by ill-disciplined levies of hastely raised soldiers. Thus, 'a powerful standing army was raised which became an admirable instrument for carrying out comprehensive schemes for the conquest of the different parts of India.'[60] The same army was also used to check the Mongol raids. However, it was a problem to finance such a big army. It would have heavily taxed the resources of the empire to do so. "The way out of the difficulty was found by giving lower salaries to soldiers but keeping them contented by providing them the necessities of life at fairly low rates. This was done by strictly enforcing the price control system. The pay of a soldier was fixed at 234 *tankās* a year and a man with two horses was paid 78 *tankās* more."[61] Thus, the Sulṭān was able to maintain a large army consisting, according to Firishtah, "of 475,000 horsemen."[62] Barani also gives a hint saying that: "in the early years of his reign, 'Alā al-Din used to take pride in his seventy thousand horses which had been stationed in the stable (*paigah*) of the capital and the *aṭrāf*".[63] These military reforms undertaken by Sulṭān 'Alā al-Din Khalji indicate the interest that he took in the well-being of the army on which the fulfilment of his ambitions for the defence of the empire depended. In this way Sulṭān 'Alā al-Din Khalji was able to encounter the Mongol onslaughts and defend his frontier.

## THE ESTABLISHMENT OF DIPLOMATIC RELATIONS WITH THE IL-KHANID RULERS OF PERSIA

Being a diplomat, Sulṭān 'Alā al-Din Khalji continued having friendly relations with the Il-Khānid rulers, Ghāzān Khān (A.D. 1295-1304) and Al-Jaitu (A.D. 1304-16) which were earlier established by Sulṭān Jalāl al-Din Khalji.[64] Barthold says; "Khwājā Rashid al-Din came to Delhi as an envoy of Il-Khān, Ghāzān Khān, and was well received by Sulṭān Alā al-Din Khalji. The Sulṭān granted a *Jāgir* to Khwājā and instructed revenue officers that the income from the *Jāgir* be properly transmitted to Khwājā through traders."[65] Howorth also records, "Relations of these friendships existed between 'Alā al-Din and al-Jaitū's predecessor Ghāzān Khān. In October, probably of 1303, Ghāzān Khān left Tabriz[66] on an elephant which had been sent as a present by 'Alā al-Din Khalji. The sight was a new one to the people of Tabriz."[67] This is also confirmed by the remarks of Waṣṣāf who hints at a message of Al-Jaitū sent to 'Alā al-Din, at the time of his accession. The message was to the effect that: "The Sultāns of Delhi had always been on good terms with the Mongol Khāqāns but it appeared strange that since the accession of Al-Jaitū, the Sulṭān had neither sent any congratulatory message nor any communication to cement the old friendship. It was time that the old friendly relations should be revived."[68] This was enough to make the Sulṭān make efforts to reestablish good relations with the Il-Khāns of Persia, who, being against the Chaghatāes of Transoxania, helped the Sulṭan to win over one branch of the Mongols as allies. Now Sulṭān 'Alā al-Dīn Khaljī could face the forces of the other Mongol branch under Davā Khān. The encounter with the second branch is described below.

## THE FIRST MONGOL INVASION (A.D. 1296)

Davā Khān, the ruler of Mawāra-un-Nahr, sent an army of 10,000 strong under the command of Kadar.[69] Amīr Khusraū depicts the Mongol raid towards India as follows: "When the subtle Tatār, accompanied by an army like a storm of torture, following their old held practice, marched towards the rivers Jhelum, Suṭlej and Beas from the Jūd mountains and the waves of these hellites set fire to the reed of huts *(talwāṛah)*[70] of the Kokars (i.e. the Gakkhars) on way that the precincts of the city also became lighted up and the building of Kaṣūr[71] were also damaged."[72] This evidence suggests that the Mongols crossed the river Indus and ravaged the Jūd hills. After this they advanced and did not ruin Lāhore but damaged Kaṣūr and reached Jallandhar. When the news of their advance reached 'Alā al-Dīn Khaljī "Ulugh Khān and Ẓafar Khān were sent against them with a large force alongwith Jalālī and 'Alāi Amīrs. The army of Islām met the accursed foe in the vicinity of Jallandhar and gained a victory. Many Mongols were captured and killed and their heads were sent to Delhī."[73] Thus the forces of Delhī defeated the Mongols.

This Mongol invasion also points out that the loyalty of the tribes of the Koh-i-Jūd had undergone a change. As this was the first time that the Mongols crushed the tribes of Jūd hills, it seems that the tribes had refused to cooperate with the Mongols against the Delhī empire. This augured well for the Delhī empire which was greatly encouraged by its victory over the Mongols. The victory also strengthened the hands of Sulṭān 'Alā al-Dīn Khaljī.

## THE SECOND MONGOL INVASION (A.D. 1299)

In the year 1299 when Ulugh Khān and Nuṣrat Khān were busy with the reduction of Gujrāt, the Mongols under the command of Ṣāldī appeared on the frontier of India as mentioned by Baranī.[74] Ṣāldī with his brother and other Mongols, invaded the western part of the country and took possession of Sīwistān.[75] Sulṭān 'Alā al-Dīn Khaljī ordered Ẓafar Khān to march post-haste to Sīwistān, invest the fortress and expel the invaders.[76] Consequently, Ẓafar Khān defeated Ṣāldī, the Mongol commandant, and brought Sīwistān under his control.[77] Ṣāldī and his followers were brought to Delhī as captive in the winter of A.D. 1299-1300.[78] Baranī comments, "This victory inspired the awe and fear of Ẓafar Khān in every heart... in consequence of his fearlessness, generalship and intrepidity, which showed that a *Rustam* had been born in India."[79] It was probably due to the proved valour of Ẓafar Khān that he received the fief of Samānā in the same year. Afterwards he mostly stayed in his fief for the Mongols were a constant source of danger in the west.[80] By this victory, the power of the Delhī empire was further strengthened and the authority of the Sulṭān was confirmed in lower Sind after the recapture of Sīwistān.[81]

## THE THIRD MONGOL INVASION (A.D. 1299-1300)

The third raid of the Mongols took place at the end of the year 1299 and ended in the beginning of the year 1300.[82] Baranī says, "At the end of the year Qatlugh Khwājā son of [the] accursed Zūd,[83] invaded Hindūstān with twenty *tumāns*."[84] Describing the reason of this Mongol invasion Baranī writes: "He probably invaded India to avenge the humiliating defeat suffered by the Mongols in Sīwistān."[85] Naturally, Qatlugh Khwājā came with full force and preparation, and was this time bent upon the conquest of Delhī. "He started from Māwāra-un-Nahr and passing the Indus with a large force, he marched on to the vicinity of Delhī. In this campaign Delhī was the object of attack, so the Mongols did not ravage the countries bordering on their march nor did they attack the forts... ."[86] Baranī further mentions, "Great anxiety prevailed in Delhī, and the people of the neighbouring villages took refuge within its walls. The old fortifications had not been kept in repair, and terror prevailed such as never before had been seen or heard of. All men, great and small, were in dismay. Such a concourse had crowded into the city that the streets and markets and mosques could not contain them. Every thing became very dear. The roads were stopped against cārvāns and merchants, and distress fell upon the people.''[87] This bold coup seems to have taken 'Alā al-Dīn Khaljī by surprise. At this critical moment, the Sulṭān held an important meeting of the council of Maliks and Amirs. In this meeting 'Alāal-Mulk said: "It would be suicidal to face the formidable enemy and the best plan would be to stand a siege and to tire out the patience of the Mongols... ."[88] The Sulṭān commended 'Alā al-Mulk's advice but did not follow it saying: "It does not become famous kings to shun war and battle."[89] 'Alā al-Dīn Khaljī, therefore, advocated a bolder plan of challenging the might of the Mongol hordes. The Sulṭān placed the treasure and his Ḥaram in the charge of *Malik al-Mulk,* and he himself marched out of the fortified city of Sirī to the plains of Kilūgharī, where a memorable battle was fought. 'Alā al-Dīn, the second Alexander, placed his army in order of battle. The right wing was entrusted to Ẓafar Khān, the greatest general of the day, who held the territories of Samānā and Multān. The left wing was assigned to the Sultān's brothers Ulugh Khān and Rukn Khān while the emperor, with Nuṣrat Khān took the charge of the centre with young and brave horsemen and many fierce elephants.[90] This was the strategy which the Sulṭān adopted to defeat his enemies. Ẓafar Khān, with the *Amīrs* who were under him, drew their swords and fell upon the enemy with such fury that the Mongols were forced to fall back. The army of Islām pursued them. Baranī comments: "Ẓafar Khān, the *Rustam* of the age and the hero of the time, pressed after the retreating foe, cutting them down with the sowrd and moving off their heads. He pursued for eighteen *kos,* never allowing the Mongols to rally."[91] 'Isāmī also points out that, "5000 of enemy had been killed."[92] The contemporary works give a graphic description of Ẓafar's bravery and 'Isāmī again records; "His horse died under him and that renowned and unmatched warrior began the struggle on foot. Having strewn his shafts on the ground before him he charged with great violence and every shaft brought one Mongol cavalier down."[93]

The Mongol commandant, Targhī, perceiving that Ẓafar Khān was leading the attack at the head of only a few thousand horsemen, laid a successful ambuscade and cut to pieces Ẓafar Khān and his followers."[94] The, Mongols, however, were considerably impressed by the valour of Ẓafar Khān and before he was surrounded and put to death he was offered the option of surrender and a high rank in the Mongol army by Qatlugh Khwājā who sent him a message saying: "Come with me and I will take thee to my father who will make thee greater than the king of Delhī has made thee."[95] But Ẓafar Khān did not swerve from his loyalty to 'Alā al-Dīn Khaljī and preferred death to dishonour. His dashing bravery, wild impetousity and steadfast loyalty made a deep impression on the Mongols and his name almost became a legend. Baranī writes: "If their [the Mongols] cattle refused to drink, they used to ask them if they saw Ẓafar Khān."[96] Under the cover of night, the Mongols retreated thirty *kos* from Delhī and returned to their country by continuous marches without stopping on way.[97] This invasion of the Mongols was one of the most formidable raids and the Sulṭān won the battle on account of his wise strategy against the Mongols, though it caused the death of a brave commander posted in the frontier region of the kingdom. These calamities forced 'Alā al-Dīn Khaljī to further strengthen the defence of the empire. Consequently, the Sulṭān made even more military reforms.

**THE FOURTH MONGOL INVASION (A.D. 1301)**

The fourth invasion of the Mongols took place in A.D. 1301.[98] Baranī has given us an immediate reason of this raid, that "the Mongol agents had informed Targhī, the Mongol commandant, about the non-presence of the Sulṭān in the capital, who had proceeded to the conquest of Chittor. By the end of the year 1302, an army was also sent to Deccan."[99] Thus Targhī availed himself of this opportunity and marching at the head of twenty or thirty thousand horsemen with all speed reached the neighbourhood of Delhī. Baranī says, "He encamped on the banks of the Jamnā, preventing all ingress and egress to the city... the Mongols were the masters of the situation, they controlled all the roads and lanes that led to Delhī."[100] Consequently, the Sulṭān left the capital and encamped at Siri where he entrenched his camp. Round the entrenchment, he built block houses and other erections to prevent the enemy from forcing a way in, and he kept his forces constantly under arms and on the watch to guard against the dreaded attack and to delay any great engagement. In every division of the army and in each line of entrenchment, there were five elephants fully armed, supported by a body of infantry."[101] 'Isāmī writes, "The patience of Targhī, who had come prepared for victory, had been well nigh exhausted and he retired to his own country."[102]

In this manner the Sulṭān succeeded in repelling this invasion of the Mongols. His success was due to some of the strategical measures which he adopted. Firstly, the Sulṭān entrenched his camp and adopted the tactics of delaying the engagement. This strategem exhausted the patience of the Mongols and forced them to go back to their country. Baranī comments, "If Targhī had continued the siege for another month, Delhī would have fallen."[103] But the real reason of the retreat was the help that came from Malik Tughlaq, the *Amīr* of Dipālpur. The author of *Tārīkh-i-Mubārak Shāhī* records: "The Sulṭān ordered off Malik Tughlaq with a big detachment. Malik Fakhr al-Dīn, *Amīr-i-Dād,* having emerged out of the citadel and joining hands with Malik Tughlaq made a night attack on the Mongols... the Mongol army was put to route and driven back. Targhī was made captive and taken to Delhī by Malik Tughlaq."[104] This authority does not explain further about the fate of Targhī and his followes whereas Barani only writes about their return to their country. However, the Mongols were harassed and there was no option for them but to beat a retreat.

## THE FIFTH MONGOL INVASION (A.D. 1305)

The Mongols had suffered at the hands of the Musalamān army on many occasions which deeply rankled in their hearts and were anxious to avenge this insult. Thus "'Alī Beg and Tartāg, the Mongol commandants, advanced towards India in A.D. 1305."[105] Baranī further says, "With thirty or forty thousand horses, they crossed the hilly region lying north-west of the Indus, crossed the Indus, and advanced towards the east."[106] When the news of their marches reached the Sulṭān, he appointed Malik Nā'ik,[107] *Muster* of the horses, with a strong force of thirty or forty thousand to deal with the Mongols. According to Baranī, "The opposing forces met in the territory of Amrohā[108] and the forces of Islām inflicted upon them a crushing defeat on Thursday, 12 Jamādī us-Sānī, 705/30 December 1305."[109] 'Alī Beg and Tartāq were taken alive and many thousand Mongols were put to death.[110] The Mongol captives were led through the mass of humanity that had gathered to watch the scene and were presented before the royal throne where they were beheaded and their heads were used in the construction of a tower of the fort of Sirī.[111] According to Firishtah, "8000 Mongol heads were used instead of stones and bricks to build the tower of Sirī which was then under construction."[112] This is also confirmed by Amīr Khusraū who writes, "They (Mongols) give blood to new building."[113] This action of the Sulṭān was a part of his strategy through which he wanted to create fear in the hearts of the invaders so that in future they would not dare to march towards the Delhī empire. However, according to 'Isāmī, "The Sulṭān pardoned 'Alī Beg and Tartāg, gave them robe of honour and provided for them all the necessities and amenities of life."[114] If this account is true, it is not surprising. For the Sulṭān sometimes adopted the policy of treating the commanders generously so that they would go back both grateful to the Delhī Sulṭān and impressed by his army. This victory of the Sulṭān also encouraged the forces of Delhī.

## THE SIXTH MONGOL INVASION (A.D. 1306)

The Sulṭān's policy of terror did not, however, deter the Mongols, and Davā Khān, the ruler of Trānsoxania, sent another expedition consisting of a strong force of the Mongols towards India to avenge the defeat of 'Alī Beg and Tartāg as well as the death of other Mongols by the forces of Delhī in A.D. 1306.[115] Kubūk, a Mongol commander, crossed the Indus with a large army and marched to Rāvī.[116] Another force of the Mongols under the command of Iqbālmanda moved southwards and arrived near Nāgaur.[117] Another contingent of the Mongols under Tā'ibū also came.[118] Amīr Khusraū writes: "... the Sulṭān ordered the Muslim armies to proceed against them... the Malik of fragrant virtues, *Kāfūr-i-Sulṭānī,* was appointed to lead the army and experienced commanders such as Malik Tughlaq, the governor of Dipalpur, and Malik 'Ālam were also sent with Malik Nā'ib."[119] Malik Tughlaq, who led the vanguard, one day suddenly sighted the Mongol scouts and immediately informed Malik Kāfūr about their location: shortly afterwards the opposing forces stood face to face on the banks of the river Rāvi. In this battle the forces of Malik Tughlaq won the day taking Kubūk as prisoner and all the followers of Kubūk were either killed or imprisoned and sent to the Sulṭān.[120] Thus the first contingent of the Mongols was defeated by Malik Tughlaq.

The second force of the Mongols under Tā'ibū also faced the Delhī forces, and, according to Amīr Khusraū; "The Sulṭān ordered Malik Kāfūr to disperse the stench of Tāi'bū, so that no trace of it may remain... the great warrior marched rapidly and crossing two stages in one night, came upon the Mongols like a storm and dispersed their wretched ranks... Taī'bū fled from the battle-field towards the rivers."[121] Thus the Muslim army won the day and the Mongols were defeated.

The third force of the Mongols under Iqbāl also faced the army from Delhī, and, according to Firishtah, "It was led by Malik Tughlaq."[122] The outcome of the battle, according to Baranī, was that: "Iqbāl was slain and thousands of the Mongols were put to sword. The Ḥazārā and Ṣadā *Amīrs* who had been caught alive were brought to Delhī and cast under the feet of the elephants."[123]

These three Mongol invasions of the year have been discussed by contemporary historians who differ from each other whether there were three different campaigns, or only one raid. Baranī speaks of the three campaigns in three different years while Amīr Khusraū mentions three generals as if they had planned a joint push: Kubūk leading the advanced contingents while the other two marched behind. This issue has not yet been decided by modern historians. It appears, however, that there was only one expedition. The ruler of Transoxania strategically sent three commanders in three different directions so that the Delhī forces should be engaged in three different places. The Sulṭān of Delhī met these forces of the Mongols successfully and defeated them. Baranī has recorded it as the last incursion of the Mongols in India.[124]

## CAUSES OF THE MONGOL FAILURE

It would be interesting to note as to why the Mongols, once a terror for the east and the west, could not succeed against 'Alā al-Dīn Khaljī. It was due to variety of causes: Firstly, the Mongol power had been considerably weakened by their internal struggle. Davā Khān, the Mongol ruler of Transoxania, fought some forty battles in Central Asia, and consequently, could not devote all his resources to the conquest of India. Secondly, the qualities of the early Mongols which had made them invincible were no more there. The agility, mobility, patience and endurance of the Mongols were gone. They now used to bring their women and children with them which seriously affected their military efficiency. Thirdly, the patience, determination and material qualities of 'Alā al-Din Khalji himself were responsible for turning the tide of the Mongol invasions. 'Alā al-Dīn Khaljī raised a huge well-disciplined and equipped army to guard the frontier and also built a chain of fortifications which has been explained in the map. Diplomatic relations maintained with the ruler of Il-Khānid dynasty in Persia also resulted in no further raid from this branch of the Mongols. This was, of course, of great help. Fourthly, after the death of Davā Khān in A.D. 1306,[125] disorder broke out in Transoxania. The throne became a bone of contention and this prevented the Mongols from invading the Subcontinent.

## FORWARD FRONTIER POLICY OF SULṬĀN 'ALĀ AL-DĪN KHALJĪ

'Alā al-Dīn Khaljī adopted a forward policy because firstly, the death of Davā Khān, the ruler of Transoxania, was followed by confusion and disorder in Central Asia; and secondly, the Sulṭān of Delhī had strengthened his power through his military reforms. Thus, the Sulṭān ordered Malik Ghāzī[126] to invade Mongol territories. Baranī records: "Ghāzī Malik who like Sher Khān before him led expedition every year to Kābul, Qandhār and Garmsīr, and plundered and ravaged those regions and levied tribute from their inhabitants. The Mongols had not the courage to come and defend their own country against him."[127] This is confirmed by Firishta and Ibn Baṭṭutah. Ibn Baṭṭutah says: "that he saw an inscription of Ghāzī Malik on the Jāmī Masjid of Multān which ran: 'I have encountered the Tātārs on twenty nine occasions and defeated them, and hence I am called Ghāzī Malik'"[128] These actions of Ghāzī Malik indicate that the Sulṭān adopted the policy of advance as the best form of defence. The Sulṭān not only sent these expeditions to the Mongol territories but he also established his influence there through getting the *Khutbah* read in his name. Amīr Khusraū says:

> ... according to the royal orders, he (Ḥajib Badr) marched with an army and after travelling through various stages, he reached the banks of the Indus. He crossed the river in boats, and proceeding onwards, arrived at Ghaznī in winter. The season was exceedingly cold. The Mongols of the place were in great alarm, from fear of the Musalmān army. But when the purport of the royal farmān was read to them, they became comforted, expressed their obedience, and were happy. As the king had ordered that the *Khutbah* of his name should be read in Ghaznī, all the Muḥammadans, who had concealed themselves in mountains and ravines, as well as the elders and the principal Musalmāns of Ghaznī, who were looking with the eye of expectation towards Delhi, assembled in the Jāmī Masjid of the city and on Friday, the *Khuṭbah* was read in the name of Sulṭān 'Alā al-Dīn. The noise of the acclamations of joy and congratulations rose high from all quarters. The vest of honour, which was sent by the king for the reader of *Khutbah*, was put on his shoulders. One of the walls of the Mosque, which was decayed and had fallen down, was newly raised. On the same Friday, before the assembly of the Muḥammadans, when the name of the king was pronounced in the *Khuṭbah*, he (Badr) offered near the pulpit, the jewels which he had brought with him and also one plate, full of gold. He threw them down on the earth and the people fell on them and picked them up. The Mongols saw this from the top of the walls of the Masjid and spoke something in their own tongue. In these days some of the infidels have embraced the Muḥammadan faith.[129]

These remarks make it clear that the influence of Sulṭān Alā al-Dīn Khaljī was established in the Mongol territory of Ghaznī. This was due to the policy of advance. Consequently, the raids of the Mongols after A.D. 1307 ceased against India. Amīr Khusraū comments, "Fear and terror now ended, their desire of coming to Hindustān was warded off from their breasts and they created no trouble till the end of Sulṭān Quṭb al-Dīn Mubarak Shāh Khaljī's reign."[130] It was a glorious achievement of Sulṭān 'Alā al-Dīn Khaljī that the Mongol problem which was once a constant headache for the Sulṭāns of Delhī, ended and perfect security was felt in the territories which had been exposed to the inroads of the Mongols, now, once again, the people of these areas carried on their agricultural pursuit in peace.

## III

## Frontier Policy of Sulṭān Quṭb al-Din Mubārak Shāh Khaljī (A.D. 1316-20)

After the death of Sulṭān 'Alā al-Dīn Khaljī, Quṭb al-Dīn Mubārak Shāh Khaljī rose to the throne of Delhī in A.D. 1316.[131] During his rule, the problem of the Mongol raids was no longer felt. Ghāzī Malik was the warden of the frontier. Malik Jūnā Khān, son of Ghāzī Malik, was made *Amīr-i-Akhūr* (Muster of horses) and Malik Mughlāti was the governor of Multān. Similarly, Muḥammad Shāh was the *Amīr* of Sīwistān. These administrative appointments indicate that the frontier policy of Sulṭān 'Alā al-Dīn Khaljī was fully followed and experienced military commanders were posted in the frontier *iqṭā's* of his empire. Besides, there was no sign of any danger from the tribes of the Koh-i-Jūd, especially the Gakkhars, as they were no longer the allies of the Mongols against the Delhī empire. In fact they too were ravaged by the Mongols as has been mentioned earlier, and were now antagonistic to the Mongols. Therefore the Gakkhars now acknowledged the suzerainty of 'Alā al-Dīn Khaljī and good terms came to exist between them. On his part Sulṭān Quṭb al-Dīn Mubārak Shāh Khaljī welcomed the opportunity of being on friendly terms with the tribes of the Koh-i-Jūd and hence enjoyed peace along his frontier *iqṭā's*. On the whole, peace prevailed in the frontier region of the empire during the reign of Sulṭān Quṭb al-Dīn Mubārak Shāh Khaljī.

1. See for details about the origin of the Khaljis in K.S. Lal, *op. cit.*, pp. 9-13. Prof. Shaikh Abdur Rashid's paper read at the I.I.H.C. at Allahabad.
2. *Jandars* were generally slaves of proven loyalty and were commanded by a trustworthy noble who was styled *Sar-i-Jandar*. I.H. Qureshi, *op. cit.*, p. 62.
3. *T.F.S.B.* (Trans.), p. 22.
4. The governors of the provinces were called *Wali, Muqti', Na'ib,* and even *Sultan*. U.N. Day, *op. cit.*, p. 77.
5. *T.F.S.B.* (Trans.), p. 194.
6. It is now situated in Patiala state and about 16 miles south-west from Patiala city.
7. He held the fief of Baran and also held the office of Muster-master-general (*'Ariz-i-Mumalik*). *T.F.S.B.* (Trans.), p. 128
8. *'Ariz-i-Mumalik* was head of *Diwan-i-arz*, ministry of war, and was responsible for maintaining the army in a state of efficiency and for the entire administration of military affairs. Qureshi, *op. cit.*, p. 197.
9. It is now called Balandshahar situated in U.P., India.
10. *T.M.S.* (Trans.), p. 57.
11. *T.F.S.B.* (Trans.), p. 56.
12. According to *Tabaqat-i-Akbari*, Firuz ascended the throne in A.H. 688. Firishta writes A.H 687 Badauni gives A.H. 689; and Barani and Amir Khusrau also record A.H. 689.
13. He was a nephew of Balban and governor of Karah, now situated in U.P., India, who raised the white canopy in Karah and had the *Khutba* read in his name. See for details, *T.F.S.B.* (Trans.), pp. 137-38.
14. *Ibid.*, p. 140.
15. *T.F.S.B.* (Trans.), p. 140.
16. Amir Khusrau, *Miftah-ul-Futuh*, (ed.) Shaikh 'Abdur Rashid, 'Aligarh, 1954, p. 8; (Trans.), Elliot, vol. III, p. 537.
17. Boyle, *op. cit.*, p. 371.
18. The terms or 'Rum Province' are used for the Roman territory, which, till the later part of the 5th century, remained an integral part of the Byzantine empire. See for details, Le Strange, p. 4.
19. Le Strange also records that the provinces of the Byzantine empire were known collectively to the Muslim as *Bilad-ur-Rum*. p. 127.
20. 'Iraq-i-Ajam means Persian 'Iraq.
21. Kumis, of which the capital was Damghan, lay in length along the north border of the Great Desert eastward of Ray, comprising the southern foot-hills of the mountain chain of Alburz which shuts off the high plateau of Persia from the Caspian Sea. Le Strange, *op. cit.*, p. 7.
22. The region of the high mountains – for the most part occupied by what, is, at the present day, known as the Alburz chain lying along the south coast of the Caspian Sea, being to the east and to the north of Kumis – was called Tabaristan by the earlier 'Arab geographers. Tabar has the signification of 'Mountain' in the local dialect, whence Tabaristan would mean 'the Mountain Land'. In the 7th (13th) century, about the time of the Mongol conquest, the name of Tabaristan appears to have fallen into disuse; being replaced by Mazandaran, which since that date has been the common appellation of this province. *Ibid.*, p. 369.
23. *Ibid.*, pp. 6, 248.

24. Ghāzān Khān first heard of Baidū's revolt at Qarā-Teppe near Sarakhs when returning from a victory gained over the Transoxania Mongols. He took no notice and proceeded on his way to Radkān, where, according to Rashīd al-Dīn, he received a message from Baidū himself formally inviting him to ascend the throne... At Khail-i-Buzrg he learnt, as Rashīd al-Din puts it, that Baidu had changed his mind and now wanted the Khānate for himself... . He despatched ambassadors to Baidū to announce his coming and ask for a safe conduct... . Baidū's reply... was to the effect that Ghāzān should turn back... . On 16 May they crossed the Safed Rūd, and three days later the two armies came face to face at Qurbān Shire... ." Boyle, *op. cit.*, pp. 377-8. For further details see, *K.T.M.G.* (text).
25. Muḥammad Ḥabīb, *op. cit.*, p. 30.
26. Contemporary as well as modern historians differ on Sunam. Baranī and 'Isamī write it as Barām. but Firishta calls it Ḥaram. Badāunī has Sunam. The modern historian K.S. Lāl says that it was Sunam. Prof. Shaikh Rashīd also takes it for Sunam. Shaikh Rashīd, "Jalāl al-Dīn Khaljī", *M.U.J.* pp. 138-9.
27. 'Isami calls it river Sind. But it cannot be Indus river because it is too far away. If the place is Sunam, the river should be Beās.
28. *T.F.S.B.* (trans.), p. 148.
29. *T.F.S.B.* (trans.), p. 148.
30. *Ibid.*, p. 149.
31. K.S. Lal says that Ulghū Khān was related to Chingīz Khān. K.S. Lāl, *op. cit.*, p. 31.
32. *T.F.S.B.* (Trans.), p. 149; *T.F.* (text), p. 94.
33. All these places lay in the suburb of Delhī. Indrapat was in the north, Kilūgharī in the middle and Ghiyāspūr in south. Mughalpūra is still the name of a village near Delhi *T.F.S.B.* (Trans.), p. 149.
34. *Ibid.*
35. Firishtah says, "In the later end of the year 696". Badāunī gives 29th Zil-Ḥijjah 695. Amīr Khusrau states that the accession took place on 16th Ramzān 695. Baranī gives no date but mentions the year 695 only. *T.F.S.B.* (text), p. 73.
36. "... the Sulṭān reached the shore before the afternoon prayer, and disembarked with a few followers. 'Alā al-Dīn advanced to receive him, and he and all his followers, showing due respect. When he reached the Sulṭān he fell at his feet, and the Sulṭān treated him as a son, kissed his eyes and cheeks and said, "I have brought thee up from infancy, why are thou afraid of me." The Sulṭān took 'Alā al-Dīn's hand and at that moment, the stony hearted traitor gave the fatal signal. Muḥammad Sālim of Samānā struck at the Sulṭān with a sword... threw him down and cut off his head... ... *T.F.S.B.* (text), p. 155.
37. Arkalī Khān was the second son of the late Sulṭān Jalāl al-Dīn and was a brave and able soldier. He was the *muqtī'* of Multān when the Sulṭān was murdered. After the accession of Sulṭān 'Ala al-Dīn Khaljī he was defeated by Ulugh Khān and Zafar Khān. *Ibid.*, p. 158.
38. *Ibid.*, p. 158.
39. *T.F.S.B.* (Trans.), p. 161.
40. *T.B.S.* (Text), p. 68.
41. Qureshī, *op cit.*, p. 59. See for details Appendix 'C'.
42. *F.M.S.* (Text), p. 69.
43. *Ibid*

44. A.N. Khan, *op cit.*, p. 71; During the days of Ghazi Malik, Dipalpur was called "Iqta'i-Buzzurg". Agha Mahdi Husain, *op. cit.*, p. 28.
45. Boyle, *op. cit.*, p. 396.
46. Boyle, *op. cit.*, p. 396.
47. Habib, *op. cit.*, p. 25.
48. See for details, Henry Howorth, *History of the Mongols*, London, 1886, vol. iv.
49. *T.F.S.B.* (Trans.), pp. 35-6.
50. *T.F.S.B.* (Trans.), Elliot, p. 171.
51. *Ibid.*, p. 191
52. *Ibid.*
53. *T.F.S.B.* (Trans.), p. 192.
54. *Ibid.*
55. His name was Malik Nusrat Jalesari and the title of Nusrat Khan was given by the Sultan.
56. He was an old general of 'Ala al-Din and his real name was Malik Hazbar al-Din.
57. *T.F.S.B.* (Trans.), p. 161.
58. *T.B.S.* (Text), p. 69.
59. *T.F.S.B.* (Trans.), p. 192.
60. *Ibid.*
61. *T.F.S.B.* (Trans.), p. 192.
62. *T.F.* (Trans.), p. 262.
63. *T.F.S.B.* (Trans.), p. 262.
64. Barthold W., *op. cit.*, p. 44. See Khaliq Ahmad Nizami, "Rashid al-Din Fazlullah as an Il-Khanid envoy to the court of 'Ala al-Din Khalji", P.I.H.C. Patiala Session, cited by Riaz al-Islam, *C.D.I.P.R.*, p. 49.
65. *Ibid.*
66. It took the first position under the later 'Abbasids as a provincial capital and retained its eminence under the Il-Khans. Le Strange, *op. cit.*, p. 160.
67. H. Howorth, *op. cit.*, p. 479.
68. *T.W.* (Text) p. 528. This event has only been mentioned by Wassaf but no Indian historian refers to it. As it concerns the affairs of Persia, Wassaf should be relied upon.
69. Barani does not give the name of the commander of the expedition but Amir Khusrau mentions his name. *T.N.* (Text), p. 18. Habib writes its date as February 6, 1298. Habib *op. cit.*, p. 126.
70. The word 'talwarah' is a common name for a village in many parts of upper Punjab.
71. This is the modern Tehsil of Qasur of the District Lahore situated south of the city itself.
72. *K.F.*, p. 18. The order given in the original text is Beas, Jhelum and Sutlej but this is erroneous.
73. Amir Khusrau names the site of the battle as Jaran Manjur. Barani says that the battle was fought within the environs of Jallandhar which lies between the rivers, Sutlej and Beas. *T.F.S.B.* (Trans.), p. 162.
74. *T.F.S.B.* (Trans.), p. 162.
75. *Ibid.*, p. 165. Siwistan implies the north-western portion of Sind known as Sehwan. P. Saran identifies it with Sivi, present Sibi in Baluchistan which commands the Bolan pass. P. Saran, *op. cit.*, p. 214.
76. *Ibid.*

77. P. Sarān, *op. cit.*, p. 214.
78. Lal, *op. cit*, p. 135. Neither contemporary nor modern works have written about the fate of Sāidī.
79. *T.F.S.B.* (Trans.), p. 165.
80. 'West' refers to the western frontier of the Delhi empire.
81. 'Alā al-Dīn appointed Nuṣrat Khān in A.D. 1296 to go with 10,000 men through the districts of Multān, Uchh, Bakar, Sehwān and Thatta to put down adverse tribes and appoint trustworthy men as governors of several towns and forts and himself return to Multān where he should make his headquarter. *T.M.M.* (Trans.), p. 16.
82. *T.F.S.B.* (Trans.), p. 165.
83. But there was no king by the name of Zūd of Zūe in Transoxania in the time of 'Alā al-Dīn Khaljī. The words, therefore, appear to be ( قتلغ بن دود لعين ) Qatlugh, son of Duā or Devā the accursed.
84. A *tumān* consisted of ten thousand men.
85. *T.F.S.B.* (Trans.), p. 165.
86. *Ibid.*
87. *T.F.S.B.* (Trans.), p. 165.
88. *Ibid.*
89. *Ibid.*, p. 122.
90. "The Sulṭān of India follows this order on the battlefield; the king stands in the centre, first surrounded by the circle of 'Ulāma and then the archers in the front and rear. The right and left wings are stretched so wide that both of them joined each other... ." *M.A.* (Text), p. 51.
91. *T.F.S.B.* (Trans.), p. 167.
92. *F.S.* (Trans.), p. 258.
93. *F.S.* (Trans.), p. 258.
94. *T.F.S.B.* (Trans.), p. 168.
95. *Ibid.*
96. *T.F.S.B.* (Trans.), p. 169.
97. *Ibid.*
98. *Ibid.*
99. *Ibid.*, p. 190.
100. Before the encampment of Targhī at Jamnā, Sulṭān 'Alā al-Dīn came back from Chittor.
101. *T.F.S.B.* (Trans.), p. 190.
102. *F.S.* (Trans.), p. 276.
103. *T.F.S.B.* (Trans.), p. 191.
104. *T.M.S.* (Trans.), p. 71. The strategical measures resulted in a strange terror that took possession of Targhī's mind, and his communication was in danger.
105. *T.F.S.B.* (Trans.), p. 198.
106. *Ibid.*
107. Amīr Khusrau says that Malik Nā'ik was a Hindū.
108. *K.F.* (Trans.), p. 26. It is now situated in U.P. (India).
109. *Ibid.*, p. 27.
110. *T.F.S.B.* (Trans.), p. 198.
111. *T.F.S.B.* (Trans.), p. 198.
112. *T.F.* (Trans.), p. 376.

113. *K.F.* (Trans.), p. 26.
114. Waṣṣāf writes that 'Alī Beg accepted Islām and that he was given the rank of a nobleman. *T.W.* (Text), pp. 326-7. *F.S.*(Trans.), p. 276.
115. *T.F.* (Trans.), p. 377.
116. *K.F.* (Trans.), p. 30.
117. It is situated in Rājasthān.
118. *K.F.* (Trans.), p. 29.
119. *K.F.* (Trans.), p. 30.
120. Lal, *op.cit.*, p. 147.
121. *K.F.* (Trans.), p. 34.
122. *T.F.* (Trans.), p. 346: Simon Digby, *op. cit.*, p. 25.
123. *T.F.S.B.* (Trans.), p. 191.
124. *Ibid.*, p. 200.
125. *T.R.* (Trans.), p. 36.
126. G͟hāzī Malik had obtained great renown in Hindustān. He held the territory of Dipālpur and Lāhore and until the end of the rule of Quṭb al-Dīn Mubārak S͟hāh K͟haljī he proved a barrier to the inroads of the Mongols occupying the position formerly held by S͟her K͟hān. *T.F.S.B.* (Trans.), p. 211.
127. *Ibid.*, No date has been mentioned by the contemporary authorities.
128. *I.B.* (Trans.), p. 97.
129. *I.K.* (Trans.), p. 566. Baranī says nothing of Alā al-Dīn's ascendancy at G͟haznī and Firis͟htah speaks only of plundering expeditions into that part and the neighbouring countries.
130. *K.F.* (Trans.), p. 30. After establishing his position, the Sulṭān dealt with iron-hands with the converted Mongols called Neo-Muslims who had rebelled against the Delhī empire. See for details, *T.F.S.B.* (Trans.), p. 206.
131. K͟husrau and 'Isāmī give the year 715 A.H., while Baranī writes 717 A.H.

## Chapter VI

# THE FRONTIER POLICY OF THE TUGHLAQS (A.D. 1320–1413)

## I

### The Frontier Policy of Sulṭan Ghiyāṣ al-Dīn Tughlaq (A.D. 1320–25)

Sulṭān Ghiyāṣ al-Dīn Tughlaq sat on the throne of Delhī on the 1st of Sha'bān, A.H. 72-/6th September 1320 A.D.[1] The Sulṭān faced troubles before he was able to mount the throne. This troublesome period proved to be a setback not only internally to the Delhī empire but it also affected the frontier arrangements. It would be interesting to know about the internal disturbance. Sultān Qutb al-Dīn Mubārak Shāh Khaljī (A.D. 1316–20) the last ruler of the Khaljī dynasty, was murdered by Khusraū Khān[2] through a conspiracy which, according to Amīr Khusraū, "Was launched with the object of removing the Sulṭān from the throne of Delhī."[3] After the death of the Sulṭān, there started a tussle between Khusraū Khān and Ghāzī Malik[4] because the latter was partial to the deceased Sulṭān's family. At this time Ghāzī Malik's son Malik Fakhr al-Dīn Jūnā was holding the post of *Akhūr-i-Bak* [Master of the horses][5] in Delhi, and Khusraū Khān gave him robes of honour and a large amount of money.[6] After a few days, Malik Jūnā mounted his horse and fled with a few of his slaves from Delhī to Dipālpur.[7] After meeting his son Jūnā Khān, Ghāzī Malik began to make preparations for war.

How a *muqṭi'* was able to raise an army powerful enough to fight the imperial army of Delhī is a problem which Baranī does not answer? But the *Tughlaq Nāmā* of Amīr Khusraū gives a detailed account of Ghāzī Malik's preparations for war. Amīr Khusraū says: "Jūnā Khān's flight dealt Khusraū Khān a straggering blow. He took counsel with his Amirs, and Yousaf Khan[8] roused Khusrau and his comrades to crush Ghāzī Malik."[9] Yousaf Khān also sent a messenger to Ghāzī Malik urging him to surrender to Khusraū and refrain from war: This made Ghāzī Malik indignant and he denounced Khusraū and killed his messenger.[10] Amīr Khusraū further says: "Ghāzī Malik sent requests through a letter to the important governors: likewise, Amīr Mughlātī, the governor of Multān, Muḥammad Shāh, the governor of Siwistān; Behrām Aiba, the governor of Uchh; Yakh Lakhī, the governor of Samānā; Hoshang, the governor of Jālor; and 'Ain-ul-Mulk for assisting him in the retaliatory war that he intended to wage."[11] When the contents of this letter reached Khusraū Khān, he sent his brother, Khān-i-Khānān, against Ghāzī Malik. After Khusraū's troops had crossed the frontier, Ghāzī Malik mobilised his army and marched towards Delhī. Malik Jūnā was placed in front of the forces and Ghāzī Malik brought up the rear.[12] Ghāzī Malik won the battle and set out triumphantly towards the capital on Sunday, 6th September, A.D. 1320.[13]

This event not only speaks of the emergence of Ghāzī Malik as a victorious Sulṭān, but also shows the strength of the warden of the frontier marches. Ghāzī Malik's *iqṭā's* of Multān, Uchh, Siwistān and Samānā thus became the frontier ramparts of the Delhī empire.

When Sulṭān Ghiyāṣ al-Dīn Tughlaq had been the warden of marches in the frontier region, as a result of his policy of advance under Sulṭān 'Alā al-Dīn Khaljī, the Mongol raids ceased. Accordingly, the assembly of Amirs and Maliks called by him after the defeat of Khusrau Khan commended him as follows: "You Ghazī Malik decidedly command our allegiance, for so many years you have been our protection against the Mongols. It is on account of you that the Mongols ceased to invade India."[14] Having had a long experience of frontier defence, the Sulṭān made administrative appointments in the frontier *iqṭā's* soon after his accession to the throne. According to Barani, "The Sulṭān appointed Kishlū Khān as governor of Multān and Sind, soon after becoming

Sulṭān."[15] 'Isāmī says, "The Sulṭān appointed Gurs͟hāsp (گرشاسپ) as the governor of Samānā."[16] These administrative arrangements in the frontier region confirm that Samānā, Multān and Sind remained the frontier *iqṭā's* of the Delhi empire. The Sulṭān further reshuffled his frontier *muqṭī's,* and Mīr Ma'sūm informs us that, "Tāj al-Dīn was appointed governor of Multān; K͟hwājā K͟hatīr, governor of Bak͟har, and Malik 'Alī Sher, governor of Siwistān."[17] Thus, keeping in view the importance of these *iqṭā's,* the Sulṭān appointed these *muqṭī's* of great repute as governors. They were responsible for guarding and maintaining peace in their respective *iqṭā's* as well as to check any Mongol advance from the west of the Indus. The contemporary as well as modern historians are silent on the question whether the Sultān had decided upon conciliating or crushing the tribes of Jūd hills who, as we have seen, had always created problems for the empire. It appears, however, that since at this time they recognised the sovereign authority of the Tughlaq Sulṭān the latter did not think of crushing them.

On the accession of G͟hiyās al-Dīn Tughlaq the political affairs beyond the Indus also took a serious turn. After Al-Jaitū's death in A.D. 1316, Abū Sa'id[18] ascended the Il-K͟hānid throne of Persia. He retained the services of C͟hobānids in the province of K͟hurāsān. Yasa'ūr, the C͟haghatāe prince, estabished in Badg͟his, had at first professed loyalty towards the young Il-K͟hān. However, his activities in K͟hurāsān were difficult to reconcile with this professed loyalty. And early in A.D. 1319 he rose in open revolt. The news of his invasion of Mazandarān was received simultaneously with a report that Oz-beg, the ruler of the Golden Horde, was approaching Darband[19] at the head of a great army.[20] According to Boyle, "It was decided that the Amīr, Ḥasan, should be sent against Yaṣa'ūr, whilst the Il-K͟hān king marched in person against Oz-beg, the ruler of the Golden Horde. Yasa'ūr's revolt was soon suppressed... in A.D. 1325, C͟hobān repulsed a second invasion of Oz-beg and even carried the war into the enemy's own territory,"[21] This situation beyond the Indus did not allow the Mongols to march towards India for the time being. However, they did invade northern India once, 'Isāmī has the following to say about the raid: "The victories of Ulugh K͟hān[22] in Deccan were in progress, when a wave of the Mongol invasions burst upon northern India. Gurs͟hāsp, the governor of Samānā, sent a message to Sulṭan Ghiyās al-Dīn Tughlaq intimating him that the Mongols had crossed the Indus and invaded Samānā. The Sulṭān sent an army commanded by some Hindū and Muslim officers. On reaching Samānā, the supreme command of the army was assumed by Gurshāsp... and two battles were successively fought and won; one in the Siwālik hills, east of Samānā, and the other to the north on the bank of the Beās. The Mongols were defeated and repulsed, and many of them were captured alive. The triumphant army then returned with its Mongol prisoners to Delhī and the Sulṭān was pleased to reward the officers handsomely."[23] According to both Baranī and, 'Afīf, "This invasion of the Mongols took place in A.H. 7[illegible]/A.D. 1324. Both these contemporary writers agree that it was an unimportant invasion which was soon repulsed."[24] But it is curious to note that none of the contemporary works has specified which branch of the Mongols, the Il-Khanid or the Chaghatae, had initiated this invasion. However, it was the only and last recorded invasion of the Mongols in India. Thereafter, the western frontier of the Delhī kingdom became quite safe from further raids of the Mongols. And it was mostly due to the strategy adopted by Sulṭān Ghiyās al-Dīn Tughlaq to safeguard his frontier *iqṭā's* that this came to pass. The Sulṭān strengthened the western frontier by building new forts and establishing garrisons on the border of Kābul.[25] These frontier arrangements confirm that Sulṭān Ghiyās al-Dīn Tughlaq was not only mindful about the defence of his western frontier but also took a step forward in implementing the realistic frontier policy of Sulṭan Ghiyās al-Dīn Balban and Sulṭān 'Alā al-Dīn Khaljī. Consequently, peace prevailed in the frontier region during his rule.

II

## The Frontier Policy of Sulṭān Muḥammad Bin Tughlaq (A.D. 1325-51)

Sulṭan Ghiyās al-Dīn Tughlaq died in A.D. 1325 and his son Muḥammad bin Tughlaq became the Sulṭān of Delhī.[26] The frontier problems of the empire, which confronted the Sulṭān were not as formidable as they had been under Sulṭān Ghiyās al-Dīn Balban and

Sulṭān 'Alā al-Dīn Khalji. Both these rulers had been troubled by foreign invasions which had taxed their resources to the utmost. The forward policy of Sulṭān 'Alā al-Dīn Khaljī had greatly minimised the Mongol danger, but the hostility of the Hindū Rājās, the overweaning claims of the native nobility, the orthodox prejudices of the clerical party and its ambition to dominate the state were dangerous portents for the future of the Delhī empire.[27] The task of the new Sulṭān, though not as difficult as that of Balban and 'Alā al-Dīn, was certainly more trying than that of his father, Sulṭān Ghiyās al-Dīn Tughlaq, who appeared on the scene at a moment in the annals of the Delhī Sultanate when the Mongols had little time or ambition to invade India. The frontier *iqṭā's*, though, were safe from Mongol invasions, were now disturbed on account of the rebellions of the *muqṭi's* which internally perturbed the Sulṭān and affected his frontier defence.

The first revolt occurred when the Sulṭān was at Daulatābād. It was led by Malik Behrām Aiba,[28] alias Kishlū Khān, who was an old friend of the Sulṭān's father and the governor of the frontier *iqṭā's* of Uchh, Sind[29] and Multān. Ibn Baṭṭūṭah records: "Kishlū Khān had incurred the Sulṭān's displeasure, for having buried the corpses of Bahā al-Dīn Gurshāsp,[30] and Ghiyāṣ al-Dīn Bahādur."[31] Firishtah records another reason of this revolt, that is, the refusal of the governor of this frontier region to send his family to the newly established capital Daulatābād and his quarrel with the messenger who brought to him the Sulṭān's order to this effect.[32] Consequently, the Sulṭān marched from the capital towards Multān and a battle was fought in the plains of Abohar.[33] Behrām Aiba was defeated and his army was completely routed. Behrām Aiba fled but was captured and executed. His head was hanged at the gate of the city of Multān as a warning to others.[34] After this the *iqṭa'* of Multān "was bestowed upon Malik Qiwām al-Mulk[35] in fiet. Later on, after a few years, the Sultān conferred this *iqṭā'* upon 'Imād al-Dīn Multānī."[36]

Baranī has recorded another rebellion which also broke out in Multān. Shāhū Afghan killed Bihzād Khān, the *Nā'ib*, and after collecting a party of Afghāns, he took possession of the city. Malik

Nawā fled from Multān to Delhī and reported to the Sulṭān about these developments.[37] The Sulṭān prepared his forces and marched towards Multān. When he was only a few marches from Multān, Shāhū submitted and appealed to the Sulṭān by saying that he repented of what he had done. Shāhū[38] fled with his Afghāns to Afghānistān.[39] The Sulṭān proceeded to Sunam.[40] In this way the rising of the Afghāns under the leadership of Shāhū was crushed.

Another frontier province was Lahore where also a rebellion broke out in A.D. 1242. Firishta has recorded that the name of the rebel was Ḥaider Khān[41] but Ibn Baṭṭuṭah and Badāūnī tell us that it was Hulājūn and that he was assisted in his enterprise by one Amīr Gul Jand or Chandar who is supposed to be a Gakkhaṛ chief.[42] However, upon receiving the news of the rebellion, Khwāja Jahān, the Wazīr raised an army by the order of the Sulṭān and marched from Delhī to Lahore. The two armies met on the banks of Beās. Ḥaider Khān was defeated and a large number of his soldiers were drowned in the river. Khwājā Jahān advanced to Lāhore where he punished all the leaders and participants in the rebellion.[43] This event clearly shows that the Sulṭān was fully prepared to control the frontier *iqṭā's* of his empire and keep them under his firm grip. He kept a vigilant watch on rebellious activities and remained always ready to deal with them with an ironhand. If the rebel chiefs were Gakkhaṛs and they rebelled in Lāhore, it also indicates that the Gakkhaṛs had advanced upto this city.

Baranī has also narrated another rebellion which broke out in the frontier *iqṭā's* of Sunam and Samānā. He records that "The Sulṭān marched to Sunam and Samānā to put down the rebels, who had formed strongholds, withheld the tribute, created disturbances, and plundered on the roads. The Sulṭān destroyed their strongholds, dispersed their followers and carried their chiefs to Delhī."[44] There the chief rebels embraced Islām and some of them were placed in the service of noblemen.

The Sulṭān, thus, succeeded in subduing all the revolts which broke out in the frontier *iqṭā's* and ultimately he was able to restore peace and order in the frontier region of the empire. He appointed loyal governors there and instructed them to keep a watch on any advance of the Mongols.

**CENTRAL ASIAN POLITICS**

The Central Asian politics, as we have seen, which always deeply influenced the frontier affairs of the Delhī empire, entered a new phase when a power struggle among the various dynasties of the Mongols reached its cilmax. Ibn Baṭṭūtah argues that religious differences were the root-cause of this struggle. According to him: "In those days the antagonism between the Sunnī and Shi'a was exceedingly acute and the rivalry between the Il-Khāns of Persia and the Chaghatāes of Transoxania became virulent."[45] There is no doubt that sectarian differences were contributary factors in widening the gulf between the antagonists. However, the gulf already existed and the real reason for its being there was the desire of both the factions to dominate the eastern parts of Central Asia. The Il-Khān ruler invaded and annexed Southern Afghanistān in A.D. 1313.[46] which provoked Kubūk Khān, the ruler of Transoxania and brother and predecessor of Tarmānshīrīn.[47] Kubūk Khān led an army and inflicted a crushing defeat on the army of the Il-Khāns.[48] The Il-Khāns lost hold eventually on their territories – Kābul, Ghazni and Qandhār, which passed into the hands of Chaghatāes.[49] It was about this time that Al-Jaitū appointed his son Abū Sā'id to the viceroyalty of Khurāsān, as already mentioned.[50] In A.D. 1316, Al-Jaitū was succeeded by his young son, Abū Sā'id.[51] After some nine years, approximately, the time when Muḥammad bin Tughlaq ascended the throne of Delhī, there started again a conflict between the Il-Khāns of Persia and the Khāns of Transoxania. Tarmānshīrīn, who ascended the throne of Transoxania, began to make preparations for an invasion of Khurāsān. With this object in view he had collected troops in Ghaznī.[52] As soon as Amīr Chobān, an Il-Khān viceroy of Khurāsān,[53] heard of this, he sent a huge army under the command of his son Amīr Ḥasan towards Ghaznī. There a battle was fought early in A.D. 1326.[54] Tarmānshīrīn was defeated and Amir Ḥasan ravaged Ghazni.[55] It was this defeat of Tarmanshirin which in all probability, compelled him to go to India to implore Sulṭān Muḥammad bin Tughlaq to help him in a joint invasion of Khurāsān.

This adventure of Tarmānshīrīn in India is explained by two contemporary writers in different ways. One account is given by

'Isāmī and another by Ibn Baṭṭūṭah. 'Isāmī under the heading of "Arrival of Tarmānshīrīn in India" records, "One day, a courtier came from Multān and announced at the royal palace that a Mongol army had made a bridge over the Rāvī river of human bodies, destroyed everything in their way, raided the Sind area and were overrunning the remotest parts of India."[56] 'Isāmī further says: "When the emperor came to know that the accursed enemies had crossed the boundary of Multān, he girded up his loins, mobilising troops in the manner of kings and commanders. He sent couriers to all parts of the country and summoned all divisions and ranks of troops... the following day, another courier came... saying, "Your Majesty: the Mongols have arrived at Mīrath and have been raiding the area for three days... . The well known Tarmānshīrīn is the commander of that wretched army... . When the emperor heard this ... . He ordered Bughrā Khān to march quickly to Mīrath with 10,000 brave cavalrymen... . The brave Indian cavalrymen put up such a heroic fight that they succeeded at last in dislocating the enemies and compelled them to take to flight... . When the Emperor came to know of the Mongols retreat from India, drums were beaten and he mounted his horses and led his troops in pursuit of the enemy... who followed them upto Indus."[57]

In the face of this evidence, it shows that Tarmānshīrīn arrived in India with warlike intentions which led to the strained relations subsequently followed between Sulṭān Muḥammad bin Tughlaq and him. Almost all the later chronicles such as Sirhindī,[58] Badāūnī[59] and Firishta[60] followed 'Isāmī. But Baranī slurs over this Mongol invasion which took place in A.H. 727/A.D. 1327.[61] Dr. S.M. Ḥaq, a modern writer, argues that it is wrong to say that Baranī does not mention this invasion because it brings discredit to the Sulṭān. In fact it was not an invasion in any sense of the word.[62] Ibn Baṭṭūṭah, a contemporary traveller, also does not agree with 'Isāmī's point of view and records, "'Alā al-Dīn Tarmānshīrīn is a great king. . . . Sulṭān Tarmānshīrīn had violated the Yasaq. ... Buzān Oghle marched against him... . Tarmānshīrīn was killed... it is also said that he was not killed. When Buzān's position became stable, BāshīOghle, the son of Tarmānshīrīn, ran away along with his sister and her husband, to the emperor of India. The emperor received them warmly and accorded them due honour in view of the friendship and correspondence and exchange of presents that he had with Tarmānshīrīn whom he used to address as brother."[63] Ibn Baṭṭūṭah's statement to this effect suggest that both Tarmānshīrīn and Sulṭān Muḥammad bin Tughlaq had cordial relations. Dismayed by his misfortunes which commenced with his adventúres in Khurāsān, Tarmānshīrīn fled to Ghaznī whence he sent his children through the good offices of Barantiya, the governor of Ghaznī, to Delhī. It is also possible that Tarmānshīrīn, after the defeat by Amīr Ḥasan at Ghaznī, might have come to India to see Sulṭān Muḥammad bin Tughlaq for reconquering Khurāsān which event has been mis-stated by 'Isāmī who calls it as Tarmānshīrīn's invasion of India. Aghā Mahdī Ḥusain, a modern historian, argues that Tarmānshīrīn's arrival in India was a friendly visit.[64] This theory is also supported by Riāẓul-Islām.[65]

## The Frontier Policy of Sulṭān Muḥammad bin Tughlaq

Taking advantage of the changed situation in Central Asian politics as discussed above, Sulṭān Muḥammad bin Tughlaq tried to adjust his frontier policy to the political exigencies of the time. This policy can be seen to be based on two fundamental principles: one, expansionism; and second, the establishment of diplomatic relations with various Central Asian rulers.

### i) THE EXPANSIONIST POLICY OF SULṬAN MUHAMMAD BIN TUGHLAQ

Sulṭān Muḥammad bin Tughlaq gave a friendly response to Tarmānshīrīn's request and planned to support him in his expedition in Khurāsān. Therefore, the Sulṭān raised a large army for the campaign against Khurāsān. According to Baranī "In that year, three hundred and seventy thousand horses were enrolled in the Muster's master office."[66] The expedition itself is described by Āghā Mahdī Ḥusain in the following words: "On reaching Transoxania, Tarmānshīrīn sent his son-in-law, Amīr Nauroz, with a large number of Mongol chieftains, to the court of the Sulṭān of Delhī. All of them joined the Sulṭān's army and Amīr Nauroz remained in Muḥammad bin Tughlaq's service until the latter's death near Thatta in A.D. 1351."[67] It was this visit of Tarmānshīrin that opened Ghazni to direct communications and negotiations with the Sulṭān of Delhī. Ghaznī was afterwards made a diplomatic centre and came within the Sulṭān's sphere of influence. In fact the Sulṭān almost took the *Qāẓi* of Ghaznī into his pay, a fact which Baranī repeatedly deplores.[68] However, the Khurasan expedition did not materialise. This could be owing to the changes that had followed in the wake of the restoration of friendly relations between Abū Sa'id of Iran and An-Nāṣir of Egypt, the deposition of Tarmanshīrin and the consequences of all these to the diplomatic and political situation prevalent in Iran, Egypt and Transoxania.

The Qarājal expedition was the second expansionist venture undertaken by the Sulṭān of Delhī. Baranī says, "It was intended as a preliminary step to the conquest of Khurāsān and Transoxania so that the passage for troops and horses might be rendered easier."[69] On the other hand Firishtah says that the Sulṭān wished to conquer the countries of China and Himāchal,[70] which does not appear to be correct. On the other it is evident that the expedition could have extended the influence of the Sulṭān to the hilly region of the Northern Himālayas. This region is actually called Himatala in the Chinese accounts.[71] Thus, the proposed Khurāsān and Qarājal expeditions of the Sulṭān show that he desired to extend his influence in the territories of Central Asia by taking advantage of the local situation.

## ii) DIPLOMATIC RELATIONS

The second trend of Sulṭān Muḥammad bin Tughlaq's frontier policy was to maintain friendly relations through the establishment of diplomatic ties with the countries of Central Asia. Sulṭān Muḥammad bin Tughlaq sent a diplomatic mission, as mentioned by Āghā Mahdī Husain, to An-Nāṣir, the ruler of Egypt, with a letter under a golden cover set with jewels, weighing two thousand *miṣqāls* which valued at three thousand dīnārs.[72] Similarly on another occasion the Sulṭān despatched to An-Naṣir a shipload of excellent Indian cloth alongwith fourteen pots filled with diamonds and gems.[73] Thus, this historical evidence confirms that there were friendly relations between the Sulṭān of Delhī and An-Nāṣir of Egypt. Ibn Baṭṭuṭah's account also describes that Sulṭān Muḥammad bin Tughlaq made a triple alliance with An-Nāṣir of Egypt and Tarmānshirin so that Khurāsān could be captured. This agreement was reached on account of sectarian differences, as mentioned by the historians. Āghā Mahdī Ḥusain says, "That during the 14th Century of the Christian era sectarian differences between the Sunnis and the Shī'as became very acute. Consequently, to the political rivalry of the Il-Khān Shī'as of Persia and the Chaghatāe Sunnīs of Transoxania was added the bitterness of sectarian hostility. Al-Jaitū Khān was a great persecutor of the Sunnīs and had, therefore, roused the enmity of his neighbouring princes. In A.D. 1316, he was succeeded by his minor son Abū Sa'id, whose accession to the throne was a signal for internal troubles in the country. When Sulṭān Muḥammad bin Tughlaq ascended the throne of Delhī, he found that the relations of Abū Sa'id, with his minister Amīr Chobān had almost reached the breaking point. It was about this time that Tarmānshīrīn marched upon Khurāsān, but he was defeated by Amīr Chobān's son Ḥasan, in a battle which was fought near Ghaznī, and compelled to make his escape into India with a small remnant of his shattered forces he reached Delhī by way of Multan."[74] It was after this visit that a triple alliance was perhaps made between Tarmānshīrīn, An-Nāṣir of Egypt and Sulṭān Muḥammad bin Tughlaq to capture Khurāsān, and mainly shatter the political stability of Abū Sa'īd, a Shī'ā ruler of Irān. But when Tarmānshirin died and the Khurāsān expedition did not materialise, the Sulṭān of Delhī also established good relations with Abu Sa'īd. The author of *Majm' al-Bahīsī* writes that in A.H. 728 the Sulṭan of Delhī sent an envoy to the court of Abū Sa'id who reciprocated his friendship and sent with the Indian envoy Sayyid al-Dīn numerous presents for the Sulṭān.[75] Thus, friendly relations were restored between the Sulṭān of Delhī and Abū Sa'īd of Irān.

These diplomatic ties of Sulṭān Muḥammad bin Tughlaq with the countries of Central Asia indicate that the Sulṭān of Delhī desired to cement good relations with those countries and extended his influence and reputation established in the territories situated beyond the frontier of his empire.

## III

## The Frontier Policy of Sulṭān Fīrūz Shāh Tughlaq (A.D. 1351-88)

Fīrūz Shāh Tughalq ascended the throne of Delhī on the 23rd of Muḥarram A.H. 752/A.D. 22nd March, 1351 after the death of Sulṭān Muḥammad bin Tughlaq.[76] After the Sulṭān's death at Thaṭṭah his large army of discordant elements, whom his personality had held together, fell apart. The Mongol cavalrymen, the *Amīrān-i-Hazārah* and *Amīrān-i-Sadah,*[77] who had come from Transoxania to assist him in his war, joined hands with the Sindhī rebels.[78] The Mongols were further provoked by Amīr Nauroz, the son-in-law of Tarmānshīrīn, who had now lost the promising and favourable position he had been enjoying at the royal court of Delhī for over twenty years.[79] Accordingly, the Mongols fell upon the Imperial camp which had already broken up, and started from Sonda[80] in the direction of Delhī with a following of India soldiers.[81] While the Mongols attacked it from the front, the Sindhī rebels plundered it from behind. But Fīrūz Shāh took a bold step and fought courageously. According to Baranī; "The Sulṭan assembled his forces of horse, foot and elephants and attacked the enemy. A fierce battle ensued, and the slaughter was great, but victory inclined to the Sulṭān, and the Mongols fled, abandoning their camp and baggage. The victory was complete."[82] This was the first victory of the reign of Sulṭān Fīrūz Shāh which not only boosted the morale of the Muslim soldiers but also strengthened the Sulṭān's power.

The Central Asian political affairs did not allow the Mongols to advance towards India any more. The Chaghatāe realm had been split up into two parts generally known as Māwarun-Nahr (Transoxania) and Mughalistān or Jatta.[83] The Chaghatāe horde had weakened. The rival houses of the Chaghatāe of Transoxania and the Il-Khāns of Persia were also engaged in mutual struggle. Moreover, the policy of advance and the influence of Sulṭān Muḥammad bin Tughlaq beyond the Indus had discouraged the Mongols from invading India. However, Baranī speaks of two Mongol raids: "On one occasion they came upto river Sodhra, and on the other occasion they made a rapid dash into Gujarāt. On both occasions they were defeated with great losses.''[84] Sirhindī, Badāunī and Firishtah are agreed that while Sulṭān Fīrūz Shāh was on a hunting visit to Samānā in A.H. 759/A.D. 1358, the Mongols invaded and came as far as Dipālpur. Malik Qābūl, the governor of Samana was deputed to oppose them but the Mongols after making considerable ravages retired before Malik Qābūl could overtake them.[85] It can be surmised from the activities of the Mongol chiefs posted beyond the Indus that they were mostly in league with the rulers of Sind. This is also confirmed in the letters of 'Ain-ul-Mulk Mahrū, the then governor of Multān.[86]

After two years the Sulṭān determined to march against the rebels of Thaṭṭah who had defied his predecessor and were a source of trouble. Their old leader Tāghī[87] was no more but the situation in Thaṭṭah, the capital of lower Sind, had deteriorated on account of the rise of Sammas, the aggressions of Jām Jūnā and his nephew Bambīna on the border of Gujarāt and the Punjāb and their alliance with the hostile Mongols across the Indus. According to 'Afīf: "The Sulṭān reached the vicinity of Thaṭṭah and arrayed the enemy in battle order. But an epidemic broke out in the Imperial camp and hence it was followed by the shortage of food and fodder. The Sulṭan retreated so that some reinforcement from Delhī should reach. He sent back with the desired reinforcements, some of which had also come from Delhī to Thaṭṭah. The Sindhīs and their rulers, Jām Jūnā and Bambīna, were taken unawares. Both Sindhī leaders were defeated and ultimately acknowledged the suzerainty of the emperor and promised to send an annual tribute.''[88] Thus the risings of the Sindhis were crushed and this too contributed towards deterring the Mongols from raiding India. Another factor which deterred them was the appointment of brave *muqṭīs* in the frontier *iqṭās*. The author of *Tārīkh-i-Mubārak Shāhī* says: "Towards Khurasan there was no Amīr capable of withstanding the attacks of the Mongols. He (the Sulṭān) was, therefore, compelled to summon *Malik ul-Shark* Nāṣir ul-Mulk from the fief of Kāṛāh and Mahobā, and to send him to Multān, in order to put down the disturbance created by the accursed Mongols and punish them for their assaults. The *iqṭā's* of the quarter and its dependencies were placed under him.''[89] This brave *muqṭī'* was perhaps appointed after the death of 'Ain ul-Mulk, the governor of Multān.

## IV

## The Frontier Policy of the Successors of Sulṭān Fīrūz Shāh Tughlaq (A.D. 1389–1414)

After the death of Sulṭān Fīrūz Shāh Tughlaq in A.D. 1388. his successors ruled the empire till A.D. 1414.[90] During this period the downfall of the empire took place. This was hastened by the civil wars started by the successors of the late Sulṭān Fīrūz, and the increased interference in the appointments of the king by the Maliks and Amīrs of the realm.[91] Party politics between the Fīrūz Shāhī slaves i.e., Khawājā Jahān[92] and the Lodī Amīrs i.e., Ẓafar Khān and his sons: Sarang Khān and Iqbāl Khān, was also a major factor which led to the disintegration of the empire.[93] In this context the *Ẓafar Nāmā* mentions that since the death of Fīrūz Shāh, two brothers, Sarang Khān and Iqbāl Khān, had obtained ascendancy over all other Amirs at the royal court.[94] Sirhindī records; "Sulṭān Nāṣir al-Dīn Mahmūd Shāh appointed Sarang Khān as governor of Dipālpur in A.D. 1394 soon after his accession to the throne of Delhī."[95] He further says, "About the same time Sarang Khān was despatched to Dipālpur for annexing the territory and suppressing the rebellion of Shaikha Kokar (Gakkhaṛ)."[96] Shaikha Gakkhaṛ, a powerful chief in Jūd hills, increased his power and captured Lāhore. Delmerick also argues and confirms that, "Shaikha Gakkhaṛ revolted during the reign of Sulṭān Māhmūd Shāh Tughlaq and occupied Lahore."[97] It is necessary to understand why Shaikha Gakkhaṛ revolted against the Delhi empire. In the *Malfūẓāt-i-Tīmūri*, it is clarified that "Malik Shaikha Gakkhaṛ was formerly the governor of Lāhore on the part of Sulṭān Maḥmūd of Delhī."[98] This informs us that Malik Shaikha was once the governor of Lāhore in the very beginning of Sulṭān Māḥmūd's reign, and, later on, his relations with the Sulṭān became strained, probably because of the appointment of Sarang Khān as the chief governor of the western provinces of the empire. Consequently, Malik Shaikha rebelled and Sarang Khān was ordered to march against him. Sirhindī records that "Sarang Khān recruited and trained the soldiers of Dipālpur to deal with the Gakkhaṛ Chief."[99] At the end of the rainy season, Sarang Khān started for Lahore with Rā'i

Diljit Bhaṭṭi of Bhaṭnīr; Rā'i Dāud of Jallandhar; and Rā'i Kamāl al-Dīn Mian of Ludhiānā. He forded the Sutlej at the village of Tihara[100] to Lāhore. Malik Shaikha carried the war into Sarang Khān's territories by advancing into the Dipālpur *iqṭā'* and laying siege to Ajodhan (modern Pākpattan), but he was defeated.[101] Shaikha Gakkhaṛ then retired towards Lāhore. Sarang Khān followed him and a well contested engagement took place between them at Samuthala[102] near Lāhore. Shaikhā was routed and in the night he fled to the hills of Jammu. Sarang Khān then placed Lāhore under 'Adil Khān, his brother, and himself returned to Dipālpur. Both Badāuni and Sirhindi have mentioned this event, but *Kai-Gohar Nāmā* is silent. This event had serious consequences for the Delhī empire. The Gakkhaṛ not only created disturbances in Lāhore but also approached Amīr Tīmūr, and requested him to invade the Delhī empire.[103] This was the most unfortunate moment for facing external aggression for the Delhī Government. Its frontier defence had become weakened because of the warfare between Sarang and Khiẓr Khān, the governor of Multan in A.D. 1395. Sarang Khān deprived him of Multan and imprisoned him. However, Khiẓr Khān escaped from confinement and fled to Bayana. Here he allied himself to Amīr Tīmūr and contributed to the invasion of India.

## THE INVASION OF AMĪR TĪMŪR (A.D. 1398/A.H. 799)

On the persuasion of the local disgruntled elements, Amīr Tīmūr[104] invaded India. But he also had his own reasons for the invasion as recorded in *Malfūẓāt-i-Tīmūri*, "About this time there arose in my heart the desire to lead an expedition against the infidels and to become a Ghāzī, ... and if he is slain he becomes a martyr. It was on this account that I formed this resolution, but I was undetermined in my mind whether I should direct my expedition against the infidels of China or against the infidels and polytheists of India. In this matter I sought an omen from the *Qur'ān* and the Verse I opened upon was this, "O Prophet: make your war upon infidels and unbelievers and treat them severely." My officers told me that the inhabitants of Hindustān were infidels and unbelievers. In obedience to the order of Almighty God I determined on an expedition against them... ."[105] These remarks of Tīmūr speak of the inhabitants as infidels and polytheists, but do not take into consideration the existence of the Muslim ruler. K.S. Lāl explains: "Indeed the conquest of India had fired the imagination of all great conquerors ever since the time of Alexander of Macedon, and Tīmūr wanted to vie with his illustrious predecessors and repeat their achievements."[106] This view is also confirmed in the letter of Prince Muḥammad Jahāngīr[107] written to Sarang Khān "I wrote a letter and sent it to him (Sarang) by an ambassador, purporting that since the fame of the great king is spread all over the world, it is certain that it must have reached him also. The great king has appointed me to the government of those provinces which lie on the borders of Hindustān and has ordered that 'if the rulers of Hindustān come before me with tribute I will not interfere with their lives, property or kingdom; but if they are negligent in proffering obedience and submission, I will put forth my strength for the conquest of India.'"[108] The substance of this letter reveals that Tīmūr, in fact, desired to establish his soveriegnty over India rather than to crush the infidels as stated earlier. The immediate cause of Tīmūr's invasion was perhaps Shaikha Gakkhaṛ's alliance with him, as mentioned by Hāji Dabīr: "Shaikha Gakkhaṛ went to Irān and waited on Tīmūr and persuaded him to capture Delhī. He acted for him as a guide and took him to India by the shortest route and the easiest path."[109] Thus, Amīr Tīmūr directed his grandson, Pīr Muḥammad, to collect the forces and march to India: The latter crossed the Indus in November, 1397 and fell upon Uchh, where 'Alī Malik, governor of Uchh on behalf of Sarang Khān, fought a battle with prince Muḥammad in A.D. 1398 but was defeated.[110] Soon Pīr Muḥammad proceeded to Multān and defeated Sarang Khān.[111]

Amīr Tīmūr left Samarqand in Rajab 800 A.H./March 1398 and set off for India with an army of ninety two thousand.[112] After a halt at Tirmīz, he crossed the Jīhūn (Oxus) and then encamped at Khulm.[113] Then passing through Ghazniyak and Samangan he arrived at Andarāb, enroute to the passes of the Hindū Kush. From Andarab he marched with a contingent of thirty thousand to punish the *Siyāh Poshes* who can be identified with the Kafirs of Nuristan.[114] After suppressing them, he resumed his march and arrived at

Naghz via Kābul from where he despatched Amīr[115] Sulaimān to join Pīr Muḥammad at Multān and himself proceeded to Bannū.[116] Tīmūr crossed the Indus and encamped on the opposite bank of the river.[117] Tīmūr, then, advanced through Chol-i-Jarad and according to the *Ẓafar Nāmā;* The Ra'is and chiefs of the Jud mountain came respectfully to pay homage to Timur and make presents."[118] Tīmūr marched forward and halted at the bank of the river Jamd (Jhelum).[119] In the middle of this stream, there was a very strongly fortified island, the ruler of which was called Shahāb al-Dīn. Tīmūr sent Amīr Shaikh Nūr al-Dīn with Ṭumāns to defeat Shahāb al-Dīn, and, later on, he personally marched and defeated Shahāb al-Dīn who fled down the river towards Uchh.[120] According to the *Ẓafar Nāmā*, "Tīmūr marched along the banks of the river Jamd (Jhelum) and after five or six days march, he came to a place in which the rivers Jamd and Chināb[121] unite, where there was a fort which was built at the confluence of the two rivers. Tīmūr halted at that place and next day he crossed the river by means of boats."[122] Tīmūr marched forward and arrived at the city of Tulambā, there he pitched his camp on the bank of the river.[123] Tīmūr himself says, "The ruler of Tulambā came out to meet him."[124] He marched from Tulambā and halted at Jal, which is on the bank of the river Beas opposite Shāhpūr, and according to the *Ẓafar Nāmā*, "In that country, there was Malik Nusrat, chief of the Kokar (i.e. Gakkhaṛ) tribe who defied the advance of Tīmūr. Tīmūr attacked and defeated Nusrat who acknowledged his authority."[125] The *Malfūẓāt-i-Tīmūrī* mentions that Malik Nusrat was the younger brother of Shaikha Gakkhaṛ,[126] but it seems that Nusrat did not have good relations with his elder brother Malik Shaikha who was guiding Tīmūr's forces, as mentioned earlier. Tīmūr left the place and halted at Shāhnawāz, a populous village on the bank of the Beās.[127] Next day Tīmūr set out from Shāhnawāz and, after crossing the river, stayed at Janjān[128] for four days where he received the news of the conquest of Multān by Pīr Muḥammad.[129] Soon, Pīr Muḥammad personally reached his camp and presented himself before Tīmūr. Then Tīmūr marched forward from Janjān and arrived at Sahiwāl. Leaving that place Tīmūr reached Jehwāl and camped there. At that place, according to the *Ẓafar Nāmā,* "Tīmūr appointed Amīr Muẓaffar Kābūlī as a *Darogha* of Dīpālpur, who was soon killed by the people of the city. The rebels had taken refuge in the fort of Bhatnir, a renowned fortress of India."[130] Consequently, Tīmūr ordered Amīr Shāh Malik and Daulat Tīmūr to march forward by way of Dipālpur towards Delhī and asked them to wait for him at Samānā , a place in the neighbourhood of Delhī.[131] Tīmūr himself marched towards Bhatnīr. The *Zafar Nāmā* mentions that "On his arrival in the neighbourhood of Ajodhan, modern Pākpattan, Tīmūr visited the tomb of Ḥazrat Farīd."[132] Leaving Ajodhan, Tīmūr marched forward and bypassing Rudhans, he halted at Khalis Kotalī, a place of ten *kos* distance.[133] Tīmūr then passed through Chol at night and reached Bhatnīr, whose ruler, Rāo Dul Chain presented himself with Shaikh Sa'd of Ajodhan.[134] Tīmūr marched forward and bypassing the fort of Fīrūz, arrived at Sirsuti and captured it. Leaving Sirsuti, Tīmūr marched eighteen *kos* and came near Fateḥabād and from Fateḥabād bypassing the fort of Rājahpur, he halted at Ahrūnī.[135] After suppressing the Hindu Jāts of Tohans in his way, Tīmūr reached the banks of the river Ghagar[136] and halted near the bridge of Kotilā.[137] Tīmūr next day marched and reached the town of Kaiteal which is situated sixteen *kos* from Samānā, where Tīmūr suppressed the infidels.[138] He then marched onwards and bypassing Pānipat, Kānbī, Gazin, Jahān Numā and Lonī, he arrived at Tughlaqābād. Tīmūr attacked Delhī and fought a battle with Sulṭān Nāṣir Al-Dīn Maḥmūd, who was assisted by his commander Iqbāl Khān in the old city of Delhī, but was defeated.[139] The Sulṭān fled to Bārān and Iqbāl Khān to Gujarāt.[140] After this victory, Tīmūr proclaimed general amnesty in the city and the *Khuṭbah* was read in his name in the mosques of Delhī. A week later some of his soldiers went into the city for buying things. Incidentally a quarrel arose and a few soldiers were killed by the inhabitants. This led to a general sack of the city which continued for three days. Tīmūr says: "By the will of God – but by no wish of mine – all the three cities of Delhī, i.e., Sirī , Jahānpanāh and old city of Delhī, were plundered. It was my earnest will that no evil should befall the inhabitants but it was ordained by God that the city be ruined."[141]

After sacking Delhī, Tīmūr went to Meeruth where the Muslim commanders Ilyās Afghān and Aḥmad Thānesrī assisted by the Hindūs resisted the invader. Tīmūr besieged and captured it in January 1399.[142] He then advanced to Hardwar, a well known place of Hindū pilgrimage on the Ganga and defeated the Hindū troopers.[143] *Ẓafar Nāmā* adds that "Timūr set out from that place on his homeward journey."[144] After subduing the inhabitants of Kutila (or Kullu) valley, Timūr reached Siwālik hills and conquered it.[145] From here Timūr sent a contingent to crush the rebellious rising of Malik Shaikhā. Timūr says, "Malik Shaikhā was formerly the governor of Lāhore on the part of Sulṭān Maḥmūd of Delhī.... From my capture of the city of Delhī till my passage of the Jamnā, he ramained in attendance on me![146] In the middle of the Doāb, he asked permission to return to his home Lāhore. When I gave him permission to go to Lahore, there he forgot the protestation of service and devotion.... He kept not the promise he made.... The defection of Malik Shaikhā had become clear to me and I had sent the princes and amirs to take that ungrateful man prisoner and to levy a ransom from the city of Lāhore. They found Malik remiss and negligent in raising the contribution and soon in compliance with my order had made him prisoner".[147] These remarks of Timūr raises the question why Malik Shaikhā, who was once a guide of his forces and faithful ally, refused to acknowledge Timūr's lordship? The contemporary works are silent on this issue but it is clear that Malik Shaikhā had sided with Timūr on account of his enmity with Sarang Khān. Now that Sarang Khān was dead and it was possible that Malik Shaikhā should establish his own authority at Lahore, he hoped that Timūr would assist him in doing so. But Timūr's action tells a different story. After subduing Malik Shaikhā, Timūr went forward and conquered Nagarkot, which was situated in between the valleys of Kaku and Siwālik hills.[148] Timūr then reached near Jammu, which was soon captured and the *Rāi* of Jammū accepted Islām.[149] It is mentioned in the *Ẓafar Nāma* that, "Timūr marched from the village of Mansir[150] and encamped on the village of Bailā[151] ( بيلا ) in the territory of Jammū. At that place he sent envoys to Sulṭān Sikandar of Kashmir, who accepted Timūr's lordship."[152] This march of Timūr must have devastated the Gakkhar country – an action which Shaikhā Gakkhar may not have foreseen – and this must have disillusioned him. Anyhow, Timūr marched onward from the Gakkhar's territory and encamped on the bank of Chināb (Chinawa). Here Timūr came to know about the suppression of Malik Shaikhā by prince Muḥammad and the other Amīrs. Tīmūr now crossed the river Chināb and after marching five *kos* he reached and encamped on the banks of the Dandanā (Jhelum).[153] During the course of his march, prince Muḥammad and other Amīrs joined Tīmūr after crushing Malik Shaikhā at Lahore, as already mentioned. Here Tīmūr held a court wherein robes and rewards were bestowed to the amīrs and according to Tīmūr, "I now appointed Khiẓr Khān, governor of Multān."[154] Tīmūr crossed the river Jhelum and after marching twenty *kos* he halted at the village of Sānbast ( سانبست ) in the Jūd mountains, which can not be identified. Next day, Tīmur travelled and reached the fort of Baruja, which might be the village of Bherā. Marching forward, Tīmūr entered the Chol-i-Jalālia and reached the banks of Indus. Then by successive marches Tīmūr returned to his native land and later on died in March, 1405.[155] The route of his invasion has been explained in the map.

Tīmūr's invasion was a fatal blow for the Delhī empire, because it not only shattered its political power, but also led to the weakening of its frontier defence and making the frontier *muqṭī's* declare independence. Sulṭān Maḥmud Shāh Tughlaq ruled from A.D. 1399 to A.D. 1414 but according to Badāunī, "The rule of the Sulṭān of Delhī is from Delhī to Pālam."[156] Khiẓr Khān, who was appointed by Tīmūr as his viceroy, availed of an opportunity from the anarchy prevailing everywhere, and he not only established his authority over the frontier *iqṭā's* i.e.. Multān. Dipālpur, Lāhore and some parts of Sind, but also defeated Mullā Iqbāl Khān after increasing his power and entered Delhī in triumph on June, 1414.[157] Consequently, Khiẓr Khān became the Sulṭān of Delhī and laid the foundation of the Sayyid dynasty (A.D. 1414–51) in Delhī.

Thus Tīmūr's march not only eclipsed the authority of Delhī but also overthrew the power of the Gakkhars. For the first time the entire area fell within the control of Central Asian empire built by Tīmūr. The frontier was wiped out from contemporary history.

## FOOTNOTES

1. *T.N.K.* (Text) verses 345-6, p. 19. This date of Ghiyas al-Din Tughlaq's accession to the throne (720/1320) has better claims to accuracy than that given by Firishtah and others. The same date, i.e. 720/1320 is also given by 'Isami. *F.S.* (Text) verse, 7404.
2. Sultan Qutb al-Din Mubarak Shah Khalji raised him to the *Wizarat*. *T.F.S.B.* (Trans), p. 391. Khusrau Khan was one of the salves of 'Ala al-Din Khalji. Lal, *op. cit.*, p. 304. According to Badauni, at first his name was Hasan Barwahbacha. The author of *Tarikh-i-Mubarak Shahi* says, 'in their younger days, Khusrau Khan and his brother fell into the hands of the Muslim army and became incorporated with the body of Sultan's personal slaves. During the rule of the late Sultan Qutb al-Din they remained near his Majesty's person and were included in his retinue. Later on, Khusrau Khan was appointed as the *Na'ib*. *T.M.S.* (Trans.), p 86.
3. *T.N.K.* (Text), p. 21.
4. .He was holding the *iqta'* of Dipalpur.
5. Akhur Bak was the superintendent of the royal stable. *T.F.S.B.* (Trans.), p. 411.
6. Agha Mahdi Husain, *op. cit.*, p. 35.
7. *T.F.S.B.* (Trans.), p. 225.
8. He was given the title of Sufi Khan by Sultan Khusrau and was an army commander. Lal, *op. cit.*, p. 313.
9. *T.N.K.* (Text), p. 89.
10. *Ibid.*, p. 58.
11. *Ibid.*, p. 63.
12. *T.N.K.* (Text), p. 89.
13. *Ibid.*, pp. 132-4.
14. *T.F.S.B.* (Trans.), p. 228.
15. *T.F.S.B.* (Trans.), p. 428. His original name was Behram Aiba.
16. *F.S.* (Trans.), p. 222.
17. *T.M.M.* (Trans.), p. 46.
18. He was the heir-apparent, still only in his twelfth year, and was in Mazandaran at the time of his father's illness. Boyle, *op. cit.*, p. 406.
19. The northernmost place in Shirvan *Bab al-Abwab*, the Gate of Gates, as the 'Arabs called Darband, the famous port on the Caspian. Le Strange, *op. cit.*, p 180.
20. Boyle, *op. cit.*, p. 408.
21. *Ibid.*, p. 409.
22. He was the eldest son of Sultan Ghiyas al-Din Tughlaq and his name was Malik Fakhr al-Din Juna Khan who became Sultan after his father's death. *T.F.S.B.* (Trans.), p. 224.
23. *F.S.* (Trans.), p. 214.
24. *T.F.S.B.* (Trans.), p. 450; *T.F.S.A.* (Trans)., p. 389.
25. *T.F.* (Trans.), p. 403.
26. Ghiyas al-Din Tughlaq had a tragic. end. He fell off the roof of a pavilion in February, 1325. *T.F.* (Trans), p. 408; *T.V.S.* (Trans)., p.97. But Barani has only given the year A.H. 725/A.D. 1325. *T.F.S.B.* (Trans.), p. 235.
27. Agha Mahdi Husain, *op. cit.*, p. 230.
28. Sultan Ghiyas al-Din Tughlaq honoured him with the title of Kishlu Khan. *T.F.S.B.* (Trans.)., p. 230.
29. According to Mir Ma'sumi, the lower Sind was conquered by the Samma tribe. *T.M.M.* (Trans.), p. 110.
30. He was the Sulgan's cousin and *Ariz-i-Lashkar* (Inspector-general of forces). *T.M.S.* (Trans.), p. 101.
31. Ibn Battutah says that he was grandson of Nasir al-Din Mahmud Bughra bin Sultan Ghiyas al-Din Balban. *I.B.R.*, f. 7, ch. 44.
32. *T.F.* (Trans.), p. 412.
33. It is now situated in Patiala State.

33. *I.B.R.* (Trans.), p. 97.
35. According to Badāunī, his name was Malik Maqbūl and was given the title of Qiwām al-Mulk. *M.T.* (Trans.), p. 130.
35. *T.M.S.* (Trans.), p. 103.
36. *T.F.S.B.* (Trans.), p. 244.
37. According to Firishtah, he was the chief of the mountain Afghāns who commenced risings in the north. *T.F.* (Trans.), p. 425.
38. Aghā Mahdī opines that Baranī uses Afghānistān in its strict literal sense, "The home of the Afghāns.., and Ibn Battutah expressly mentions Cambay, Gujarāt and Nahrawala as the home of the Afghāns. Aghā Mahdī, *op. cit.*, p. 283.
39. *T.F.S.B.* (Trans.), p. 245.
40. Delmerick suggests that Haider Khān was a Gakkhar chief. J.G. Delmerick, *op. cit.*, p. 35. But Barani has recorded his full name as Mubārak Khān Halājūn. *T.F.S.B.* (Trans.), p. 164.
41. Firishtah says that he was a chief of the Gakkhars, but Aghā Mahdī records that
42. "Qul Jands" is the Arabic form of Gul Chand, the name of a Hindū Amīr. Aghā Mahdi, *op. cit.*, p. 246.
43. *T.F.* (Trans.), p. 425.
44. *T.F.S.B.* (Trans.), p. 245.
45. *I.B.* (Trans.), p. 256. *M.S.* (Trans.), p. 45.
46. Boyle, *op. cit.*, p. 405.
47. *Ibid.*
48. *Ibid.*
49. *Ibid.*
50. *Ibid.*
51. *Ibid.* Abū-Sa'id, at the age of thirty-one, died without male issue, the realm fell into pieces. Michael Prawdin, *The Mongol Empire,* London, 1940, p. 379.
52. It was an outpost of strategic importance.
53. It is important to note that the mediaeval writers apply the name of Khurāsān to the area north-west of the Indus including Ghaznī. *T.R.* (Trans.), p. 30.
54. 'Abdul Razzāq, *op. cit.*, pp. 22-3; Ḥamdullāh Musṭaufī, *op. cit.*, p. 607.
55. *H.S.* (Text) p. 703.
56. *T.S.* (Trans.), p. 462.
57. *F.S.* (Trans.), p. 462.
58. *T.M.S.* (Trans.), p. 200.
59. *M.T* (Trans.), p. 138
60. *T.F.* (Trans.), p. 340.
61. *T.F.S.B.* (Trans.), pp. 240-88.
62. S. Mo'īn al-Haq, *Baranī's History of the Tughlaq*, 'Alīgaṛh, 1944, p. 46.
63. *I.B.R.* (text), p. 58.
64. According to Aghā Mahdī Ḥusain, the man who appeared in Sind claiming himself to be Tarmānshīrīn was the pretender who was mistaken by 'Isāmī and even by Baṭṭuṭah for Tarmānshīrīn. Aghā Mahdī Husain, *op.cit.*, p. 135.
65. Riāẓ-ul-Islām, *op.cit.*, p. 7.
66. *T.F.S.B.* (Trans.), p. 340.
67. Aghā Mahdī Ḥusain, *op. cit.*, p. 143. Baranī mentions Amīr Nauroz as Nauroz Kūrgan. *Ibid.*, p. 533.
68. *Ibid.*
69. *T.F.S.B.* (Trans.), p. 533.
70. *T.F.* (Trans.), p. 369
71. See S. Beal: *Buddhist Records of the Western World,* Delhī Reprint 1969, p. 156.
72. Naṣir al-Dīn Muḥammad bin Qalaun known as An-Naṣir was the ninth Sulṭān of the Mamluk dynasty of Egypt and a contemporary of Sultan Muhammad bin Tughlaq. Agha Mahdi Husain, *op. cit.*, p. 103.

73. *Ibid,*
74. Aghā Mahdī Husain, *op. cit.*. p. 103.
75. *Majm' al-Fasihī* (MS), Bankipore, f. 209. This is also evident from the *Masālik ul-Absar*, which recounts, in the first instance on the authority of *Qazi ul-Qazat* Abū Muhammad Hasan bin Muhammad Ghorī Hanafī, how Muhammad bin Tughlaq sent one of his private secretaries named Baighsan as an ambassador of Sultan Abū Sa'īd, with a sum of ten lakhs of tankas to be given away in charity at the sacred shrines in 'Iraq. *M.A.*, p. 120.
76. On the demise of Muhammad bin Tughlaq, the army that had been led by him to Thattah fell into the utmost disorder, and was assailed by the Mongols in front and the rebelts of Thattah in rear. As there was no one possessing the ability to redeem the soldiers from the hands of the Mongols, the chiefmen of the army entreated Firūz to ascend the throne. *T.B.S.* (Trans.), p. 121.
77. The Mongol commanders of thousands and captains of hundreds. Hodivala, *op. cit.*, p. 120.
78. Sultan Qazan who ruled over Transoxania from A.H. 733/A.D. 1334 to A.H. 760/A.D. 1361, was a friend of Sultan Muhammad bin Tughlaq. *S.A.* (Trans.), p. 377.
79. *T.F.S.A.* (Trans.), p. 278.
80. It is near Thattah in Sind.
81. *T.F.S.A* (Trans.), p. 278.
82. *T.F.S.B.* (Trans.), p. 266.
83. To the Chaghatāes of Mawarun-Nahr and the west, Mughalistān was known in the 13th and 14th centuries by the name of Jattah, which was a "steppe" or pastoral country, and the homeland of the dominant tribe. *T.R.* (Trans.), p. 52.
84. Transoxania was contiguous to India as its dominion spread eastward to beyond
85. Herāt and Ghaznī, and southward to Makrān. *T.R.* (Trans.), p. 30.
86. *T.F.S.B.* (Trans.), p. 268.
*Sīrat*, f, 272, *I.M.* (Text), pp. 19-21.
87. Taghī had fled from Thattah toward Gujarāt where he was killed. *T.A.* (Trans.), p. 227.
88. *T.F.S.A.* (Trans.), pp. 329-36.
89. *T.M.S.* (Trans.), p. 127. According to Firishtah, Nāsir ul-Mulk, the youngest son of Malik Mardān Dowlat, was made the governor of Punjab and the country as far as Kābūl. *T.F.* (Trans.), p. 456.
90. Sultān Tughlaq Shāh (A.D. 1388-9), Sultān Muhammad Shāh (A.D. 1389-94), Sultān 'Alā al-Dīn Sikandar Shāh (A.D. 1394), Sultān Nasir al-Dīn Mahmud Shāh (A.D. 1394-1414) were the successors of Sultān Fīrūz Shāh. *Ibid.*, pp. 148-86.
91. Aghā M. Husain, *op. cit.*, p. 444. Lāl, *op. cit.*, p. 15.
92. He was a leader of the Fīrūz Shāhi slaves, who bore the name of Malik Sarwar. Aghā M. Husain, *op. cit.*, p. 455.
93. Lal., *op. cit.*, p. 15.
94. *Z.N.* (Text), p. 14.
95. *T.M.S.* (Trans.), p. 149.
96. *Ibid.*, p. 156; Firishtah calls him a Gakkhar Chief. *T.F.* (Trans.), p. 479.
97. Delmerick, *op. cit.*, p. 356.
98. *M.T.* (Trans.), p. 474.
99. *T.M.S.* (Trans.), p. 156; Delmerick, *op. cit.*, pp. 67-107.
100. Fort of Tihara is situated on the bank of the Sutlej to the west of Ludhiānā. *'Ain-i-Akbarī* (Trans.), vol. ii, p. 295.
101. *T.M.S.* (Trans.), p. 157.
102. It is situated at a distance of twenty one miles from Lāhore. *Ibid.*, p. 165.

103. Thomas, *op. cit.*, p. 326.
104. Timūr was born on Tuesday 9 April 1336/25 Sha'bān 736 in the town of Sabzwār about 40 miles south of Samarqand. His father, Amir Turkhay was a chief of the Gurgān branch of the Barlās tribe, and his mother was Taghina Khātūn. He ascended the throne on Wednesday 9 April 1370/12 Ramzān 771 A.H. *Akbar Nāmā* (Trans.), Beveridge, p. 205; Sykes, *History of Persia*, ii, p. 199.
105. *M.T.T.* (Trans.), pp. 394-5.
106. Lal, *op. cit.*, p. 15.
107. Pīr Muḥammad (d. 809 A.H./1406) was the son of Ghiyāṣ al-Dīn Jahāngīr, the son of Timūr. Lanepool, *The Muḥammadan Dynasties*, p. 268. He was holding the provinces of Qunduz, Balaqan, Kabul and Qandhar. *Z.N.* (Text), p. 14.
108. *M.T.T.* (Trans.), p. 499.
109. *Z.W.* (Text), p. 904.
110. Āghā M. Ḥusain, *op. cit.*, p. 461.
111. Sarang Khān was imprisoned and killed by prince Muḥammad. *M.F.T.* (Trans.), p. 418; S.A. Ḥalīm, "Relation of Delhī Sulṭanate with the Kingdom of Multān", *M.V.J.*, April, 1941, p. 72.
112. Sykes, *op. cit.*, p. 207; *Z.N.* (Text), p. 18.
113. Khulm lay about 50 miles east of Balkh. Holditch, *op. cit.*, p.270.
114 *J.A.S.B.*, vol. ii, 1833, pp. 305-7.
115. *Z.N.* (Text), p. 47.
116. *Ibid*
117. *Ibid.*
118. *Jamad* means an open country and *Chol* means desert. Hence it is also called Chol-i-
119. Jalalia. *Ibid*, p. 48; (Trans). Dowson, vol. III, p. 482.
120. *Ibid.*
121. *Ibid.*
122. *Z.N.* (Text), p. 53.
123. Tulambā is an ancient town in Multān division and is situated seventy miles from Multān. *ibid.*, p. 54. See for details, Hodivala, p. 350.
124 *M.T.T.* (Trans.), p. 53.
125 *Ibid.*, p. 474.
126. *Z.N.* (Text), p. 56.
127. *Ibid.*
128. *Ibid.*, p. 58.
129 *Z.N.* (Text), p. 58.
130. *Ibid.*, p. 63.
131. *Ibid.*, p. 64; Āghā M. Ḥusain, *op. cit.*, p. 463.
132. *Ibid.*, p. 63.
133. *Ibid.*, p. 64.
134. Bhatnir was a Rajput stronghold, which was considered impregnable as it was surrounded by a desert for about fifty kos, in which no water could be obtained. Lal., *op. cit.*, p. 20.
135. *Z.N.* (Text), p. 77.
136. *Ibid.*, Samana was near this place.
137. It is ancient structure over the river Ghagar. *Ibid.*, p. 81.
138. *Ibid.*
139. *Ibid.*, p. 94.
140. *Ibid.*, p. 110.
141. *M.T.T.* (Trans.), p. 445.
142. Malik Ilyās Afghān was the governor of Meeruth. *Ibid.*, p. 155.
143. A.M. Ḥusain, *op. cit.*, p. 486.
144. *Z.N.* (Text), p. 110.

145. *Ibid.*, p. 149.
146. *M.T.T.* (Trans.), p. 474.
147. *Ibid.*
148. *Z.N.* (Text), p. 154.
149. *Ibid.*
150. *Ibid.*, p. 162. It is near Jammu. See for details, Hodivala, pp. 357-8.
151. *Ibid.* It is also in Jammu. Hodivala, p. 357.
152. *Ibid.*, p. 162.
153. *Ibid.*, p. 170.
154. *Z.N.* (Trans.), p. 474.
155. According to A.M. Ḥusain, Tīmūr fell ill and died on 19th January, 1404/10th S̲h̲a'ban 807, *Ibid.* (Text), p. 467.
156. *M.T.B.* (Text), vol. i, p. 266. Pālam is a village about six miles south-west of modern Delhī.
157. *T.M.S.* (Text), p. 189.

## Chapter VII

# CONCLUSION

The frontier policy of the Delhī Sulṭāns has been viewed in the perspective of the state formations in the great valleys of the Oxus and the Ganges. Throughout the mediaeval period, before the formation of the Mughal empire, the Indus zone remained fragmented and could not put up a united system of government that could hold sway over this entire valley, particularly after the death of Sulṭān Maḥmūd of Ghāzni. However, there were zones in the Indus region that played a significant part in the formation of the frontier policy. As the main theatre of activity was around Ghazni and Ghor, which now forms a part of Afghānistān, the main thrust of the Central Asian hordes was along that route which infringed on to the Indus river either across the Gomal plain or the Bannū plain. It is only in these early years that Peshāwar[1] and Hund[2] are seen to attract the attention of the intending contestants. As a result the Pothwar region, which was then the home of the Gakkhars[3] and many other tribes of the Koh-i-Jūd, practically served as a buffer zone. All attention was diverted south of the Salt Range and the main defence line stretched across Bannū, Multān, Dipālpur, Pākpattan or Lāhore and across the gap between the desert and the Siwālik hills to Delhī. The Sulṭāns of Delhī strengthened their strongholds along this line of march and by keeping strong garrison in these places they hoped to defend the empire which they had built with Delhī as their capital.

This line of defence lay mostly through the southern Punjab i.e. to the south of Lāhore. Both the cities of Lāhore[4] and Multān[5] bore the real brunt of attacks. But in the south of Multān the position of deltaic Sind was precarious. The hold from Delhī was inconsequential. The local governor of Multān could push his authority southward and put up a semblance of power over the local rulers who could easily profit by diplomatic friendship with a power strong in Afghānistan. Such was the position of the Samma rulers of Sind[6] who very often courted friendship with the Mongols. On the other hand the position of the Koh-i-Jūd was very vital not only for the defence of Delhī but also for any power from the west that intended to press hard towards the east. It is here that the *qabā'il* of Koh-i-Jūd were asked to play a decisive role. Among these tribes, the name of Kokar (Gakkhaṛ), comes out prominently. Since the time of Rā'i Sankirān, who gave a daughter in marriage to Jalāl al-Dīn Mangbarnī[7] to the time of Shaikhā Gakkhaṛ who incited Amīr Tīmūr to invade the Delhī empire,[8] this tribe played a definitive role in deciding the fate of the fighting armies.

It is very strange that the Delhī Sulṭāns did not crush the power of the Kokars or Gakkhaṛs who were generally seen in league with the Mongols and exploited the situation by giving aid to the invaders and joining them in the general loot and plunder. It is probable that the terrain of their country was too difficult to be brought under the direct control of the Delhī Sulṭāns. On the other hand, it is also possible that their territory lay outside the main defence line and hence to waste energy on controlling them was not thought prudent. In any case these tribes of the Koh-i-Jūd, although sometime they bore the fury of the Delhī Sulṭāns, yet remained independent and were in a position to be on the bargaining side. Hence we find some of their chiefs, at least in the Tughlaq period, becoming governors at Lāhore.[9] It may be that at that time various Gakkhaṛ settlements were made on this route to Lāhore.

It has been earlier shown that the frontier policy of the Delhī Sulṭāns was not just limited to their attitude towards the Mongols, although the Mongols became a strong power in due course in Central Asia.[10] The emergence of the Mongols in Central Asia divided the Turks and made them seek new homes and build new empires. In the early years it was the Turks who were fighting among themselves to establish stable power or powers in this vast region. The appearance of the Mongols in Central Asia drove many Turkish tribes towards the subcontinent.[11] These tribes coalesced and built up the Delhī empire. Those Turks who were left behind in Central Asia wooed the Mongol overlords and later intermingled with them to maintain their hold in Transoxania.

It is unfortunate that the Mongols in Central Asia have been studied only from the point of view of the Mongol menace and no attempt has been made to understand a type of feudal government that was built in the vast Central Asian belt spreading from the heart of Mongolia to Irān. This vast experiment in state building created new forces of strength that loomed large for centuries. As long as this state power was strong, it stood as a great challenge to the neighbouring empires. The Sulṭanate of Delhī was one such empire which, though it did not stand as a challenge to the Mongols, existed on a great fertile region and occupied the proverbial treasure land of India over which the Central Asian hordes had always cast avaricious eyes. It was beyond the power of the Delhī Sulṭāns to go outside the boundary of the subcontinent and challenge the Mongols in their own home country in Central Asia. And hence all through the period of the Delhī Sulṭanate the frontier policy has been defensive – a measure to strengthen their own home against the marauding hordes.[12] of Central Asia. The invading armies were met within the subcontinental boundary and the attempt to destroy the source of power in their own home was never made.

However, the policy was not merely to maintain a simple line of defence nor was it always a glorious retreat into the fastnesses of the Sulṭān's fortified cities. A deeper study of the frontier policy brings out intricate diplomacy that was involved in the relations of the ruling powers of the time. Although the details of these diplomatic relations are not always available owing to the interest of the contemporary chroniclers in the fate of kings and their armies rather than diplomacy. Yet small pieces of information which are interspersed in the sources do make up a more or less clear story of diplomacy and statesmanship that were pushed by the rulers of the time. The greatest achievements of the Delhī Sulṭāns was that were able to lay the foundation of a Muslim Sulṭanate against the opposition of the Hindūs and were also able to maintain the independence of the Sulṭanate against the recurring pressures of the mighty powers of Central Asia.

Looked at from the angle of the Delhī Sulṭāns the role of the tribes of Koh-i-Jūd[13] and that of the Samma rulers of Sind may be called unpatriotic because they courted the friendship of the Central Asian powers. But this action on their part should be judged from the view point of their own position as well. As they were not a part of the Delhī Sultanate, their actions were motivated by considerations of their own self preservation. It is unfortunate that the history of the tribes of the Koh-i-Jūd and of the Sammas is not much detailed and hence the main contribution that they made in the development of their respective regions is today hidden from our eyes. Yet their place in the northern and southern flanks of the main line of defence of the Delhī Sulṭanate was vital and important. This vast area on either side of the Indus should be regarded as much more than a mere buffer zone between the powerful states that were emerging in Central Asia and in the Delhī Sulṭanate. It is probably their own inner strength that kept them alive and enabled them to play a role that was decisive in Asian history.

The beginning of the frontier policy was formulated in the birth pangs of the Delhī Sulṭanate when Quṭb al-Dīn Aibak was called upon to set his house in order against the challenges of Yaldūz and the growing strength of Khwārizm Shāh.[14] Although Aibak dashed to Ghaznī,[15] this proved to be a vain venture as it was not well planned. Lahore remained the bulwark of his strength.

It was Iltutmish who came out as a great successful diplomat against the encroaches of Jalāl al-Dīn Mangbārnī.[16] Although Jalāl al-Dīn allied himself through marriage with a Gakkhaṛ chief named Rae Sankīrān by matrimonial relationship,[17] Iltutmish was wise enough not to advance into the Gakkhaṛ territory with the hope that they would be destroyed by the Mongols sitting on the other side of the Indus. On the other hand Iltutmish, was waiting to see the destruction of his foes Yaldūz and Qubācha, whose strength was much weakened by their clashes with Jalāl al-Dīn. In due course Jalāl al-Dīn met his own fate and Iltutmish had the satisfaction of consolidationg the Delhī Sulṭanate and keeping the tribes of the Koh-i-Jūd as well as a new power of Hasan Qarlugh[18] in between himself and the Mongols.

The Mongol incursions following the death of Iltutmish were severe but the Sulṭanate survived the onslaughts. It was left to Ghiyas-ud-Din Balban to devise a policy of internal strength by keeping a drilled army always ready to meet the challenge of the Mongols at the several defensive posts built all along the frontier of his empire.[19] This policy of military strength and preparedness was the only measure to meet the challenge of the power that was being built by Chingiz Khān and his successors in Central Asia.[20] Balban sacrificed his own son Muḥammad[21] in the defence of the empire but the memory of his name and the policy of strength continued to inspire the coming generations.

This system of military strength was inherited by Jalāl al-Dīn Khaljī, whose experience as a warden of the western marches,[22] earned him fame as the defender of the empire. However, it was 'Alā al-Dīn Khaljī who pushed this strength forward and made his presence felt not only in Sind and the Koh-i-Jūd but also in Ghaznī, where his name was read from the pulpit of the Mosque[23] although very briefly. This was the only time when a Delhī Sulṭān could show his power felt so far away in Ghaznī.

It was now time for following up this show of strength with actual participation in the politics of Central Asia. This opportunity came in the time of Muḥammad bin Tughlaq when Tarmanshirin, the Mongol ruler of Transoxania,[24] sought his assistance in regaining his position at home. The credit of taking advantage of this situation and making the diplomatic move of going ahead and pushing forward in the war theatres of Central Asia must be given to Muḥammad bin Tughlaq. Although all preparation was made, yet new developments in Central Asia prevented the plan from being executed. Both the diplomacy and the military strength failed to have any positive result in face of the new power that was then arising in Transoxania.[25] The real cause of this was the weakness caused by internal frictions which sapped the strength of the Delhī empire. This weakness could not be overcome even by the efforts of an able ruler like Fīrūz Shāh Tughlaq.

The rise of Amīr Tīmūr in Central Asia created a new power structure in Central Asia.[26] Before such a power could be contained, the Delhi Sulṭanate was already facing internal disintegration. Shaikhā Gakkhar, who was the governor of Lāhore, was dissatisfied with the administrative change which had been impered from Delhī. He, therefore, invited Amīr Tīmūr to give a death blow to the

Delhī Sulṭanate in the fond hope that he could be spared his own territorial possession. Timūr's advance wiped out the frontier and effaced the remaining strength of the Sulṭanate. The Timūrid empire now claimed territorial right of conquest over the Sulṭanate. The war asserted by his later successor, Ẓāhir al-Dīn Muḥammad Bābar,[27] who laid the foundation of the Mughal empire.

## FOOTNOTES

1. Before the advent of the Turki S'āhī rule (Po-lu-sha-pu-lo), Peshāwar was the capital of Gandhāra. Raḥman, *op. cit.*, p. 16.
2. It was the capital of S'āhī rule. *Ibid.*, p. 143.
3. *K.G.N.* (Text), p. 25.
4. It was a frontier *iqṭā'* of the Delhī empire.
5. It was a frontier post of the Delhī Sulṭanate.
6. *T.M.M.* (Trans.), p. 32.
7. *T.J.G.* (Trans.), p. 147.
8. *Z.W.* (Trans.), p. 904.
9. *M.T.* (Trans.), p. 473.
10. Boyle, *op. cit.*, pp. 303-322.
11. *F.M.* (Text), p. 47. He gives a list of sixty four Turkish tribes.
12. It means the Mongol forces.
13. See in Appendix for details.
14. *T.N.* (Trans.), pp. 513-29.
15. *Ibid.* (Text), p. 54.
16. *T.J.G.* (Trans.), p. 145.
17. *Ibid.*
18. He was a Khwārizmian noble who after the departure of Mangbarnī carved out his own principality of Binian.
19. It has been termed as a realistic frontier policy.
20. After the death of Chingīz Khān, the power he had established in Central Asia was further split up into various dynasties. Among them, one was established by his son Chaghatāe in Transoxania which became famous as the Chaghatāe dynasty of the Mongols and the other was founded by Halākū Khān in Irān called the Il-Khānid dynasty of Persia. See for details Boyle, *op.cit.*, pp. 303-22.
21. He was the eldest son and the heir-apparent of the Sulṭān. He was posted in Multān and Sind as governor and died in 1285 while fighting a battle with the Mongols near Multān.
22. *T.F.S.B.* (Trans.), p. 178.
23. Amīr Khusrau speaks only of this event in his work, *'Ijāz-i-Khusravī*, which is also called *Inshāi Amīr Khusrau* on account of a collection of farmans, despatches and letters. See for details, *I.K.* Book IV, Sec. iii, Letter 3.
24. *I.B.* (Trans.), pp. 257-8.
25. *Z.N.* (Text), p. 44.
26. *T.R.* (Trans.), pp. 15-43.
27. He defeated Ibrāhīm Lodī, the Delhi Sulṭān, in A.D. 1526 at Panipat and became the founder king of the Mughal dynasty in South Asia.

# APPENDICES

## Appendix-A

### THE KOH-I-JŪD AND ITS TRIBES

The study of the Koh-i-Jūd and its tribes is of vital importance for understanding the problem of the frontier of the Delhī Sulṭāns. This region played a definite role in the formation of the frontier policy by the Sulṭāns. However, a student of mediaeval Indian history comes across only a passing reference to the Koh-i-Jūd and its tribes in contemporary sources. This study attempts to throw light, first of all, on the historical geography of the Koh-i-Jūd and, secondly, on the political history of its tribes.

I

The Jūd hills are very important hilly region of South Asia. The word 'Jūd' ( ) was first used by mediaeval Indian historians in such works as *Tāj-ul-Ma'āṣir*, *Jāmi-ut-Twārīkh*, *Tabaqāt-i-Nāṣiri* and *Tārīkh-i-Jahān Gusha*, which are, therefore, the first chronicles throwing light on the Jūd hills. They are followed by Ziā al-Dīn Baranī, Yahyā Sirhindī, Badāūnī and Firishta. The earliest distinct mention of Jūd occurs in *Tāj-ul-Ma'āṣir*, a history written in A.H. 620/A.D. 1205 which says, "The Kokars (کوکر) razed the country between the Sodhrā (modern Chināb) and the Jhelum and defeated the Muslim governor of Sangwān,[1] who held a fief within the border of Multān, but was defeated by Quṭb al-Dīn Aibak, and one of the sons of Kokar Rā'i escaped to a fort in the hills of Jūd, which was captured on the following day by the Sulṭān."[2] The Kokars mentioned here are obviously the Gakkhars who ravaged the area between the Jhelum and the Chināb, and when Quṭb al-Dīn Aibak advanced, retreated to Jhelum. One of the sons of the Rā'i, however, entered the Jūd hills.

Next, Rashīd al-Dīn gives a reference to Jūd hills in his work,

*Jami'-ut-Twārīkh*, when he speaks of a battle fought between Sulṭān Muḥammad bin Sām and the tribes of Jūd hills. He records: "... the Kokars fled to the highest ranges of the Koh-i-Jūd after their defeat."[3] Similarly, Minhāj al-Dīn Sirāj in his book, *Ṭabaqāt-i-Nāṣirī*, mentions, "the Kokars and the tribes of Koh-i-Jūd (کوه جود) had broken out into revolts when Sulṭān Muḥammad bin Sām was engaged in preparing his expedition against Turkistān."[4] Juvainī also says in his work, *Tārīkh-i-Jahān Gushā*: "When the weather became hot the Sulṭān Khwārizm Shāh left Uchh for summer quarters in the mountains of Jūd, and Balālā and Nikālā."[5] Another mediaeval historian, Ẓiā al-Dīn Baranī, also writes, while recording the account of Balban's expedition against the tribes of Koh-i-Jūd: "Balban accordingly marched thither with suitable forces and inflicted chastisement upon the hills of Jūd and the vicinity."[6]

These references to the Jūd hills in the mediaeval works prove that they were not unknown in the mediaeval age. It is important to note however, that earlier historians of Sulṭān Maḥmūd of Ghaznī's period have not mentioned the name of Jūd hills. Al-Berunī, who visited India and remained in the fort of Nandanā, situated in the Jūd hills, does not give the name of Jūd. It seems that the hilly area was then better known by the name of Nandanā which was not only a province of the Hindu Shāhis but also a 'national capital' at the beginning of Ānandpāla's reign as mentioned by Al-'Uṭbī.[7] Though there is a reference to the hills in the contemporary works but the name of the hills is not given. Al-'Uṭbī in his work, *Tārīkh-i-Yamīnī*, says, "Bīgī Rā'i of Bhetāi (Bhīrā) escaped after the defeat and sought refuge on the top of some hills of Bālanāt."[8] Al-'Uṭbī further says: "Maḥmūd did not advance beyond the hills of Bālanāt, a mountain overhanging the Jhelum and now generally called *Tilla*, which means a hill."[9] Later on when Sulṭān Maḥmūd captured Nandanā from Trilocanapāla, son of Ānandpāla, in A.H. 404/A.D. 1013, there is again no mention of Jūd hills.[10] At the time of Sulṭān Maḥmūd of Ghaznī's invasion of India, Jūd hills were known by the importance of Nandanā and its one peak Bālanāt, and hence these names occur in the contemporary books of history. The name of Jūd hills became more well-known during the reign of Sulṭān Muhammad bin Sām and later in the time of the

Delhī Sultāns and the Mughal rulers. This happened after the destruction of Nandanā.

Later chronicles i.e. *Tārikh-i-Mubārak Shāhi*, *Muntakhab-ut-Twārikh*, *and Gulshan-i-Ibrāhimī* of Firishtah have also mentioned the Jūd hills. Similarly Sharf al-Dīn in *Zafar Nāma* also tells us about the Jūd hills. He says: "When Timūr crossed Indus, all the *Rājās* and *Zamindārs* of Koh-i-Jūd submitted their allegiance to Timūr."[11] Bābar, the founder of the Mughal dynasty in India, also visited the Jūd hills and has mentioned in his work, *Tuzuk-i-Bābarī*, about the Jūd hills and their tribes. He records: "Fourteen miles (seven kos) north of Bhirā lies the mountain range written in *Zafar Nāmā* and other books as the Koh-i-Jūd."[12] After Bābar, Abūl Fazl also writes in *Akbar Nāmā*: "Seven kos from Bhirā towards the north, there is a mountain called the hill of Jūd."[13] These accounts of the Sultanate and the Mughal periods clearly show that the name of the Jūd hills was well known at that time. Modern historians and travellers i.e. Cunningham, Elphinstone, and Wolseley Haig and others have identified Jūd hills with the salt range[14] of today.

After studying all these accounts of mediaeval writers, the question why they called it the Jūd hills arises. It is astonishing to observe that none of the mediaeval historians and geographers have answered the question. Bābar is the first person, who has tried to provide an explanation in, *Tuzuk-i-Bābarī*. He says:

> "I had not known why (the) Koh-i-Jūd was called this?
>
> Now I know. On it dwell two tribes, descendants from the one parent-source, one is called Jūd, the other Janjū'a. These two from of old have been the rulers and lawful commanders of the peoples and hordes of the range and of the country between Bhirā and Nīlāb... . On one half of it are the Jūd, the Janjū'a on the other. People call it Koh-i-Jūd through connecting it with Jūd tribes."[15]

This observation of Bābar shows that it was famous because of the Jūd tribes dwelling therein but he has not spoken of its early history and also of the origin of Jūd. A few modern British writers have tried to trace its origin. Griffin, a modern British traveller, says:

> The traditions of the Janjū'a trace their descent from a Rājā Mal, a descendant of the Pāndūs of the Rāthor Rājpūt race, who about A.D. 980 migrated to the Punjāb from Jodhpur. Hearing that the Pāndūs had once taken shelter in the hills to the north of Jhelum, he journeyed there with his followers and founded the village

> of Rājgarh now famous as Malot, where he ruled in peace till the invasion of India by Sulṭān Maḥmūd... . He adopted Islām after being forced by Maḥmūd... . He left five sons and among these only two sons, Jodh and Wīr, got importance. On the death of their father, they determined to divide the country, the Malūkī Dhan, between them. Jodh took the Salt range near about the Makrocḫ and captured the town of Makshath... . He changed its name to Makhiālā and built there a fort and two tanks for rain water. Wīr, the second son of Rājā Mal, took the possession of Kura near modern Pind Dāden Khān... .[16]

These remarks of Griffin indicate that Jūd hills were known because of the territory of Jodh, son of Rājā Mal, a contemporary of Sulṭān Maḥmūd of Ghaznī. But this tradition is not supported by any contemporary chronicle. Another opinion expressed by Erskine and Leydon, is that, "This hill got the name Jūd from a supposed resemblance between the lofty isolated Arārāt and a spur of the Salt range."[17] Beveridge further suggests that "Jūd is probably the Sanskrit word *Yuddha* meaning war."[18] Beveridge's argument is based on the fact that the dwellers in this hilly range have fought wars either with the original inhabitants for capturing the region or with the outside invaders to safeguard their territory.[19] Thus on account of these wars (in Sanskrit *Yuddha)* the hilly region got the name of Jūd hills.

After discussing the historical background of Jūd hills and the literal meaning of Jūd as far as it is possible to trace it, we now turn to its geography. Bābar was the first writer to throw light on the geographical position of the hills. He records: "The Koh-i-Jūd runs for fourteen miles along the Bhīrā country, taking off from those Kashmīr mountains that are one with the Hindū-Kush, and it draws out to the south-west as far as the foot of Din Kot on the Sind river."[20] According to this observation of Bābar, Jūd hills extended from Din Kot or Dan Kot near modern Kālābāgh to the borders of Kashmīr probably near the present Mangla Dam. Firishta, a historian of the Mughal period, also describes the location of Jūd hills while speaking of the Gakkhaṛs. He says: "The Gakkhaṛs who inhabited the country along the banks of the Nīlāb to the foot of the mountains of Siwālik, exercised unheard of cruelties... ."[21] This is certainly the region of the Gakkhaṛ tribe, which lies between Nīlāb and the hills of Siwālik, which, according to Firishta, is identified with the Jūd hills. The name of the Koh-i-Jūd was used till the reign of Akbar, and then its importance decreased because the frontier of the Mughals now came to extend upto Qandhār and Kābul. As modern British travellers and geographers have identified the Jūd hills with the Salt range, it is pertinent to understand their reasons as well. According to Elphinstone, "It is a branch of Safed Koh and may be called the Salt range as shooting out from the Safed Koh and extending in a south-easterly direction by the South of Teerce to Kālābāgh where it crossed the Indus, stretches across part of the Punjāb and ends at Jalālpur on the right bank of Jhelum becoming lower as it gets further from the mountains of Sulaimān."[22] Another British geologist Wynne records: "The Salt range forms a prominent physical feature of the northwest of India, rising between the outworks of the Himālaya, Hindū-Kush and Afghan mountain..."[23] Similarly another geographer, Spate writes: 'Salt range ramparts, sensuous in outline and exceeding complex in detail, sharply mark off the region from the Punjab plains. They reach nearly 5000 feet at Sakesar, but in general the summits are at 2500–3500 feet... .'[24] These accounts of the experts fully describe the physical features of the Salt range. Similarly the Salt range has been defined by other British experts like Garret, Thomas and Cunningham but it is not necessary here to refer to their accounts. However, these descriptions of the Salt range show the physical position which the Salt range is holding today. However, we are concerned with the location of the Jūd hills of the mediaeval age and for this the description of Babar about the Jūd hills is more relevant. According to this description, the Koh-i-Jūd was limited only to the eastern side of the Indus. Thus the Koh-i-Jūd is apparently a part of the Salt range described by the modern geographers.

This account about the historical geography of the Koh-i-Jūd explaining its exact location will be of great help in understanding the role it played in the history of the region. We can now move to the history of the tribes which inhabited this area.

## Tribes of the Koh-i-Jūd

The tribes of the Koh-i-Jūd played a dominant role in the mediaeval period. The contemporary chronicles have mentioned the Janjū'a and the Gakkhar as the main tribes of the Jūd hills but they do not throw much light upon their history. During the Ghaznavid rule, Nandanā, situated on the Jūd hills, was the capital of Ānandapāla, whom modern writers include among the Hindū Shāhi rulers, as mentioned by Al-Beruni.[25] After the end of the Hindu Shāhi rule, this region became a part of the Ghaznavid kingdom.[26] Probably, at this time, the Gakkhaṛs (or Kokars) got their footing in this region under the leadership of Gakkhaṛ Shāh.[27] After the decline of the Ghaznavids, the Ghorids established their political power and advanced towards India. At this time, there is a reference to the tribes of the Koh-i-Jūd ( کوہ جود ). Minhāj mentions that the "Kokars ( کوکر ) and the tribes of the Koh-i-Jūd ( قبائل کوہ جود ) had broken out into revolts when Sulṭān Muḥammad bin Sām was engaged in preparing his expedition against Turkistān... ."[28] The author of the *Jami'-ut-Twārikh* also supports this event and says: "The ruler of the Koh-i-Jūd, at which the frontier of Hind commences, who had turned Musalmān, and subsequently relapsed, and the Kokars (or Gakkhaṛs) who also used to pay tribute to the Sulṭān, in consequence of these reports of Sulṭān's death also rose... ."[29] According to the *Tarīkh-i-Alfī*.

> Among other enemies, one named Rāi Sāl, who lived in the mountains between Lahore and Kabul, having united with a number of Kokars, who dwelt in those parts and paid tribute to the treasury of Shihāb al-Dīn, excited a rebellion, began to plunder that tract, and intercepted the communications between Lāhore and Ghazni, so that no one could pass from one to the other.[30]

These contemporary references show that Rā'i Sāl belonged to a tribe different from that of the Kokars. It is possible that he was a ruler of the Janjū'ā tribe. Thus both Rā'i Sāl and the Kokars were the main dwellers of the Koh-i-Jūd at the time of Sulṭān Ghorī's invasion of India. But Bābar mentions Jūd, Jāts and Gujars in addition to the Janjū'ā and the Gakkhar as the tribes of the Koh-i-Jūd.[31] However, we will discuss the political history of the tribes of Koh-i-Jūd i in the following pages as far as it is possible to trace it in the light of the contemporary as well as modern works.

### i) THE GAKKHAR TRIBE

There is some controversy about the origin of the Gakkhaṛs among the historians though much has been written about it and about the history of this tribe. General Court tried to connect the

Gakkhars with the Greeks[32] but without any firm basis. According to Cunningham, the Gakkhars reperesent the *'savage Gangaridae'* of Dionysius and are descendants of the great Yuechi Scythians, who entered India from the north west in the early centuries of the Christian era.[33] But Denzil Ibbetson and Thomson argue that though the Turanian origin of the Gakkhars is highly probable, the rest of Cunningham's theory is merely a plausible surmise.[34] These controversial opinions about the origin of this tribe are a feature of modern scholarship about them. As far as the early historians, they have written much about them, but consensus is lacking among them too.

A mediaeval book *Taj-ul Ma'āṣir* says.

> The Kokar tribe, rising in rebellion, entertained the idea of becoming independent, and obtaining dominion... . On hearing this Shihāb al-Dīn Ghorī wrote to his slave, Quṭb al-Dīn who was the commander of the forces of Hind, to assemble the troops of Hindustān and march against the Kokars... . When the command reached Quṭb al-Dīn, he assembled and made ready his forces and was about to move against that tribe... . Shihāb al-Dīn himself also set out from Ghaznī towards Hindustān. When the Sulṭān reached Peshāwar, he found that the Kokars in large number, had taken up a position between Jhelum and Sodhrā. On hearing this news, the Sulṭān made a forced march from Peshāwar on Thursday, the 25th of Rabī-ul-Awwal, 602 A.H., and fell upon them unawares, and from break of day till the time of afternoon prayers he kept up the flames of battle and conflict, and the Kokars fought in such wise, that with all that grandeur and power, the Sulṭān had nearly been forced back from his position, when, unexpectedly, at that juncture, Quṭb al-Dīn Aibak, with the forces of Hindustān arrived and commenced slaughtering the Kokars. As Quṭb al-Dīn's troops were fresh and vigorous, the Kokars were unable to resist them, and they took to flight.[35]

This evidence proves that the Kokars were the local rulers of the Koh-i-Jūd during the time of Sulṭān Shihāb al-Dīn Ghorī's invasion of India. Raverty in his translation of the *Ṭabaqāt-i-Nāṣirī* has tried to identify the Kokars with Khokhars. Raverty asserts this on the basis of his linguistic study,[36] but the factual position is somewhat different. There is hardly any Khokhar living in the vicinity of the place of the murder of Sulṭān Muḥammad bin Sām,[37] which lies six *kos* from the present village of Sohāwā in the district Jhelum. This whole area is occupied by the Gakkhars but Raverty would like to substitute the word Gakkhar for Khokhar and take them to be the murderer of Sulṭān Shihāb al-Dīn Ghorī. Raverty's reading of

Khokhar does not appear to be sound. The Kokar mentioned in this account can more plausibly be taken for the Gakkhars as they have been living in this part in the past. This is supported by several contemporary chronicles. Juvainī records; "Prince Jalāl al-Dīn crossed the Indus with seven hundred followers after his defeat at the hands of Chingiz Khān and sought refuge in the Koh-i-Jūd. As the number of the followers went on increasing by his presence in their region, the neighbouring chiefs of the Koh-i-Jūd felt threatened, and one of them decided to turn him away. The Rājā led an army of six hundred soldiers against the Sulṭān but was defeated."[38] Juvainī further says: "After refusal of asylum by Iltutmish, Jalāl al-Dīn Khwārizm Shah returned to the hills of Balālā and Nikala,[39] where the total number of his followers amounted to 10,000 men. He now sent Tāj al-Dīn Khaljī with an army to the mountain of Jūd. They ravaged the country and carried off much booty."[40] Now after ravaging Jūd, Jalāl al-Dīn made friendly overtures to the Raja of this region . Once again according to Juvainī: "Jalāl al-Dīn also sent an embassy to Rāi Kokar Sankin ( سنکن ) and sought his daughter in marriage, who agreed and likewise sent his son to Sulṭān Jalāl al-Dīn with an army. The Sulṭān conferred upon the son the title of Quṭlugh Khān."[41] The name Rāi Kokar Sankin also poses problems of identification. It is possible that it is a corrupted form of Mang Khān. This conjecture is supported by Dunī Chand's narrative.[42]

After the departure of Jalāl al-Dīn from India, his chief Ḥasan Qarlugh of the Indian territories made alliances with the chiefs of the Koh-i-Jūd and established his rule in this region.[43] After the end of the Qarlugh rule in this region, the chiefs of the Koh-i-Jūd made alliances with the Mongols and acted as guide to them in their raids into the frontier *iqṭā's* of the Delhī empire. Minhāj refers to an expedition which was led by Sulṭān Shams al-Dīn Iltutmish to crush the tribes of the Koh-i-Jūd, but the Sulṭān could not do this on account of his illness and subsequent death. Soon another expedition was launched by Sulṭān Nāṣir al-Dīn Maḥmūd and Ulugh Khān Balban against the rulers of the region of the Koh-i-Jūd and the *Khiṭṭāh* of Banīān. Having crossed the river Ravi near Lāhore, Sulṭān Nāṣir al-Dīn encamped on the bank of the river Sodhrā (Chināb) and then ordered Ulugh Khān (later Sulṭān Balban) to march towards Nandanā in the Koh-i-Jūd and Baniān for the chastisement of their local rulers. On Ulugh Khān's march the local people destroyed the cultivation, so that the Delhī army did not get fodder for its troops. Consequently, Ulugh Khān plundered the tract upto the territory of Rāi Jaspāl who had fled away with his followers and Ulugh Khān retreated."[44] Here Minhāj refers to Jaspāl, another tribal chief of the Koh-i-Jūd. This event also confirms that the Gakkhars were the main tribes in this region who always remained active and were a perpetual source of trouble for the Delhī Sulṭāns.

During the rule of 'Alā al-Dīn Khaljī, the region of the Koh-i-Jūd was ravaged for the first time by the Mongols because it seems that the tribes of this region, perhaps, refused to act as a guide to the Mongol forces for their raids into India. During the reign of Sulṭān Muḥammad bin Tughlaq, the Afghāns under their leader Shāhū crossed the Indus and ravaged Multān and Lāhore. Taking advantage of this disturbance, the Gakkhaṛs, rose against the Delhī empire. Firishta says: "In the year 743 A.H./A.D. 1342, Malik Ḥaidar, a chief of the Gakkhaṛs, invaded the Punjāb and slew Tātār Khān, the viceroy of Lāhore, in action. Khwājā Jahān was sent but the Gakkhaṛs seem to have maintained their position and completed the ruin of the province."[45] Till the invasion of Tīmūr in A.D. 1398, the Gakkhaṛs established their position. During the short reign of Nāṣir al-Dīn Tughlaq, the Gakkhaṛs revolted under their chief Shaikhā and occupied Lāhore. But Tīmūr records in his *Malfūzāt-i-Tīmūrī* that Shaikhā Gakkhaṛ was the governor of Lāhore on the part of the Delhī Sulṭān."[46] Hence it is possible that he was removed by the Delhī Sulṭān from the governorship of Lāhore. As a result, Shaikhā raised the banner of revolt against the Delhī Sulṭān. Firishta records, "Sārang Khān, the governor of Dipalpur, in the succeeding reign of Maḥmūd Tughlaq, after collecting a large force from the country round about Multān, went out to meet them and a great battle was fought about 24 miles from Lāhore. Shaikhā was utterly defeated and having hastily removed his wife and family from Lāhore, he fled and took refuge in the Jammū hills."[47] On account of these events Shaikhā was antagonistic to the Delhī Sulṭān, and consequently he approached Amīr Tīmūr. Ḥājī Dabīr says, "Shaikhā went to Irān and waited on Tīmūr and persuaded him to capture Delhī. He acted as a guide for Tīmūr and took him to India by the shortest cut and easiest path.''[48] Shaikhā was succeeded by his brother Jasrat after his death, who resolved to extend his conquests as far as Delhī. Jasrat seized Lāhore, Ruper, Ludhiānā and Sirhind, which forced Mubārak Shāh, the king of Delhī, to lead personally with a force against Jasrat. Jasrat without giving battle fled and the Sulṭān pursued him as far as Jammū. Though a large number of Gakkhaṛs were killed still Jasrat escaped by flight to the hills.[49] Jasrat formed a friendly compact with Mīr Shaikh 'Alī, the governor of Kābul. During the reign of Sayyid Muḥammad, the Gakkhaṛs under Jasrat joined Bahlūl Lodī, governor of Punjab.[50] Thus the Gakkhaṛs developed cordial relations with the Lodīs and remained peaceful till the invasion of Bābar. This is also verified by Bābar who records in the *Tuzuk-i-Bābarī* that "Tātār Gakkhaṛ had waited on Daulat Khān and was in a certain way subject to him.''[51] At the time of Bābar's invasion, Tātār Gakkhaṛ and Hātī Gakkhaṛ of the same family were the rulers of the Koh-i-Jūd. According to Bābar:

> In amongst the mountains of Nīlāb and Bhira which connect with those of Kashmīr, there are, besides the Jūd and Janjūha tribes, many Jāts, Gujars and others akin to them, seated in villages everywhere on every rising ground. These are governed by headmen of the Kakar tribes, a headship like that over the Jūd and Janjūha. At this time (925 A.H.) the headmen of the people of these hillskirts were Tātār Kakar and Hatī Kakar, two descendants of one forefather, being paternal uncle's sons.[52]

This account of Bābar confirms that the Gakkhaṛs were prominent in the hilly region between the Indus and the Jhelum. Bābar established good relations with them and consequently the Gakkhaṛs sided with Ḥumāyūn after Bābar's death while the former was chased by Sher Shāh Surī. 'Abbās Sherwānī writes that "Sher Shāh determined to crush the Gakkhaṛs and built a fort at Rohtās situated in the Gakkhaṛ territory. He also marched with his forces to meet Sārang Khān, a Gakkhaṛ chief, who was defeated and killed.''[53] After the death of Sārang Khān, his brother Ādam Khān took up the banner of the Gakkhaṛ leadership and faced the forces of Salīm Shāh, the successor of Sher Shāh. After regaining power, Ḥumāyūn, the Mughal emperor, estabished friendly relations with the Gakkhaṛs, which were continued throughout the Mughal rule in India. Thus, the Gakkhaṛs governed the hilly region between the

Indus and the Jhelum under various Gakkhaṛ chiefs for many generations, which is proved by the genealogies given by Abūl Faẓl and Dunī C̲h̲and.[54] After their settlement in the Koh-i-Jūd, the Gakkhaṛs were split up into several branches. According to Rose, these branches are six in number and are spread in various principal areas: Admāl in Sulṭānpurā; Iskandrāl in Lehrī and Bakrālā; Bugiāl in Domelī, Pandhrī and Baragowah; Frozāl near Jhelum and lastly Tuliāl near Dīnā."[55] This settlement also shows that they were the old inhabitants of the Koh-i-Jūd. At present, the Gakkhaṛs are found in the Jhelum, Hazara and Rāwalpindī districts.

## ii) THE JANJU'A TRIBE

The next important tribe of the Koh-i-Jūd to be considered is the Janju'a tribe who connect themselves with the Rajpūts. They once held almost the whole of the modern Salt range tract, but were gradually dispossessed by the Gakkhaṛs in the north and by the A'wāns in the west. Ultimately, they were left in possession of the central and eastern parts of the Koh-i-Jūd which they held at the time of Bābar's invasion. There are different views regarding their origin. According to Clauson, "In A.D. 540, the tribes identified with *Juan-Juan* who ruled the eastern parts of the steppes from the Chinese frontier in the east to Ṭurfān in Chinese Turkistan and a line running roughly north from that point to the western tip of Lake Baikal in the west... . About A.D. 552 their empire was destroyed by the Turks."[56] This theory of Chinese origin of the Janjū'as was rejected by Grousset, who talks of the Mongoloid origin of the Janjū'as.[57] The 'Arab writer Mas'ūdi has an important piece of information on this point. He says: "The king of Kandahar, who is one of the kings of Sind and its mountains, is called Ḥaḥaj; this name is common to all sovereigns of that country. From his dominions comes the river Raid, one of the five rivers which form the Mihran of Sind. Kandahar is called the country of the Rāhbūt (or Rājpūt)."[58] Here there are three important things to be noted; firstly Mas'ūdī has given the name of the contemporary Hindū dynasty which ruled in "Kandahar", secondly this dynasty is called by him J-Ḥaj ( جج ) or Ḥ-Ḥaj ( حج ), and thirdly the country is said to be of the Rājpūt. In other words, the ruling dynasty were Rājputs. From Al-Berūnī we learn that the ruling dynasty was Hindū Shāhī, which name is more a title than the actual name of the dynasty. Here for the first time Mas'ūdī gives the name of the dynasty as J-Ḥaj or Ḥ-Ḥaj. This interpretation was also given by Elliot.[59] It is because of this reading that Cunningham equated J-Haj with Janjū'ā.[60] This equation is corroborated by the fact that the ruling dynasty was called Rājpūt – a claim still made by the Janjū'ās of today. Hence it is probable that the real name J-Ḥaj was Janjū'ā. If this is acceptable, the history of the Janjū'ās can be pushed back to the time of the Hindū Shāhis, who put up a formidable fight against the Ghaznavid Sulṭāns but ultimately got defeated and had to remain unnoticed for some time. Juvaini's account about the battle between Chingiz Khān and the Rānā of Jūd hills is helpful in understanding the origins of the Janjū'ās too. Juvainī says: "Chingiz Khān despatched an envoy to the Rānā of the Jūd hills also, who at first accepted submission but did not remain constant. The Khān sent an army which seized and slew him."[61] Juvainī does not name the Rānā of Jūd hills here but it is possible that this unnamed Rānā was the chief of the Janjū'a tribe since the name Rānā is very common among the Rājpūts. There is again a reference of Minhāj that Ulugh Khān (later Sulṭān Balban) led an expedition and plundered the tract upto the territory of Rāe Jaspāl who fled away with his followes to the Koh-i-Jūd.[62] This Rāe Jaspāl may be a Janjū'ā chief because his name resembles the names of Hindū Shāhī rulers of this region. Sulṭān Jalāl al-Dīn Khalji refers to them as an important tribe of the Koh-i-Jūd, and says,"... how, at another time, I made the blood flow in Janjū'ā, so that a boat might have glided within the hills of Jūd."[63] This reference is important since it speaks of the power of the Janjū'ās, and how their power was crushed by Sulṭān Jālāl al-Dīn Khaljī. We do not hear about them any more until we come to the time of Bābar who says, " The Janjū'ās were the rulers, from old times, of the Koh-i-Jūd and of the tract between Nīlāb and Bhirā. Langar Khān and Sangar Khān are the rulers of this region."[64] From Bābar we learn that the Janjū'ās were supreme in the eastern parts of the Koh-i-Jūd. Later on Sher Shāh Sūri also mentions the Janjū'ās. It was with their help that he was able to build the fort of Rohtās and crush the Gakkhars.[65]

Similarly, Abūl Fazl calls them the old settlers of the Sind Sāgar Doāb.[66] At present, the Janjū'ās also live in the eastern and central parts of the Salt range.

### iii) THE JŪD TRIBE

The early history of the Jūd tribe is quite obscure. Mediaeval works, though they mention the Koh-i-Jūd and its tribes, do not give any detail about the Jūd tribe. Bābar's account is the only source which says, "The hill of Jūd was held by two tribes of common descent, the Jud and Janjū'ā."[67] This account of Bābar suggests that the Jūd and the Janjū'ā were of the same family. Bābar further records, "Seven kos north of Bhira lies the mountain range written in the *Zafar Nāma* and other books as the Koh-i-Jūd. I had not known why it was called this: I now know. On it dwell two tribes, descendants from one parent-source, one is called Jūd, the other Janjū'ā. These two from of old have been the rulers and lawful commanders of the peoples and hordes *(ulus)* of the range and of the country between Bhira and Nilab... The Jūd and the Janjū'ā both are divided into several clans... On one half of it are the Jūd, the Janjū'ā on the other. People call it the Koh-i-Jūd through connecting it with the Jūd tribe."[68] This description of Bābar shows that this hilly region became famous due to this tribe and is known as Jūd hills most probably after their name. This tribe may represent the modern Jodhrā tribe[69] who are settled in the Jhelum district.

Besides the Gakkhars, the Jūd and the Janjū'ā there were other tribal hordes like that of the Awans,[70] Gujars[71] and the Jats[72] etc. in the Jūd hills during the mediaeval age but they were not in a ruling position.

Summarising the political history of the tribes of the Koh-i-Jūd, it is found that the Gakkhars and the Janjū'ās were the main tribes who played a dominant role during the mediaeval age in this hilly region which served as a buffer zone between the territories of the Mongols and the Sulṭāns of Delhī. This comprehensive study of the Koh-i-Jūd and its tribes, thus, enables a student of mēdiaeval Indian History to grasp correctly the frontier policy of the Delhī Sulṭāns. But it is astonishing to note that we do not get any information about the social and cultural history of these tribes of the Koh-i-Jūd.

However, a detailed study of a number of forts that exist in this region can throw further light on the military strategy and war tactics of these people. A sociological analysis of the different branches of these tribes will reveal the actual social condition of these people. All of them have preserved long genealogies and traditional history about their origin. For example, the Gakkhars call themselves the Kianis. It will be worthwhile to examine how and why they associate themselves with this old Persian tradition. However, all these tribes today have become part and parcel of the Pothwār plateau and adopted this region as their homeland, accepted the local language as their own, imbibed local rituals and customs and certainly contributed to the rich cultural tradition of the Pothwār. Their detailed history remains to be written.

1 This place of Sangwān has not been identified by the contemporary as well as modern historians. It is possible that the tract between the Jhelum and the Chīnāb was known as Sangwān.
2. *T.M.N.* (Trans.), Elliot, vol. ii, p. 145.
3. *J.T.*, cited by Raverty (Trans.), *T.N.*, at page 482 as *Jabl-i-Jūd* (جبل جود).
4. *T.N.*, pp. 482, 538, 606, 609.
5. *T.J.G.* (Trans.), Boyle, p. 15. Balālā may be identified with Bālanāt, a hilly peak near Jhelum, and Nikālā can be Makhiālā on the Salt range.
6. *T.F.S.* (Text), Shaikh 'Abdur Rashid, p. 150.
7. Al-'Utbī, *Kitāb-i-Yamīnī*, (Trans.), James Reynolds, London, n.d., p. 266: Also cited by 'Abdur Rahmān, *op. cit.*, p. 151.
8. Bālanāt is today called Jogī tilla, and is one of the peaks on the Salt range. *Ibid.*, p. 151.
9. Al-'Utbī, *op. cit.*, p. 226.
10. 'Abdur Rahmān, *op. cit.*, p. 159.
11. *Z.N.* (Trans.), p. 482.
12. *T.B.* (Trans.), p. 379.
13. Abūl Fazl, *Akbar Nāmā*, (Trans.), H. Beveridge, Calcutta, n.d., vol. i, p. 237.
14. Ranking says that the Koh-i-Jūd is apparently a part of the Salt range (Lat. 32 Long. 71). Ranking, *op. cit.*, p. 128.
15. *T.B.* (Trans.), p. 379.
16. Lepel H. Griffin, *Chiefs and Families of Note in the Punjab*, Lahore 1910, vol. ii, p. 254.
17. Beveridge, *op. cit.*, p. 237. fn.
18. *Ibid.*
19. Describing the battle of Nandanā, 'Utbī says that the conflict continued as before until God blew the gale of victory on his friends and the enemies were slain on the tops of the hills, and in the valleys. al-'Utbī, *op. cit.*, p. 152.
20. *T.B.* (Trans.), p. 379.
21. *T.F.* (Trans.), p. 182.
22. Elphinstone, *Account of the Kingdom of Kabul and its Dependencies*, London, 1915, p. 4.
23. Wynne, *Geology of the Salt range in Punjab: Memiors of the Geological Survey of India*, Calcutta, 1878, p. 36.
24. Spate, *op. cit.*, p. 451.
25. *T.H.* (Trans.), p. 258.
26. Bosworth, C.E., *The Later Ghaznavids*, New York, 1977, pp. 126-30.
27. *K.G.N.* (Text), p. 46.
28. *T.N.* (Trans.), p. 482. The upper route of the North-west frontier region was not safe. The tract was known Jūd hills. It was inhabited by the hill tribes known as Kokars, A'wān, and Janjū'as who were turbulent and used to plunder the neighbouring cities. G.D. Gulati, "Multān as a Trading Centre during thirteenth and fourteenth century", *P.P.H.C.* Patiala, 1978, p. 58.
29. *J.T.* (Text), p. 192. Sewakpāl or Sukhpāl a near relation of Jaipāl, who had been made prisoner alongwith Jaipāl in A.D. 1002, and who had subsequently embraced Islām, was appointed governor of Multān by Mahmūd. But no sooner had Mahmūd turned his back, then Sukhpāl turned Hindu.... Gulshan Rā'i, "The Struggle of the Hindū S'ahī Rulers of Kābul and Punjāb against the Central Asian Turks", (870-1027 A.D.), *J.P.H.S.*, Lahore, 1919, p. 126.
30. Maulana Ahmad, *Tārīkh-i-Alfī* cited by Raverty, *op. cit.*, p. 382; (Trans.), Dowson, vol. V, pp. 163-4.
31. *T.B.* (Trans.), p. 387.

32. General Court cited by Rose, *op. cit.*, p. 274.
33. Cunningham, *op. cit.*, pp. 22-3.
34. Denzil Ibbetson, *Punjab Census Report,* 1891, p. 483; Thomasan, *Jhelum Settlement Report,* p. 57.
35. *T.M.* as cited by Raverty, pp. 482-3.
36. See for details, Raverty, *op. cit.*, pp. 361-71.
37. Hodivala says that the persons into whose hands, the Sulṭān fell were not the infidels or Khokhars, who were defeated in the battle, but were Malahida ( ملاحده ) as mentioned by Minhāj, Ḥājī Dabīr and Ḥasan Niẓāmī. Here Malaḥida means Qarāmatā or Isma'īli. Hodivala, *op. cit.*, p. 204.
38. *T.J.G.* (Trans.), p. 412.
39. Hodivala identifies Balālā with Bugial which lies under the lofty hills of Bālanāt on the Salt range, and Nikālā with Makhiāla on the Salt range. See for details, Hodivala, *op. cit.*, pp. 233-4.
40. *T.J.G.* (Trans.), p. 146.
41. As the Kokar chief had some quarrel with Qubācha, the ruler of Sind, therefore, he willingly entered into an alliance with the Sultān. *T.J.G.* (Trans.), p. 146: J.T. (Trans.), p. 26.
42. The word Mang may have been originally San and similarly the word Kin or Kan may have been Khān. Thus it seems that with the passage of time Sankan was changed into Mang Khān and later writers like Dunī Chand, therefore, use this later variant of the name.
43. *T.N.* (Trans.), pp. 730-1; U.N. Day, "The North-West Frontier of the Sulṭanate during the 13th Century", *I.H.Q.*, March, 1941, p. 62.
44. *T.N.* (Trans.), p. 732. The text runs as follows:

برلب آب لوهور عبره کرد و لشکر اسلام را بسبب کوه جود و اطراف سند فرمان داد و الغخان اعظم خلدت سلطنت در مرتبت امیر حاجبی بود
بر سر آن حشم نامزد شد و سلطان با بنه و فیلان برلب آب سودره مقام فرمود و الغخان اعظم آن لشکر ببرد و به فضل و نصرت آفریدگار کوه جود
را نهب کرد و جیلم و کوکران و کفار متمردان را مبالغ بعد و زخم فرستاد و تا لب آب سند براند و آن اطراف نهب کرد و از آنجا مراجعت نمود

ص ۱۱۷

45. *T.F.* (Trans.), p. 245.
46. *M.T.T.*, (Trans.), p. 459.
47. *T.F.* (Trans.), p. 279.
48. Āghā Mahdī Ḥusain's view is that Shaikhā went to Samarqand where Tīmūr at that moment was present. It was from Samarqand that Tīmūr started for India in April 1398/Rajab 800 A.H. Aghā M. Ḥusain, *op. cit.*, p. 467.
49. *T.F.* (Trans.), p. 306.
50. *Ibid.*, p. 420.
51. *T.B.* (Trans.), p. 389; R.C. Verma, "The Relations of the Mughals with the Tribes of the North-West", *I.C.*, October, 1950, p. 256.
52. *T.B.* (Trans.), p. 387.
53. *T.S.S.* (Trans.), p. 104.
54. See for details *'Ain-i-Akbarī* (Trans.), p. 414 and *K.G.N.* (ed.) p. 49.
55. Rose, *op. cit.*, p. 275.
56. G. Clauson, *Acta Orentalia,* Vol. xxxii, 1970, p. 54. Samolin says that the Juan-juan, after their defeat, took refuge at Ch'ang-an, the capital of the western Wei. They were pursued by the Turks who arrived before the capital with a powerful force and demanded that the Chinese deliver the fugitive over to them. The ruler of Juan-juan and three thousand of his followers were turned over to the Turks who decapitated them outside the city. W. Samolin, *East Turkestan Down to the Twelfth Century,* London, 1954, p. 55.
57. Cf. Rene Grousset, *The Empire of the Steppes,* (Trans.), Naomi Walford, New Jersy, 1970, p. 80.

58. *M.D.* (Trans.), Egypt, A.H. 1346, p. 103, (Trans.), Elliot, p. 22. The text runs as follows:
59. Elliot, *op. cit.*, p. 22.
60. A. Cunningham, *Later Indo-Scythians,* Indian reprint. 1962, p. 94.
61. *T.J.G.* (Trans.), p. 412. North Indian title of Rāna was the proper name.
62. *T.N.* (Trans.), p. 732.
63. Amīr Khusraū, *Miftāḥ al-Futūḥ,* (Trans.), Elliot, p. 537.
64. *T.B.* (Trans.), p. 146.
65. Sherwānī, *op. cit.*, p. 104.
66. Abūl Fazl, *op. cit.*, pp. 326-8.
67. *T.B.* (Trans.), p. 390.
68. *T.B.* (Trans.), pp. 379-80.
69. "Thomson's Account of the Tribe in Jhelum", cited in Rose p. 355.
70. The A'wāns are an important tribe chiefly found in the Salt range. About the origin of the A'wāns, Cunningham says that the Janjū'ās and the A'wāns were within historical times one race while Brandreth's theory suggests that the A'wāns, though recent immigrants into the Punjab, are descended from the Bactrian Greeks. But in the best available account of the tribe the A'wans are indeed said to be of 'Arabian origin and descendants of Quṭb Shah, who ruled Herat and joined Maḥmud of Ghaznī when he invaded India. Cunningham, *op. cit.*, p. 17; Brandreth's Account cited by Rose, p. 26; Talbot, W.S., *Jhelum Gazetteer,* 1905, pp. 102-3.
71. There are different theories regarding the origin of Gujars. It is said that they are descended from White Huns or Ophthalites. Their dwelling place was Gujarāt, the country or tract of the Gujars. Popular local traditions assign its foundations to Rājā Bachan Pal in A.D. 1910. *J.R.A.S.*, 1905, pp. 1-4; Rose, *op. cit.*, p. 304. At the present day the Gujars are found in great numbers in every part of the north-west of India from the Indus to the Ganges, and from the Hazara mountains to the Peninsula of Gujarāt. Cunningham, *op. cit.*, p. 82.
72. The Jāts, of the Koh-i-Jūd were the ancient dwellers of the area and they were one of the important hordes of the hills when Bābar invaded India. *T.B.* (Trans.), p. 380.

Appendix-B

## CHRONOLOGY OF THE MONGOL INVASIONS

| | |
|---|---|
| A.H. 618/<br>A.D. 1221 | Jalāl al-Dīn Mangbārnī's flight to Afghānistān to place in this year. He was favoured by Chingiz Khān who overtook him on the banks of the Indus. Battle beside the Indus. When Mangbārnī's force had been surrounded, he flung himself once more against the Mongols at the head of the 700 men of his body-guard, cut through ranks, recaptured the colours that had been taken by the enemy, turned about, again forced his way through the Mongols, and, then, seated on his charger, leapt from the top of a sixty feet cliff into the Indus and swam across the river bearing the banner in his hand. After gaining this victory, Chingiz Khān followed the Indus for some distance upstream, and then turned off into the valley of the upper Kurram. He despatched Chaghatāe in the pursuit of Mangbārnī whilst proceeding himself with the main army to winter quarters in a region probably to be identified with the Swāt valley. |
| A.H. 621/<br>A.D. 1224 | The Mongol commander named Torbāe with two tūmāns invaded Multān and laid siege to the city. The Muslim forces at Multān resisted and consequently the Mongols raised the siege and went back. |
| A.H. 633/<br>A.D. 1234–5 | The Mongols headed by General Hoqūtqar appeared and plundered Kashmīr and made a |

large number of people captive. Ḥasan Qarlugh, ruler of Baniān and Koh-i-Jūd region, acknowledged the suzerainty of the Mongol emperor Ogetāe.

A.H. 636/ A.D. 1238 — The Mongols under a leader named Makānū ( مکانو ) marched towards India and Kashmīr. The Mongols attacked Ḥasan Qarlugh who was defeated and fled towards Multān. After ravaging the frontier of India, they went back.

A.H. 639/ A.D. 1241 — The Mongols under Bahādur Ṭāir marched towards India. They invaded Multān where Kabīr Khān, the Delhī *muqṭi*ʻ, successfully held out against the invaders. Finding it difficult to capture Multān, the Mongols raised the siege and turned towards Lāhore. Malik Qarāqash, the *muqṭi*ʻ of Lāhore, defended the city for a few days and then fled, leaving the city to be sacked completley by the enemy. After a few months, the Mongols left the city and went back.

A.H. 643/ A.D. 1245 — The Mongols headed by Mangūtah invaded Uchh. Ḥasan Qarlugh fled to Debul and Siwistān. The Mongols laid siege around the town of Uchh and ravaged its environs. The people of Uchh successfully defended the city and killed the Mongols in large numbers. Sulṭān ʻAlā al-Dīn Masʻūd Shāh also started from Delhī to relieve Uchh. As soon as the Mongols received intelligence of the advance of the Delhī forces they raised the siege and returned to Khurāsān.

A.H. 651/ A.D. 1257 — Sālī Bahādur was directed by the Mongol emperor to proceed to India alongwith prince Jalāl al-Dīn, the brother of Sulṭān Nāṣir al-Dīn Maḥmūd. He and the prince came to Lāhore. The prince held Lāhore under the Mongol protection till the end of Sulṭān Maḥmūd's reign.

| | |
|---|---|
| A.H. 655/ A.D. 1257 | Sālī Bahādur, the Mongol Nū'in, came to India. After plundering the *iqṭā'* of Multān upto the Sutlej river, the Mongols returned to their base in Ghaznī |
| A.H. 656/ A.D. 1258 | Halākū Khān sent his emissaries alongwith Jamāl al-Dīn Khaljī, the *Ḥājib,* to the court of Delhī. The Wazīr went out to meet him in haste with a train of 50,000 foreign horses, then in the service of the Delhī government, 2,000 elephants, and 3,000 carriages of fire works. Having exhibited some feats of horsemanship in sham fights, and having made a very splendid display before the ambassador, the latter was conducted in state through the city direct to the palace. There the court was arranged in the most gorgeous and magnificent style. All the nobles, and public officers of State, the *Qāẓīs,* the *'Ulamā*, and the great men of the city were present, besides twenty five princes of 'Irāq-i-'Ajam, Khurāsān, and Māwāraan-Nahr with their retinues, who had sought protection at Delhī from the armies of Chingiz Khān, which sometime before had overrun most part of Asia. |
| A.H. 678/ A.D. 1279 | A Mongol force was sent by Prince Arghūn, who invaded India and crossed Biāh (modern Biās). The Sulṭān of Delhī sent prince Muḥammad from Multan, Bughrā Khān from Samānā and Malik Bārbak from Delhī to meet the forces of the Mongols. As a result, the Mongols were unable to advance beyond the Biāh and went back. |
| A.H. 684/ A.D. 1285 | Samar, the bravest man of the Mongols, invaded Multān. Prince Muḥammad, the *muqṭi'* of Multān, fought bravely, but was slain. Amir Khusraū was also taken away as a captive. The Mongols went back after doing great destruction. |

A.H. 685/ A.D. 1286 Tātārs under the command of Tamar Khān invaded Lāhore. When the army of the Delhī Sulṭan under Shaikh Bārbak *Khān-i-Khānān,* reached near Lahore, the Mongols ran away, but ravaged the suburb of Lāhore while retreating to their own territory.

A.H. 691/ A.D. 1291 'Abdullāh, the grandson of Halākū Khān, invaded India. The battle ended with a peace treaty. Ulugh Khān, a relative of Chingiz Khān, with his followers opted to stay in India. Sulṭān Jalāl al-Dīn Khaljī gave one of his daughters in marriage to Ulugh Khān.

A.H. 696/ A.D. 1296 The Mongol commander Kadar under the command of 10,000 army invaded India and ravaged Koh-i-Jūd and Kasur. Bypassing Lahore, the Mongols reached Jalandhar. Ulugh Khān and Ẓafar Khān were sent by Sulṭān 'Alā al-Dīn Khaljī to meet the forces of the Mongols who defeated them.

In the same year, Amīr Dāwood, king of Transoxania, had prepared an army of 100,000 Mongols with a design to conquer Multān, Lāhore and Sind. He then advanced with great expedition and carried every thing before him with fire and sword. Sulṭān 'Alā al-Dīn Khaljī despatched his brother, Alp Khān, to oppose the invaders, and the two armies met in the districts of Lahore. In that battle the Mongols were defeated with the loss of 12,000 men including many of their chiefs. In the same year again, the Mongols under their leader Saldi appeared on the frontier of India, and took possession of Siwistān. Ẓafar Khān was sent to meet the Mongols who defeated Saldī. Saldī and his followers were brought to Delhī as captives.

| | |
|---|---|
| A.H. 699/ A.D. 1299-1300 | Qutlugh Khwājā, the Mongol leader, invaded India with twenty tūmāns and reached the vicinity of Delhī. This sudden appearance of the Mongols embarrassed the Sulṭān and the masses. The Sulṭān faced them boldly, and defeated them with the help of Ẓafar Khān and Ulugh Khān. Unfortunately, Ẓafar Khān was killed by the Mongols but they were forced back with great destruction. |
| A.H. 703/ A.D. 1303 | Targhi, the Mongol leader, invaded India and reached the neighbourhood of Delhī. Consequently the Sulṭān left the capital and encamped at Sirī where he entrenched his camp. The Sulṭān was able to repel this invasion of the Mongols. |
| A.H. 705/ A.D. 1305 | 'Alī Beg and Tartāq, the Mongol commandants, advanced towards India. They passed to the north of Lahore and skirting the Siwalik hills, penetrated without opposition to Amroha. Malik Tughlaq was sent by the Sulṭān who defeated the Mongols. 'Alī Beg and Tartāq with 9000 of their troops were made prisoners and sent in chains to the Sulṭān who ordered the chiefs to be thrown under the feet of elephants, and the soldiers to be put to death. As a reward of his services, Tughlaq Malik was made the *muqṭi'* of Dipālpur. |
| A.H.706/ A.D. 1306 | Kubūk, the Mongol leader, crossed Indus and reached near river Rāvī. Tughlaq Malik defeated the Mongols. Another force of the Mongols under Iqbalmanda arrived near Nagaur but was defeated by Malik Kāfūr. Similarly, another contingent of the Mongols under Tae-bū came but was also defeated by Malik Tughlaq. |

| | |
|---|---|
| A.H. 724/<br>A.D. 1324 | The Mongols invaded India. Gurshāsp, the *muqṭi'* of Samānā informed the Sulṭān that the Mongols had crossed the Indus and invaded Samānā. The Sulṭān sent an army and Gurshāsp defeated the Mongols. |
| A.H. 727/<br>A.D. 1327 | Arrival of Tarmānshīrīn in India. According to 'Isāmī, Tarmānshīrīn invaded India, but Ibn Baṭṭūṭah opines that Tarmānshīrīn sent his sons to the court of the Sulṭān of Delhī for help after his defeat by Amīr Ḥasan, son of Amīr Chobān and governor of Il-Khānid dynasty at Ghaznī. Aghā Mahdī Ḥusain, a modern historian, suggests that Tarmanshirin had come to India after his defeat by Amir Ḥasan at Ghazni. |
| A.H. 760/<br>A.D. 1358 | The Mongols invaded and reached near Dipalpur. Kabul Khān, the governor of Samānā, defeated the Mongols. |
| A.H. 799/<br>A.D. 1398/ | Tīmūr sent prince Pīr Muḥammad, his grandson, to invade India. Pir Muhammad captured Multan. Tīmūr crossed river Indus and came to Tulambā from where he proceeded to Delhī. A battle was fought at *Hauz Khās* near old Delhī between Tīmūr and Sulṭān Nasir al-Dīn Maḥmūd. The Sulṭān of Delhī fled to Baran after defeat. Tīmūr proclaimed general amnesty in the city and had the *Khuṭbah* read in his name in the mosques. After a few days, Tīmūr started his return march via Jammū and Kashmīr. He appointed Khizr Khān as governor over his Indian conquered territories and he himself left for Samarqand on March 28, 1399. He crossed the Indus and went back to his country where he died in A.D. 1404. |

Appendix-C

## GLOSSARY OF IMPORTANT TERMS

*'Ajami:* non-Arab

*Amir:* *'amil* of the province who commanded ten *Sipah-sālārs*

*Amir-i-Akhūr* or *Akhūr-i-Bak:* superintendent of the imperial stables

*Amir-i-dād:* an officer who enforced the decision of judges and brought culprits before the Qaẓis and presided over the *Diwān-i-Maẓālim*.

*Amir-i-hazārah: amir* of one thousand men

*Amir-i-Ṣadah: amir* of one hundred men

*Amir-i-Shikār:* the 'grand huntsman' (i.e. master of the hunting expeditions)

*Amir-ul-Umarā:* chief of the *amirs*

*Arẓ-i-mumālik:* head of the *Diwān-i-Arẓ* or the military organisation of the State.

*Arrada:* a machine which throws stone balls or missiles at fortified places.

*Aṭrāf:* suburb

*Bahādur:* commander of the Mongol army

*Balistā:* machine throwing stone-missiles on the enemy soldiers in the battle.

*Bilād:* country

*Chual:* uncultivated or desert tract

Deputy *Wakil-dār*. an officer who assisted the *wakil-dār*

*Hiṣṣār:* a fortified wall

*Jāgir:* land or estate bringing in revenue

*Jamādār:* royal wardrober

*Jang-jū:* warrior

*Khān:* an officer who commanded ten thousand horsemen or had authority over ten Maliks

*Khān-i-Khānān:* the greatest Khān
*Khāqān* or *Qa'an:* title of the Mongol ruler
*Khāzin:* an officer who kept the cash of the Empire (the treasurer)
*Khwājah:* head of the provincial finance and also the assistant of the governor of a province
*Kotwāl:* head of the police
*Kuriltāe* or *Quriltāe:* grand national assembly of the Mongol princes
*Malik:* an officer who commanded a thousand horsemen and had an authority over ten amīrs
*Malikah-i-Jāhān:* senior queen of the Empire
*Manjanīq:* machine throwing stone balls - missiles
*Mūqṭi':* *iqṭā'*-holder or governor of a province
*Na'ib:* Deputy
*Nā'ib-mumlikat* or *Nā'ib ul-Mulk:* regent of the empire or Lord-lieutenant of the empire
*Nū'in* or *Noyan:* Title used by the Mongols both for civil and military chiefs, governors and commanders in the field
*Paigah:* stable
*Rāi* : title of local tribe's leader in Koh-i-Jūd
*Ra'is:* title of local chief in Koh-i-Jūd
*Rānā:* title of the Rājpūt clan or the title of the rulers of the Rajpūts.
*Shāhnah:* superintendent of various departments
*Shāhn'agān:* a Mongol resident at the court of Indian local chiefs
*Sar-i-Jandār:* chief of the Royal bodyguards
*Talwārah:* huts
*Tankā:* a coin used by the Sulṭāns of Delhī
*Tūmān:* A Mongol body of ten thousand soldiers
*Wakīl-i-dār:* master of the court ceremonies. He was also styled the *Amīr-i-ḥājib-i-barbak*. He also controlled the entire household and supervised the payment of allowances and salaries to the personal staff of the *Sulṭān*
*Wālī*: Governor of the province having extraordinary powers
*Yarlugh* or *Yāsū:* a personal order of the Great Khān or orders of the Mongol ruler

# BIBLIOGRAPHY

## Contemporary Works

### (i) MANUSCRIPTS (UNPUBLISHED WORKS)


Anonymous, *Sīrat-i-Fīrūz Shāhī,* MS, Aligaṛh Muslim University Library, Aligaṛh (Transcribed copy of Jadunath Sarkar's collection).

Baranī, Ẓiā al-Dīn, *Tārīkh-i-Fīrūz Shāhī*, MS, Aligaṛh Muslim University Library, Aligaṛh. See also under published works.

Firishtah, Muḥammad Qāsim Hindū Shāh Astarābādī, *Tārīkh-i-Firishtah*, MS, Punjab University Library, Lahore (Pe I 14A: V 1-2). See also under published works.

Juzjānī, Minhāj al-Dīn Sirāj, *Ṭabaqāt-i-Nāṣiri,* MS, Punjab University Library, Lahore (Pe I 4B 2357). See also under published works.

Khān, 'Abdullāh, *Tārīkh-i-Dāūdī,* MS, Punjab University Library, Lahore (AP e I 16-53). See also under published works.

Khusraū, Amīr, *I'jāz-i-Khusravī*, MS, Punjab University Library, Lahore. See also under published works.

Multānī, A'in al-Mulk, *Inshā-i-Māhrū*, MS, Aligaṛh Muslim University Library, Aligaṛh. See also under published works.

Musṭawfī, Ḥamdullāh, *Tārīkh-i-Guzīdā*, MS, Punjab University Library, Lahore (AP e I 5-47). See also under published works.

Mā'ṣūm, Muḥammad, *Mīrāt-i-Mā'ṣūmī*, MS, Punjab University Library Lahore (Pe III-9-2304). See also under published works.

Niẓāmī, Ḥasan, *Taj al-Mā'aṣir,* MS, Aligaṛh Muslim University Library, Aligaṛh. See also under published works.

Raizādā, Chatarman, *Chahār Gulshan*, MS, Punjab University Library, Lahore (Pe I 44-863).

Rashīd al-Dīn Fazlullāh, *Jami' al-Twārīkh*, MS, Punjab University Library, Lahore (Pe I 55-2035).

Samarqandī, 'Abdur Razāq, *Matla'-us-S'adain*, or *Majma'-i-Bahrain* MS, Aligarh Muslim University Library, Aligarh.

Shāh, Fakhr al-Dīn Mubārak, *Ādāb al-Harb wa Shuja'ah*, MS, Aligarh Muslim University Library, Aligarh. See also under published works.

Sirhindī, Yahyā bin 'Abdullāh, *Tārīkh-i-Mubārak Shāhī*, MS, Aligarh Muslim University Library, Aligarh. See also under published works.

Thattawī, Mullā Ahmad, *Tārīkh-i-Alfī*, MS, Aligarh Muslim University Library, Aligarh.

Tīmūr, Amīr, *Malfūzāt-i-Tīmūrī*, MS, Punjab University Library, Lahore (Pf. IV 1-481).

Tughlaq, Fīrūz Shāh, *Futūhāt-i-Fīrūz Shāhī*, MS, Aligarh Muslim University Library, Aligarh. See also under published works.

Wassāf, 'Abdullāh bin Fazl'ullāh, *Tārīkh-i-Wassāf*, MS, Punjab University Library, Lahore, (PPe II 15-1547).

## (ii) PUBLISHED WORKS

'Afīf, Shams Sirāj, *Tārīkh-i-Fīrūz Shāhī*, ed., Maulvi Wilayat Hussain, Calcutta, 1890. See also Elliot and Dowson.

Al-Bīnāgitī, Abū Sulaimān Dā'ūd, *Rauzatul-Auli'l Albāb fī Twārīkh-i-Akhbār wal Ansāb*, London, n.d.

Al-Berūnī, Abū Raihān Muhammad bin Ahmad, *Kitāb al-Hind* or *Kitāb fī Tahqīq Ma'lil Hind*, Hyderabad (Deccan) 1958. See also Sachau and Dānī.

Al-Kūfī, 'Alī bin Hamīd bin Abī Bakr, *Chach Nāmā* or *Fateh Nāmā Sind*, Persian Trans., Daud Pota, Umar bin Muhammad, Hyderabad (Deccan), 1939.

Al-'Umarī, Shihāb al-Dīn, *Masālik al-Absār fī Mamālik al-Amsār*, Aligarh Muslim University, Aligarh. n.d. See also Siddique.

Al-'Utbī, *Kitāb-i-Yamīnī*, Arabic text, Cairo, 1280 A.H.; Persian text, Tehran, 1272 A.H.

Anonymous, *Ḥudūd al-'Ālam*, ed., Manoochihr Sotoodel, Tehran, 1962; See also Minorsky V., Eng. Trans.

Anonymous, *The Secret History of the Mongol Dynasty*, Eng. Trans., We-kwei, Sun, Aligarh, 1957.

'Awfi, Nūr al-Dīn Muḥammad, *Jawāmī al-Ḥikāyāt*, ed., Muḥammad Ramẓan, Tehran, 1956. See also Elliot and Dowson.

Baihāqī, 'Abul Faẓl, *Tārīkh Subuktīgīn*, ed., Moreley, W.H., Calcutta, 1862; Tehran, 1319 A.H.

Baranī, Ẓiā al-Dīn, *Tārikh-i-Fīrūz Shāhī*, ed., Syed Aḥmad Khān, Calcutta, 1860; W.N. Lees and Maulvī Kabīr al-Dīn, Calcutta, 1890; 'Shaikh 'Abdur Rashīd, Aligarh, 1954.

Faẓlullāh, Rashīd al-Dīn, *Jamī' al-Twārīkh*, Tehran, 1310 A.H., Russian Trans., N. Berezin, 1858; Karl Yan, London, 1940; See also Boyle.

Ibn al-Aṣīr, 'Abū al-Ḥasan 'Alī bin 'Abd al-Karam Moḥammad bin Moḥammad bin 'Abd al-Karam bin 'Abd al-Wahāb ash-Shaibānī, *Al-Kāmil fi'l-Tarīkh*, ed., C.J. Tornberg, Leiden, 1867; Cairo, 1301 A.H.; Beirut, 1955 (reprint).

Ibn Baṭṭūṭah, *Kitāb al-Reḥlā* or *Tuḥfātul Nazar fi Gharā'ib al Amṣār*, Cairo, 1870; Arabic text with French Trans., Defremery and Sanguinetti, Paris, 1874-9. See also Gibb, H.A.R.

'Iṣāmī, 'Abd al-Malik, *Futūḥ-us-Salāṭīn*, ed., Usha, A.S., Madras, 1948; Agha Mahdi Ḥusain, Agra, 1938; (Trans.), Bombay, 1967.

Juvainī, 'Alā al-Dīn 'Aṭā Malik, *Tārīkh-i-Jahān Gushā*, ed., Mirzā Muḥammad bin'Abdul Wahāb Qazvīnī, London, 1911; See also Boyle, J.A.

Juzjānī, Minhāj al-Dīn Sirāj, *Ṭabaqāt-i-Nāṣirī*, ed., W.N. Lees, Khādim Ḥusain and 'Abdul Ḥaiy, Calcutta, 1864. See also H.G. Raverty.

Kalhana, *Rājatarangini*, 1185 A.H.; See also Stein.

Khusraū, Amīr, *Khazā'in al-Futūḥ*, ed., S.M. Ḥaq, Aligarh, 1927. See also M. Ḥabib.

——, *Ijāz-i-Khusravī*, Lucknow, 1876.

——, *Qirān-us-Sa'dain*, Lucknow, 1883; Aligarh, 1918.

——, *Tughlaq Nāmā*, ed., Sayyid Hashmī Farīdābādī, Aurangābād, 1933.

——, *Nūḥ Sipihr*, ed., Waḥīd Mīrza, Calcutta, 1950.

——, *Miftāḥ al-Futūḥ*, Aligarh, 1954.

——, *Dewal Rānī*, Aligarh, 1917.

Multānī, 'Ain al-Mulk 'Abdullāh bin Māhrū, *Inshā-i-Māhrū*, ed., Shaikh 'Abdur Rashid, Lahore, 1965.

Mustawfī, Ḥamdullāh Qazvīnī, *Tārīkh-i-Guzīdā*, ed., E.G. Brown, London, 1913; 'Abdul Ḥasan Navai, Tehran, 1960.

Mas'ūdī, Abul Ḥasan bin Al-Ḥusain bin 'Alī, *Murūj al-Dhahab*, ed., 'Abdur Raḥman, Muḥammad, Cairo, 1346 A.H.; Paris. 1916. See also A. Sprenger, Eng. Trans.

Nasawī, Shihāb al-Dīn, *Sīrat-i-Jalāl-al-Dīn Mangbārnī*, ed., Minovi. Tehrān. n.d.

Shāh, Fakhr al-Dīn Muddabbir Mubārak, *Adāb al-Ḥarb wa al-Shuja'ah*, ed. Aḥmad Suhaili Khwarsari, Tehrān, 1967; E.D. London, 1927.

Shīrāzī, 'Abdullāh Waṣṣāf, *Tajziāt al-Amṣār wa Tajriyāt al-Āṣār* or *Tārīkh-i-Waṣṣāf*, ed., Muḥammad Mahdi Asfahānī, Bombay, 1327 A.H./A.D. 1877.

Sirhindī, Yaḥyā bin Aḥmad bin 'Abdullāh, *Tārīkh-i-Mubārak Shāhī*, ed., Hidayat Ḥussain, Calcutta, 1931. See also K.K. Basu, Eng. Trans.

Tīmūr, Amīr, *Tuzuk-i-Tīmurī*, ed., Fazal Ḥussain, Hyderabad, Deccan, n.d. See also Dowson.

——, *Malfūẓāt-i-Tīmūrī*, Persian Trans., 'Abu Ṭālib Ḥussain, Tehran, 1662. See also Elliot and Dowson.

Yazdī, Sharf al-Dīn 'Alī, *Ẓafar Nāmā*, ed., Maulvi Muḥammad al-Hadad, Calcutta, 1884 Calcutta, 1887. See also Elliot and Dowson.

**Later Published Works**

'Abul Fazl, *'Ain-i-Akbarī*, Persian text, Calcutta, 1877; ed., Sayyid Aḥmad Khan, Delhī, n.d. See also Blochmann, Eng. Trans.

Bābar, Ẓahīr al-Din Muḥammad, *Tuzuk-i-Bābari*, Tehran, n.d. See also A. Beveridge, Eng. Trans.

Badāūnī, 'Abdul Qādir, *Muntakhab al-Twārīkh*, ed., W N. Lees and Aḥmad Alī, Calcutta, 1940. See also G.S. Ranking, Eng. Trans.

Bakhshī, Niẓām al-Dīn Aḥmad, *Ṭabaqāt-i-Akbarī*, ed., B.De and M. Ḥidāyat Ḥussain, Calcutta, 1927; Lucknow, 1875. See also Beni Prasad, Eng. Trans.

Bhandari, Sujān Rāi, *Khulasat al-Twārīkh*, ed.; Ẓafar Ḥussain, Delhī, 1918.

Chand, Dunī, *Kai-gohar Nāmā*, ed., Muḥammad Bāqir, Lāhore, 1965.

Daughlat, Mīrzā Muḥammad Ḥaidar, *Tārīkh-i-Rashīdi*. See also E.D. Ross and N. Elias, Eng. Trans.

Firishtah, Muḥammad 'Abul Qāsim Hindū Shāh Astarābādī *Gulshan-i-Ibrāhimi* or *Tārīkh-i-Firishta*, Bombay, 1831-32; Lucknow, 1864. See also J. Briggs, Eng. Trans.

Hāji, Dabīr al-Dīn, *Ẓafar al-Walih bi-Muẓaffar wa alih* (An Arabic History of Gujarat), ed., E.D. Ross, London, 1928.

Kanbū, Muḥammad Sālih, *Madan-i-Akhbār-i-Aḥmadī*, Calcutta, n.d.

Khān, 'Abdullāh, *Tārīkh-i-Dāūdī*, ed., Shaikh 'Abdur Rashīd, Aligarḥ, 1954.

Khān, 'Alī Muḥammad, *Mīrāt-i-Aḥmadī*, Bombay, 1307 A.H.; ed., Syed Nawāb Ali, Calcutta, 1928; Baroda, 1927-28.

Khwānd, Mīr, *Rauẓāt al-Ṣafā*. Tehran, 1274 A.H.; Trans. E. Rehatsek, Calcutta, 1893; Bombay, 1250 A.H./A.D. 1850; Lucknow, 1911.

Ma'ṣūm, Syed Muḥammad, *Tārīkh-i-Mā'ṣūmī*, or *Tārīkh-i-Sind*, Poona, 1938; ed., Daud Pota. See also Elliot, Eng. Trans.

Mirzā, Ulugh Beg, *Shajrāt al-Aṭrāk* or *Ulus-i-Arbāb-i-Chingīzī*, ed., W. Miles, London, 1938.

Ni'amat Ullāh, *Tārīkh-i-Jahānī wa Makhzan-i-Afghānī*, ed., Muḥammad Imām al-Dīn, Calcutta, 1960. See also B. Dorn.

Sarwānī, 'Abbās, *Tārīkh-i-Sher Shāhī*. See also Elliot and Dowson, Eng. Trans.

## Modern Works

### (i) ENGLISH

Adami, J., *National Frontier in relations to Frontiers*, Rome, 1919.

Aḥmad, Jamāl al-Dīn, Co-author, *Afghanistān* Bombay, 1936.

Aḥmad, Q.M. and Siddique, I.H., Eng. Trans., *A 14th Century Arab Account of India under Muḥammad bin Tughlaq*, Aligaṛh, n.d.

Aḥmad, 'Aziz, *Studies in Islamic Culture in the Indian Environment*, Oxford, 1964.

Aḥmad, Muḥammad, Aziz, *Political History and Institutions of the Early Turkish Empire*, Lahore, 1949.

Aiyanger, S.K., *South India and Her Muḥammadan Invaders*, London, 1921.

Alastair, Lamb, *Asian Frontiers*, London, 1968.

Andrew, C.F., *Challenge of the North West Frontier*, London, 1937.

Arberry, A.J. *The Legacy of Persia*, Oxford, 1953.

Arthur, Swinson, *North West Frontier*, London, 1967.

'Azīz, Muḥammad 'Abdul, Co-author, *Afghanistan*, Bombay, 1936.

Banerjee, J.M., *History of Fīrūz Shāh Tughlaq*, Delhī, 1947.

——, The Age of Imperial Guptas, Delhī, 1924.

Barthold, W., *Turkestan down to the Mongol Invasions*, London, 1958.

Basu, K.K., Eng. Trans., *Tārīkh-i-Mubārak Shāhī*, Baroda, 1932.

Beveridge, A.S., *A Comprehensive History of India*, London, n.d., Vol. I.

——, *Tuzuk-i-Babarī*, Eng. Trans. Lahore, 1976.

Bhattacharya, S.N., *History of the Mughal North Eastern Frontier Policy*, Calcutta, 1929.

Bhuyan, S.K., *Annals of the Delhī Badshāhate*, Assam, 1947.

Blochmann, H., *'Ain-i-Akbarī*, Eng. Trans., Calcutta, 1873.

Bosworth, C.E. *The Ghaznavids: Their Empire in Afghanistān and Eastern Iran*, Edinburgh, 1963.

——, *The Later Ghaznavids*, New York, 1977.

Boyle, J.A., *The Cambridge History of Iran*, Cambridge, 1968, Vol. I.

——, *The History of the World Conqueror*, Eng. Trans., Manchestor, 1958.

Briggs, J.E., *History of the Rise of the Muḥammadan Power in India*, Eng. Trans., Calcutta, 1920.

Caroe, Olaf, *The Pathans*, London, 1958.

Cornish, W.B., *Modern Geography of Asia*, London, 1949.

Crooke, W., *The North West Frontier of India*, London, 1972.

Cunningham, A., *Ancient History of Indiā*, London, 1871.

——, *Later Indo-Scythians*, London, n.d.

Dames, M. Longworth, *The Baluch Race*, London, 1904.

Dānī, A.H., *Peshawar: Historic City of the Frontier*, Peshawar, 1961.

——, *Ancient Pakistan*, Peshawar, 1973.

Davis, C. Collin, *The Problems of North West Frontier*, London, 1932.

Day, U.N., *Administrative System of Delhī Sulṭanate*, Allahābād, 1959.

——, *Studies in Medieval India*, Delhī, 1965.

Delmerick, J.G., *History of the Gakkhaṛs*, Bengal, 1871.

D'Ohsson, *Historie des Mongols*, Amsterdom, 1835; Paris, 1824.

Dorn, B., Eng. Trans., *History of the Afghans*, London, 1836.

Edward Thomas, *Chronicles of the Pathan Kīngs of Delhi*, London, 1971.

Ellias, N., Eng. Trans., *A History of the Mongols of Central Asia*, London, 1889.

Elliot and Dowson, ed. and Trans., *History of India as told by its own Historians*, London, 1867. 8 Vols.

Elphinstone, M., *The History of India*, London, 1880.

Fraser Tytler, W.K., *Afghanistān: A Study of Political Developments in Central Asia*, London, 1953.

George MacMunn, *The Romance of the Indian Frontier*, London, 1931.

Gibb, H.A.R., Eng. Trans., *Ibn Baṭṭuṭah's Travels in India and Africa*. London, 1929.

Gonkovsky, Yu. V., *The Peoples of Pakistān*, Lāhore, 1971.

Gorgon. East W., Gen. ed., *The Changing Map of Asia*, London, 1950.

Ḥabibullah, A.B.M., *The Foundation of the Muslim Rule in India*, Allahābād, 1961.

Ḥabib, Muḥammad, *Campaigns of 'Alā al-Din Khaljī*, Eng. Trans., Bombay, 1933.

——, *The Political Theory of the Sulṭanate of Delhī*, Delhī, n.d.

——, *Life of Ḥaẓrat Amir Khusrau*, Aligaṛh, 1927.

Haq, S.M., *Barani's History of the Tughlaqs*, Karachi, 1940.

Hardy, P., *Historians of Medieval India*, London, n.d.

Hilda Hockman, *Tamerlane: The Conqueror*, London, 1962.

Hodivala, S.A., *Studies in Indo-Muslim History*, Bombay, 1939.

Holdich, T.M., *Political Frontiers and Boundary Making*, London, 1918.

——, *The Gates of India*, Quetta, 1977.

Howorth. H., *History of the Mongols*, London, 1886.

Hughes, A.W., *The Country of Baluchistan: Its Geography, Topography, Ethnology and History*, London, 1877.

Ḥusain, Agha Mahdī, *Tughlaq Dynasty*, Calcutta, 1933.

—, *The Rise and Fall of Muḥammad bin Tughlaq*, London, 1938.

——, *The Reḥla of Ibn Baṭṭuṭah*, Eng. Trans., Baroda, 1953.

——, *'Isami's Shahnama-i-Hindustan*, Eng. Trans., Vol. I, Aligarh, 1938; Vol. II, 1978.

Hunter, W.W., *The Indian Musalmāns*, London, 1871.

Ibbetson, D., *Glossary of the Punjab Tribes and Castes*, Lāhore, 1911.

Kalichbeg Faridunbeg, Trans., *Chachnama*, Karachi, 1900.

Kazī, S. Aḥmad, *A Geography of Pakistan*, Karachi, 1965.

Keene, H.G., *History of India*, Edinburgh, 1906.

Lal, K.S., *Twilight of the Ṣulṭanate*, London, 1963.

——, *History of the Khaljis*, Karachi, 1950.

Lane Poole, S., *Muḥammadan Dynasties*, London, 1894.

——, *Medieval India under Muḥammadan Rule*, London, 1926.

Ḳureshy, K.U., *A Geography of Pakistān*, Karachi, 1977.

Lyall, D., *The Rise of British Dominion in India*, London, n.d.

Lyde, L.W., *The Continent of Asia*, London, 1933.

Majumdar, R.C., *The Arab Invasion of India*, Lahore, 1974.

Malet, C.C., Trans. *History of Sind,* Bombay, 1955.

Malleson, G.B., *History of Afghanistān*, London, 1878.

Martin, R. Montgomery, *Our Indian Empire*, London, n.d., Vol. I.

Minorsky, V., Eng. Trans., *Ḥudud al-Alam*, London, n.d.

Mirzā, M.W., *Life and Works of Amīr Khusrau*, Lahore, 1962.

——, Eng. Trans., *Khazā'in al-Futuḥ*, Lahore, 1975.

Mookerjee, R.K., *The Gupta Empire*, Bombay, 1937.

Narain, A.K., *The Indo-Greeks*, Oxford, 1957.

Nāẓim, Muḥammad, *The Life and Times of Sulṭan Mahmud of Ghazna*, Lahore, 1973.

Nirodlhusan Roy, *Niamatullah's History of the Afghāns*, Bengal, 1958.

Niẓāmī, K.A., *Studies in Medieval Indian History and Culture*, Allahābād, 1966.

——, *Religion and Politics in India during 13th Century*, Aligarh, 1961.

——, *Politics and Society during the Early Medieval Period*, ed., Vol. I, Aligaṛh, 1974.

Norman, J.G., *Political Geography*, New York, 1963.

Oliver, E.E., *Across the Border of Pathan and Baloch*, London, 1890.

Orlich, C.L. Von, *Travels in India*, Lahore, 1976.

Pandey, Awadh Bihari, *The First Afghān Empire in India*, Bombay, n.d.

Patricia Kendal, *India and the British*, London, n.d.

Pennel, T.L., *Among the Wild Tribes of the Afghān Frontier*, Karāchī, 1975.

Percival Spear, *India: A Modern History*, New York, 1961.

Prasad, Benī, *Ṭabāqāt-i-Akbarī*, Trans., Calcutta, 1913.

Prasad, Ishwari, *Politics in Pre-Mughal Times*, Allahabad, 1938.

——, *Medieval India*, Allahabad, 1945.

——, *History of the Qurunah Turks*, Allahabad, 1936.

Prawdin, Michael, *The Mongol Empire: Its Rise and Legacy*, London, 1940.

Qureshī, I.H., *The Administration of the Sulṭanate of Delhī*, Lāhore, 1942.

Raḥman, Abdur, *The Last Two Dynasties of Sahis*, Islamabad, 1979.

Ranking, G.S., *Muntakhab al-Twārikh*, Eng. Trans., Calcutta, 1898.

Raverty, H.G., *Notes on Afghanistān and Baluchistān*, Quetta, 1976.

——, *Ṭabaqāt-ị-Nāṣiri*, Eng. Trans., Calcutta, 1873.

Riaẓ-ul-Islām, *Indo-Persian Relations*, Karachi, 1976.

——, *A Calendar of Documents on Indo-Persian Relations* (A.D. 1500-1750), Vol. I., Karachi, 1982.

Riẓvī, Mujtāba, *The Frontier of Pakistān*, Karachi, 1970.

Robertson, George Scott, *The Kāfirs of Hindū Kush*, London, 1974.

Romila Thapar, *Ancient India*, Cambridge, 1916.

Rose, H.A., *A Glossary of the Tribes and Castes of the Punjab and North West Frontier Province*, Lahore, 1978.

Ross, E. Denison, *A History of the Mongols*, Eng. Trans., London. 1895.

——, *An Arabic History of Gujarat*, Eng. Trans., London, 1921.

Ross, Davis, *The Land of the Five Rivers and Sind*, London, 1883.

Saran, P., *Studies in Medieval Indian History*, Delhi, 1952.

Sachau, E.C., *Al-Berūni's India*, Eng. Trans., London, 1888.

Sen, S.K., *People and Politics in Early Medieval India*, Calcutta, 1963.

Shaikh, 'Abdur Rashīd, ed., *Tārīkh-i-Fīrūz Shāhī*, Aligarh, 1956.

——, *Afif's Tārīkh-i-Fīrūz Shāhī*, (Unpublished).

——, *Jalāl al-Dīn Fīrūz Shāh Khaljī*, Aligarh, n.d.

——, *Inshā-i-Māhrū*, ed., Lahore, 1967.

Shaikh, M. Ikram, *History of Muslim Civilization in India and Pakistan*, Lahore, 1961.

Simon Digby, *War-horse and Elephant in the Delhī Sulṭanate: A Study of Military Supplies*, Oxford, 1971.

Smith, V.A., *Early History of India*, Oxford, 1924.

Spate, O.H.K., *India and Pakistan*, New York, 1954.

Spain, James W., *The Ways of the Pathans*, New York, 1962.

Spuler, Berthold, *History of the Mughals*, London, 1972.

Stein, M.A. Eng. Trans., *Rajatarangini*, West minster, 1900.

Strange G. Le, *The Lands of the Eastern Caliphate*, London, 1905.

Syed, Muḥammad Latīf, *The Early History of Multān,* Lāhore, 1963.

Sykes, Sir Percy, *A History of Persia,* London, 1951.

Ṭayyab, A., *A Political Geogrraphy of Pakistan,* Toronto, 1968.

Tripathi, R.P., *Some Aspects of Muslim Administration,* Allahabād, 1936.

Vyre, Griffin, W., *Southern Afghānistān and North West Frontier of India,* London, 1881.

William Miles, Eng. Trans., *Shajra-tul-Atrāk,* London, 1838.

Wolsley Haig, *The Cambridge History of India,* Vol. III, Cambridge, 1928.

Younis, Muḥammad, *Frontier Speaks,* Bombay, 1947.

(ii) **URDU**

Muḥammad Hafiz-ur-Raḥmān, *Tārikh-i-Uch,* Delhī, 1931.

Maulvī, Muḥammad Ẓakā Ullāh, *Tārikh-i-Hindustān,* Aligaṛh, n.d.

Nadvī, R.A., *Tuzuk-i-Bābarī,* Trans., Lahore, 1968.

Nadvī, Sayyid Abū Ẓafar, *Tārikh-i-Sind,* Azamgarh, 1947, pt. I.

Nadvī, Sayyid Rīāsat 'Alī, *'Aḥd-i-Islāmī kā Hindustān,* Patna, 1950.

Sayyid, Aḥmad Khān, *Asār-us-Ṣanādid,* Delhī, 1854.

Sayyid Sabaḥ al-Dīn 'Abdur Raḥmān, *Hindustān; 'Ahd-i-Islāmi ki aik Jhalak,* Azamgarh, n.d.

Shaikh, M. Ikrām, A'ab-i-Kausar, Lāhore, 1953.

(iii) **THESES**:

Aḥmad, Niāz, "The Bolan Pass: Political and Strategical Importance", Punjab University M.A. Thesis, 1962.

Karamat, S.K., "The Western Frontier of West Pakistān," New York Ph.D. Thesis, 1958.

Peter Jackson, "Mongols in India, 1221-1351", Cambridge University Ph.D. Thesis, 1976.

Rīāẓ-ul-Islam, "A History of Firuz Shah Tughlaq," Aligaṛh Muslim University Ph.D. Thesis, 1946.

Raḥman, Khalīl 'Abdur, "An Account of the Khaljī Sulṭān of Delhī: Jalāl al-Dīn Fīrūz Shāh," Eng. Trans., Punjab University M.A. Thesis, 1965.

(iv) **GAZETTERS**

*Baluchistan District Series*, vol. iv., 1906.

*District and States Gazetteers of the Punjab*, vol. i, *Dera Ghazī Khān District*, Lahore, 1976.

*District and States Gazetteer of the Punjab*, vol. i., *Jang District*, Lāhore, 1976.

*District and States Gazetteer of the Punjab*, vol. i., *Rawalpindi District*, Lāhore, 1976.

*District and States Gazetteer of the Punjab*, vol. i., *Jhelum District*, Lāhore, 1976.

*District and States Gazetteer of the Punjāb*, vol. i., *Attock District*, Lāhore, 1976.

*Gazetteer of Dera Ismāil Khān District*, 1883-4, Lahore, 1884.

*Gazetteer of Multān District*, 1902, Lahore, 1902.

Holdich, T.M., *The Imperial Gazetteer of India*, vol. i, Oxford, 1909.

*N.W.F.P. Gazetteer, Peshawar District*, vol. i, 1931.

Ludwing W. Adamis, *Historical and Political Gazetteer of India*, Australia, 1972.

*Punjāb District Gazetteers*, vol. vii, part A, *Multān District*, Lahore, 1926.

*Punjāb District Gazetteers*, vol. xxxvi, *Jullandhar District*, Lāhore, 1902.

*Punjāb District Gazetteers*, vol. xxxvi, *Patiala District*, Lahore, 1902.

*Punjāb State Gazetteers*, Vol. xxxvi, *Bahawalpur State*, Lahore, 1904.

(v) **ATLAS**:

Charles Joppen, *Historical Atlas of India*, London, 1914.

Longmans, *A New Historical Atlas of India*, Delhi, n.d.

*Map of West Pakistan*, Survey of Pakistān, Government of Pakistān, Rawalpindī, 1968.

Sita Ram Kohli, *Historical Atlas of India*, Lahore, 1936.

*The Imperial Gazetteer of India:* Atlas, vol. xxvi, Oxford, 1909.

## (vi) ARCHAEOLOGICAL AND GEOLOGICAL REPORTS

Cunningham, A., *Archaeological Survey of India: Report for the year, 1872-73*, vol. v., Calcutta, 1875.

——, *Archaeological Survey of India: Report for the year 1881-82*, vol. v., Calcutta, 1875.

Wynne, *Geology of the Salt Range in Punjab: Memiors of the Geological Survey of India*, Calcutta, 1878.

## (vii) ENCYCLOPAEDIA

*Encyclopaedia of Islam*, vol. iii, Leiden, 1967.

## (viii) JOURNALS

Aḥmad Nabi Khān, 'Dipalpur through the Ages', *Journal of the Research Society of Pakistan*, University of the Punjab, Lahore, vol. iii, No. i, January, 1970, pp. 71-2.

Anṣārī, B., 'Bannu', *Encyclopaedia of Islām*, vol. i., Leiden, 1967, p. 1020.

Banerjee, A., 'Proceedure of Succession of the Delhī Sulṭanate', *Journal of Indian History*, vol. xv, part. i., Madras, 1937, p. 111.

Bāqir, M., 'Lahore during the Pre-Muslim period', *Islamic Culture*, (Quarterly), vol. xxii, no. 3, Hyderabad (Deccan), pp. 295-305.

Bonamy, J. (Capt.), 'Memoranda on the North West Frontier of British India and on the importance of the Indus river connected with its defence', *The Punjab: Past and Present*, vol. ii, October 1970, pp. 254-66.

Borah, M.I., 'The Life and Works of Amīr Ḥasan Dehlavī', *Journal of the Royal Society of Bengal*, vol. vii, No. 1, Calcutta, August 1941, pp. 7-12.

Dānī, A.H., 'Ancient Peshawar', *Journal of the Research Society of Pakistan*, University of the Punjab, Lahore, vol. iii, No. 4, 1966, pp. 1-30.

'Al-Beruni and City of Lahore', *Journal of Central Asia*, Islamabad, vol. i, No. 2, December, 1978, pp. 81-7.

Day, U.N., 'The North West Frontier of the Sulṭanate during the 13th Century', *The Indian Historical Quarterly*, Calcutta, vol. xvii, No. 1, March, 1941, pp. 59-69.

Dharam, Pal, 'Ala al-Dīn Khalji's Mongol Policy', *Islamic Culture*, Hyderabad (Deccan). vol. xxi, July, 1954, pp. 255-61.

——, 'North West Frontier Policy of Lord Lawrence', *Indian Historical Quarterly*, Calcutta, vol. xxii, No. 2, June, 1946, pp. 40-52.

Faṭimī, S.Q., 'First Muslim Invasion of the North West Frontier of the Indo-Pakistan Subcontinent', *Journal of the Asiatic Society of Pakistan*, Dacca, vol. viii, No. 1, 1963, pp. 32-40.

Gulati, G.D., 'Multan as trading centre during 13th and 14th century', *Proceedings of the Punjab History Conference*, Punjab Historical Study Department, Punjab University, Patiala, 1978, pp. 23-31.

Garret, H.L.O., 'An Early Scientific Travellers in Punjab', *Journal of the Punjab Historical Society*, Lahore, vol. ii, part ii, December, 1933, pp. 121-6.

Ḥabībullah, A.B.M., 'Provincial Government under the Mamlūk Sulṭāns of Delhī', *Indian Historical Quarterly*, Calcutta, vol. xix, No. 1, March, 1843, pp. 250-5.

Khān, Ḥusain, 'The Identification of place where Sulṭān Khwārizm Shāh crossed the Indus', *Journal of Asiatic Society of Pakistan*, Dacca, April, 1961, pp. 23-31.

Khān, Yār Muḥammad, 'The Use of Artillery During the Sulṭanate Period', *Islamic Culture*, (Qaurterly), Hyderabad, (Deccan), vol. xxxv, No. 3, July, 1961, pp. 16-23.

Majumdār, R.C., 'The Arab invasion of India', *Journal of Indian History*, Delhī, vol. x, part 1, reprint in Dacca University Supplement, 1931, pp. 30-7.

Martin Honigher, 'Journal of the Route from Dera Ghazi Khān through the Vizirī country to Kābul', *Journal of Asiatic Society of Bengal*, Calcutta, vol. iii, April, 1934, pp. 175-8.

Maulvi, 'Abdul Kādir, 'Memorandum of the route between Delhī and Kābul', *The Punjab: Past and Present*, ed., Ganda Singh, Department of Punjab Historical Studies, Punjab University, Patiala, vol. xii, April, 1978, pp. 15-28.

Nasim al-Dīn, Aḥmad M., 'Early Cultural contacts between Pakistan and Persia' paper read at the R.C.D. Seminar, Tehran, March, 1965, pp. 19-30.

Rai, Gulshan, 'The Struggle of the Hindu Shahī Rulers of Kābul and Punjāb against the Central Asian Turks', *Journal of the Punjab Historical Society*, Lahore, vol. vii, No. 2, 1919, pp. 115-129.

——, 'The Mughal Province of Multān and its subsequent history', *Journal of the Punjab University Historical Society*, Lahore, vol. iii, part i, April, 1933, pp. 350-55.

——, 'Ancient courses of the Punjāb rivers', *Journal of the Punjab University Historical Society*, Lahore, vol. iii, part 1, No. 5, April, 1934, pp. 81-5.

Siddique, I.H., 'Qarlugh Kingdom in the North Western India During the 13th Century', *Islamic Culture*, Hyderābād, (Deccan), vol. iiv, No. 2, April, 1980, pp. 45-60.

——, 'Relations between Sulṭān Jalāl al-Dīn Khwārizm Shah and the Turkish rulers of North India'' *Indian Historical (Quarterly)*; Indian History Congress, Calcutta, 1971, pp. 81-89.

——, 'The Army of the Afghan kings in North India: A.D. 1451-1555', *Islamic Culture*, (Quarterly), Hyderabad, (Deccan), vol. xxxiv, No. 33, July, 1965, pp. 233-43.

Srivastava, A.L., 'A Survey of Indian Resistance of Medieval invaders from the North-West: Causes of eventual Hindu defeat', *Journal of Indian History*, Kerala, vol. xliii, part ii, No. 128, August, 1965, pp. 249-68.

Stein, Aural, 'Notes on the Routes from the Punjab to Turkistan and China recorded by William Finch: A.D. 1611', *Journal of the Punjab University Historical Society*, Lahore, vol. vi, No. 2, January, 1917, pp. 60-73.

Stow, A.M., 'The Road between Delhī and Multān', *Journal of Punjab Historical Society*, Lahore, vol. iii, No. 1, 1914, pp. 26-37.

Syed, Maqbul Aḥmad, 'Road System of India as described by Al-Berūnī', *Medieval India: A Miscellany*, Aligaṛh Muslim University, Aligaṛh, part i, 1972, pp. 1-8.

Varma, R.C., 'The Relations of the Mughals with the tribes of the north-west', *Islamic Culture*, (Quarterly), Hyderabad, (Deccan),

vol. xxiv, No. 4, October, 1950, pp. 249-60.
'The tribal policy of the Mughals', *Islamic Culture* (Quarterly), Hyderabad, (Deccan), vol. xxvi, No. 3, July, 1952, pp. 13-24.

Yasin Mazhar Siddique, 'Military Organisation under the Sulṭāns of Delhī', *Proceedings of Indian National History Conference*, 1965, pp. 19-30.

Ẓahoor 'Ali, Khan, 'The Quest for a Scientific Frontier: A study of North Western frontier of medieval Indian empires', *Indian History Congress*, Waltair, 1979, (used photo-copy of the original paper), pp. 1-15.

# INDEX

1

# NORTH WEST FRONTIER OF INDIA

## A.D. 1206 – 1526

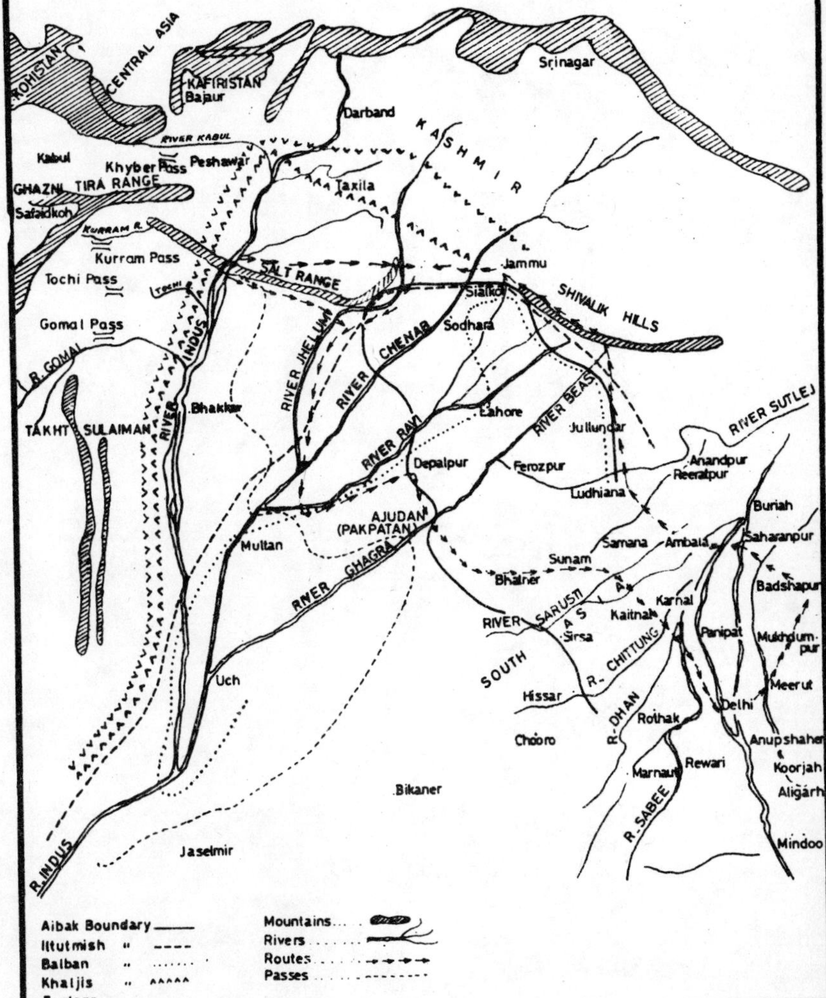

(2)

# ROUTES BETWEEN CENTRAL ASIA AND SOUTH ASIA

## A.D. 1200 – 1526

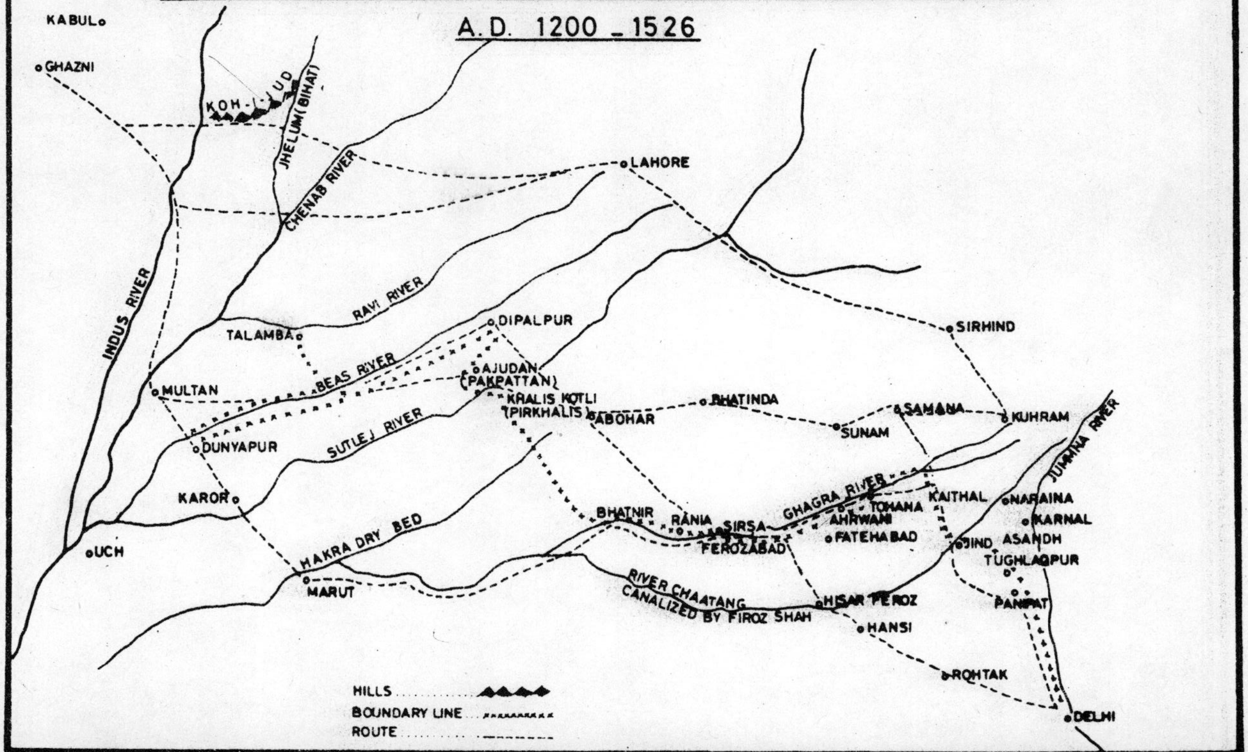

3

## ROUTE OF YALDUZ AND BATTLE WITH AIBAK

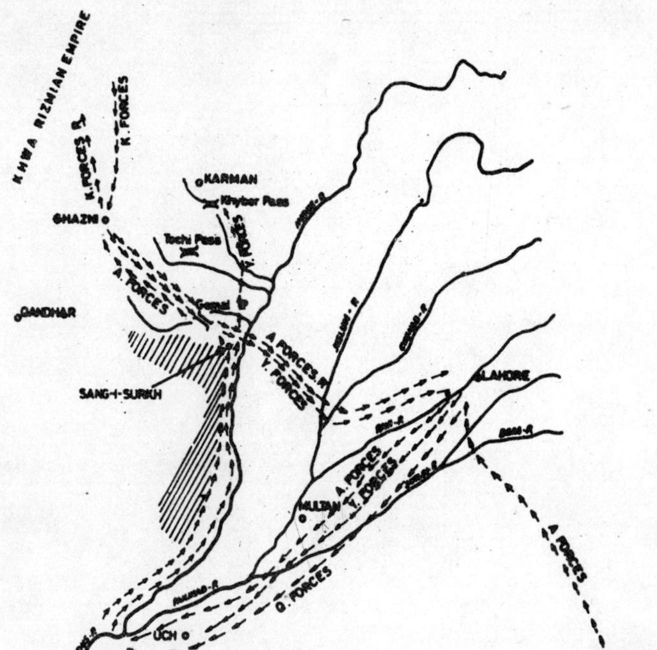

4

## QARLUGHS & OTHER MONGOL'S ALLIES DOMINIONS

### A.D. 1220-1286

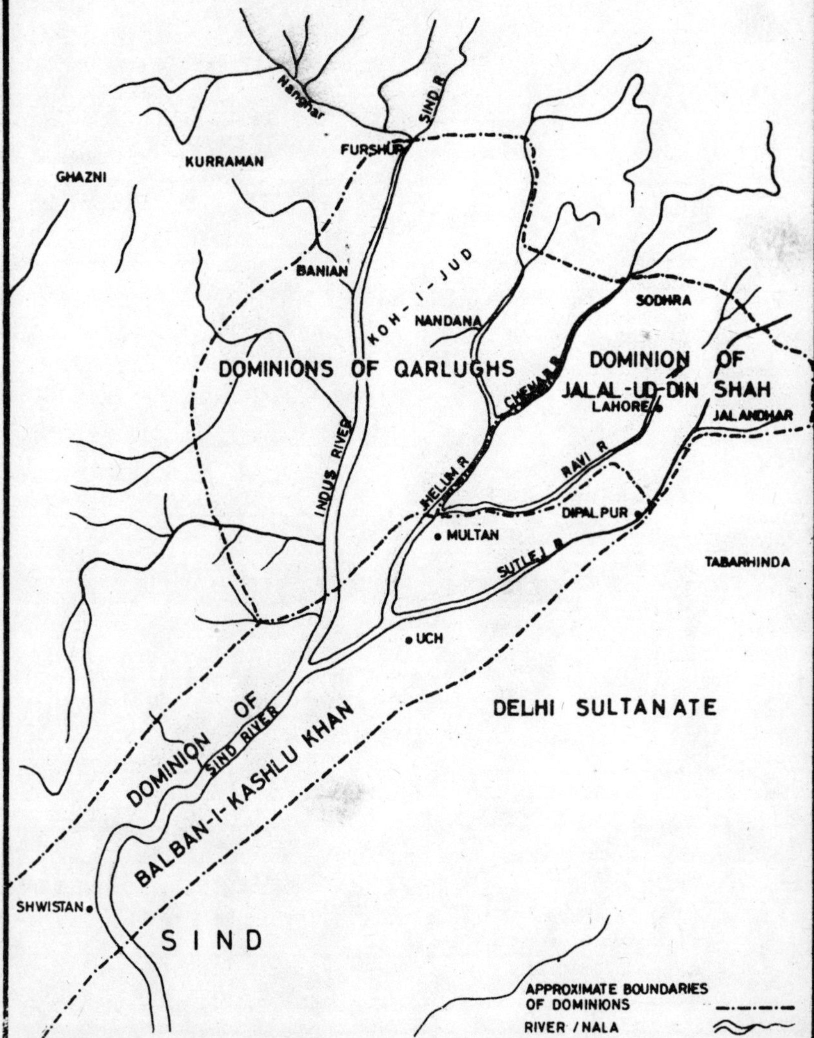

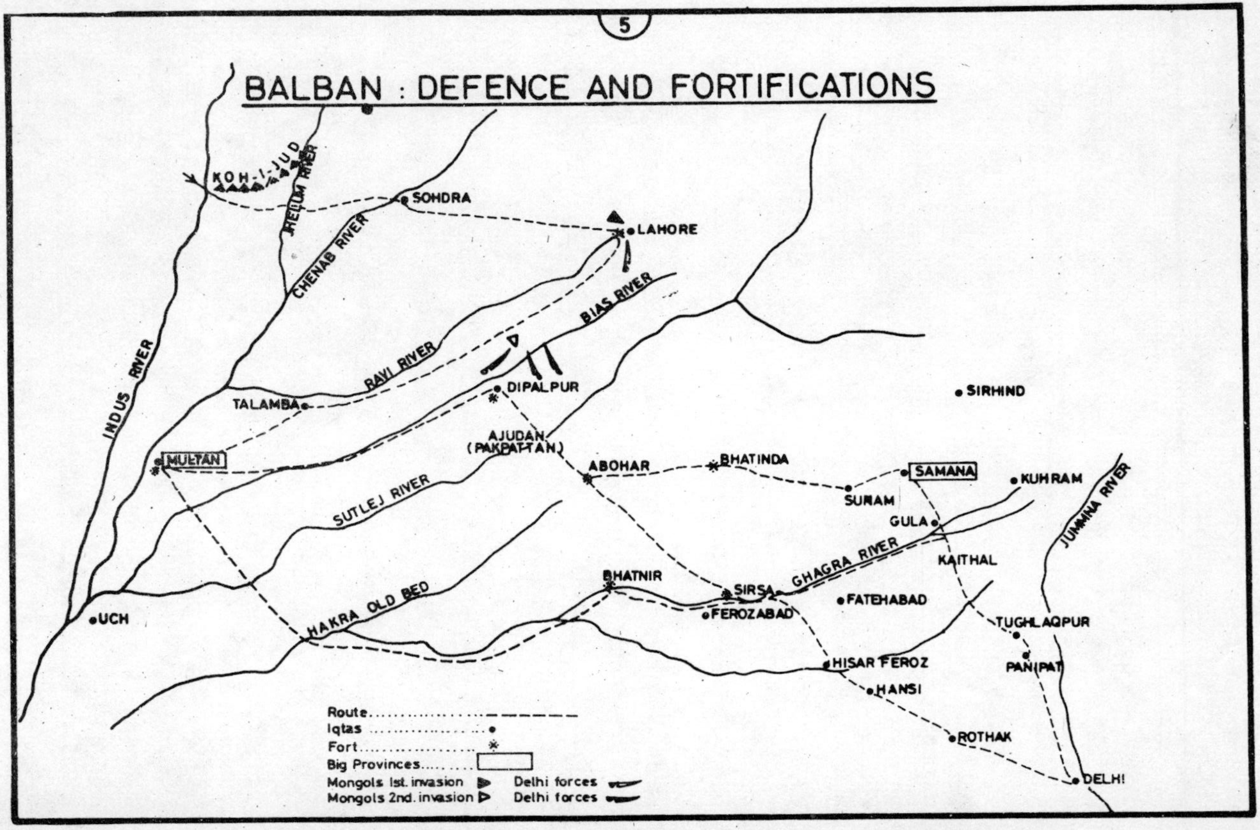
5
BALBAN : DEFENCE AND FORTIFICATIONS
KOH-I-JUD
JHELUM RIVER
SOHDRA
CHENAB RIVER
LAHORE
BIAS RIVER
RAVI RIVER
INDUS RIVER
DIPALPUR
TALAMBA
SIRHIND
AJUDAN
(PAKPATTAN)
MULTAN
ABOHAR
BHATINDA
SAMANA
KUHRAM
SURAM
SUTLEJ RIVER
GULA
JUMMNA RIVER
KAITHAL
GHAGRA RIVER
BHATNIR
SIRSA
FATEHABAD
HAKRA OLD BED
UCH
FEROZABAD
TUGHLAQPUR
HISAR FEROZ
PANIPAT
HANSI
ROTHAK
DELHI
Route
Iqtas
Fort
Big Provinces
Mongols Ist. invasion
Mongols 2nd. invasion
Delhi forces
Delhi forces

6

# KHALJIS : DEFENCE AND FORTIFICATIONS

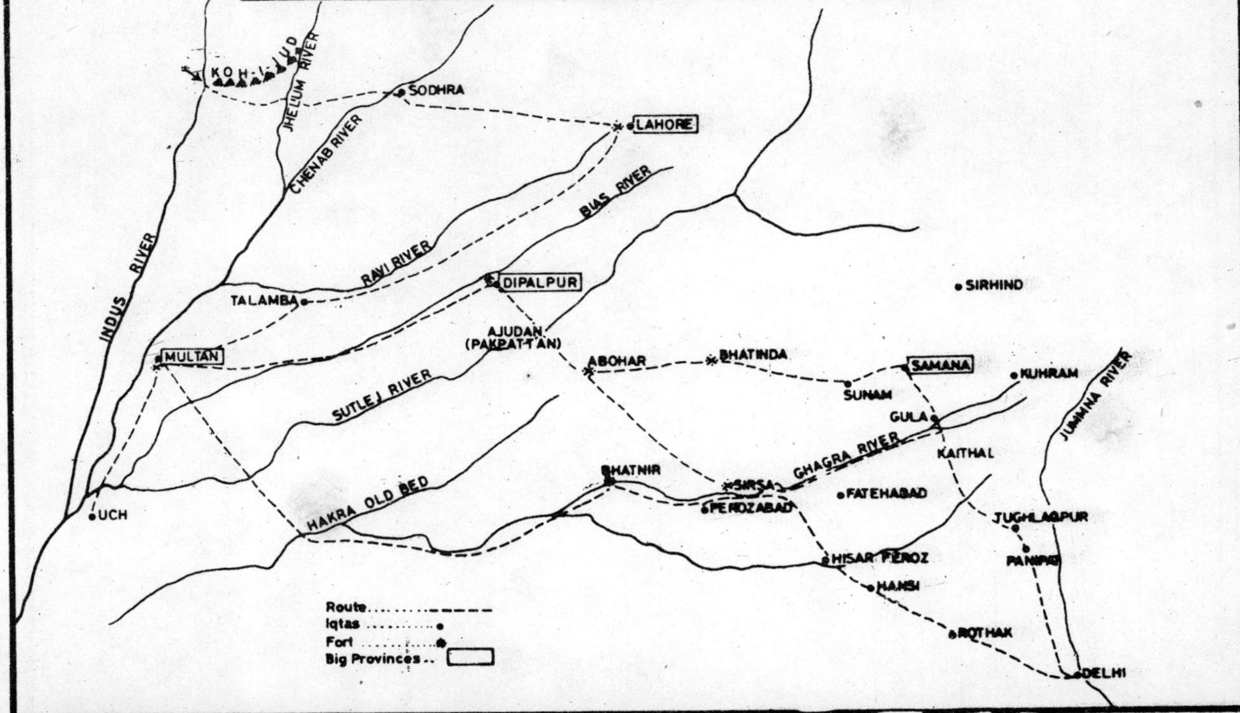

7

# ROUTE OF TIMURS INVASION

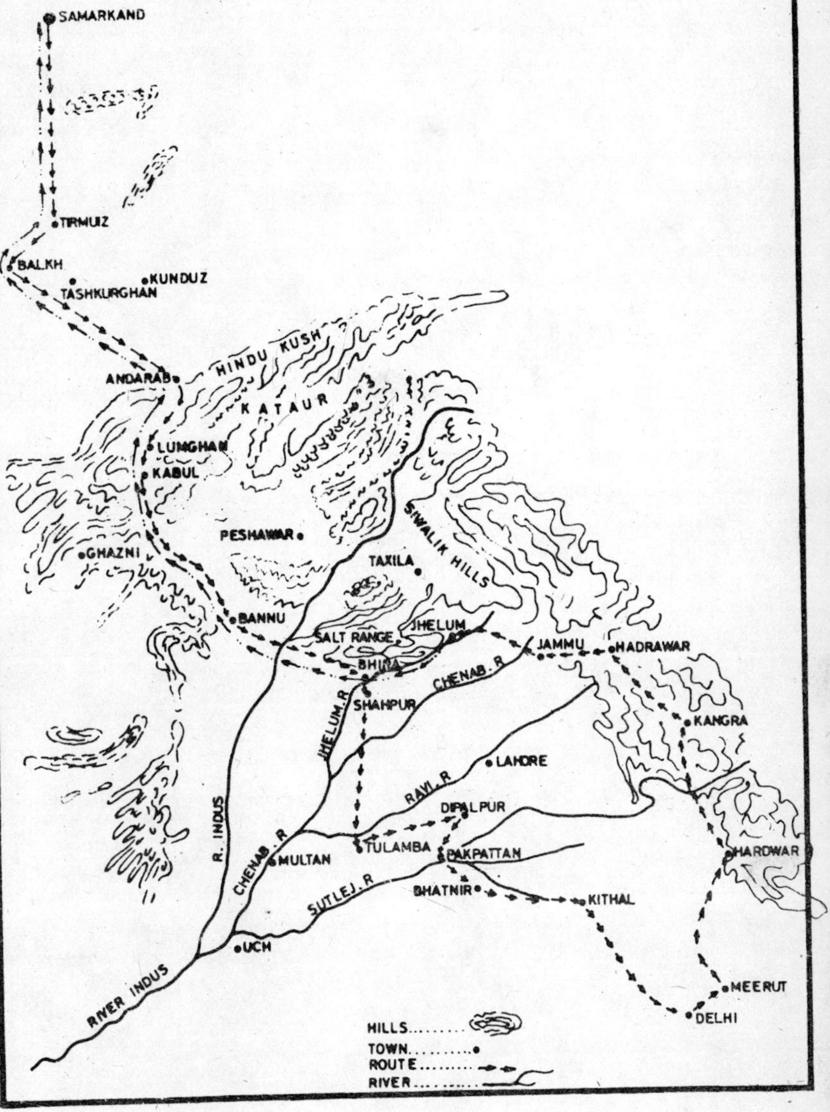

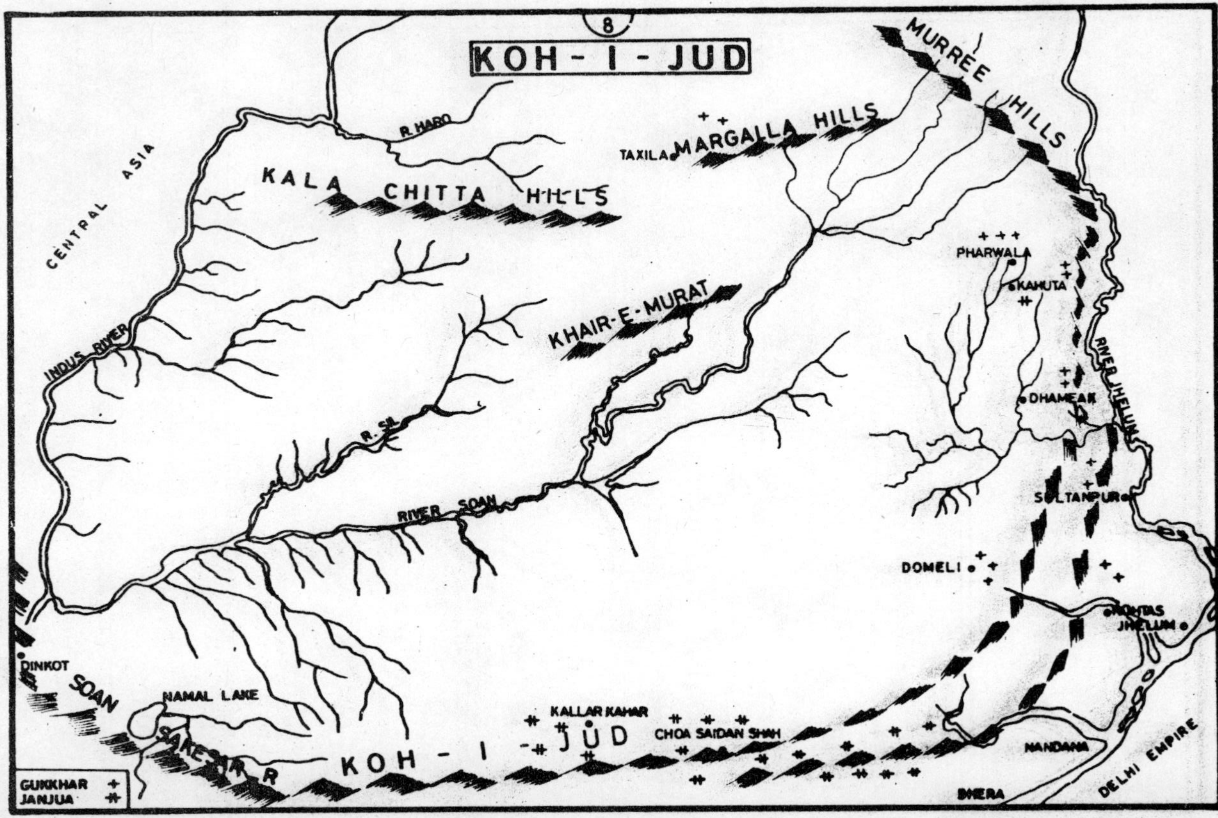

8
KOH - I - JUD
MURREE HILLS
MARGALLA HILLS
TAXILA
KALA CHITTA HILLS
R. HARO
CENTRAL ASIA
INDUS RIVER
KHAIR-E-MURAT
R. SIL
RIVER SOAN
PHARWALA
KAHUTA
DHAMEAK
RIVER JHELUM
SOLTANPUR
DOMELI
ROHTAS
JHELUM
DINKOT
SOAN
NAMAL LAKE
SAKESAR R
KALLAR KAHAR
JUD
CHOA SAIDAN SHAH
KOH - I
NANDANA
BHERA
DELHI EMPIRE
GUKKHAR
JANJUA

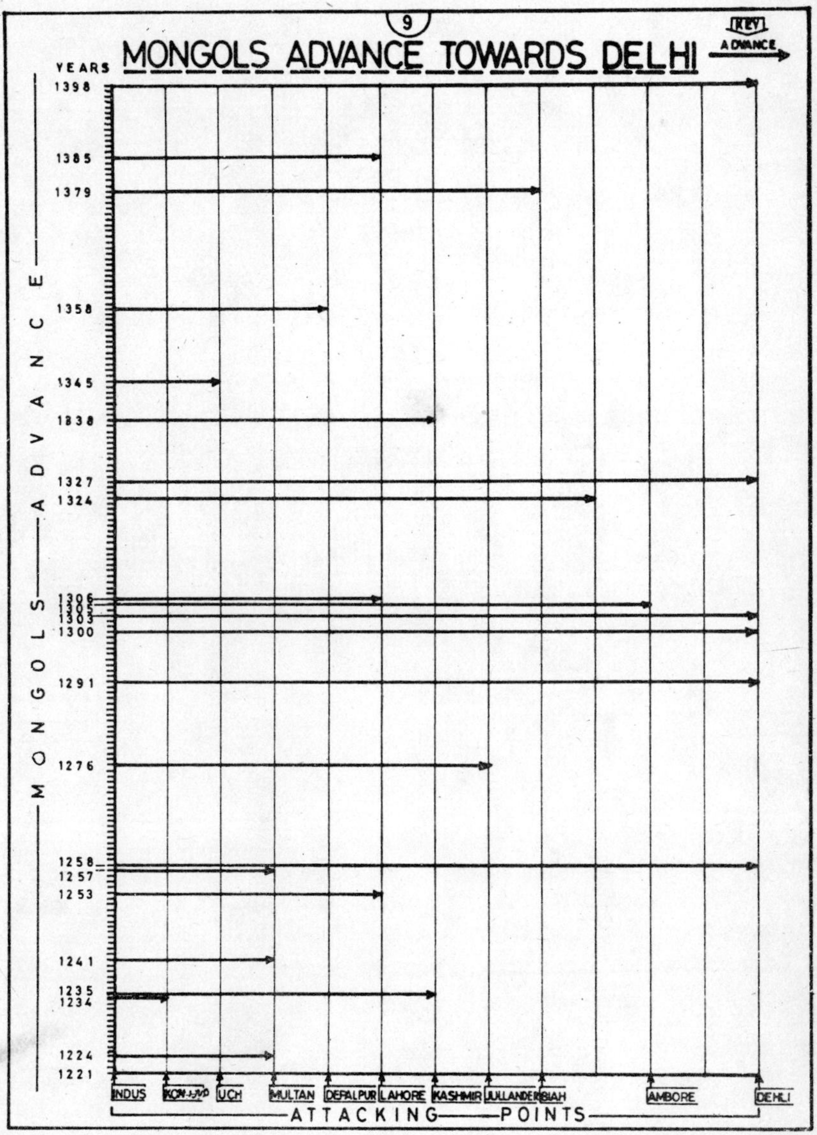
9
MONGOLS ADVANCE TOWARDS DELHI
KEY
ADVANCE
YEARS
MONGOLS ADVANCE
1398
1385
1379
1358
1345
1338
1327
1324
1306
1305
1303
1300
1291
1276
1258
1257
1253
1241
1235
1234
1224
1221
INDUS
UCH
MULTAN
DEPALPUR
LAHORE
KASHMIR
JULLANDER
BIAH
AMBORE
DEHLI
ATTACKING POINTS